ENTREPRENEURSHIP IN THE RAW MATERIALS SECTOR

Entrepreneurship in the Raw Materials Sector

Edited by

Zoltán Bartha
Associate Professor, Faculty of Economics/University of Miskolc/Miskolc, Hungary

Tekla Szép
Associate Professor, Faculty of Economics/University of Miskolc/Miskolc, Hungary

Katalin Lipták
Vice Dean, Associate Professor, Faculty of Economics/University of Miskolc/Miskolc, Hungary

Dóra Szendi
Assistant Professor, Faculty of Economics/University of Miskolc/Miskolc, Hungary

CRC Press
Taylor & Francis Group
Boca Raton London New York Leiden

CRC Press is an imprint of the
Taylor & Francis Group, an **informa** business

A BALKEMA BOOK

CRC Press/Balkema is an imprint of the Taylor & Francis Group, an informa business

© 2022 selection and editorial matter, Zoltán Bartha, Tekla Szép, Katalin Lipták & Dóra Szendi; individual chapters, the contributors

Typeset by Integra Software Services Pvt. Ltd., Pondicherry, India

Library of Congress Cataloging-in-Publication Data

A catalog record has been requested for this book

First published 2022
by CRC Press/Balkema
Schipholweg 107C, 2316 XC Leiden, The Netherlands
e-mail: enquiries@taylorandfrancis.com
www.routledge.com – www.taylorandfrancis.com

ISBN: 978-1-032-19596-4 (Hbk)
ISBN: 978-1-032-19597-1 (Pbk)
ISBN: 978-1-003-25995-4 (eBook)
DOI: 10.1201/9781003259954

Table of contents

Preface

LIMBRA ('Decreasing the negative outcomes of brain drain in the raw materials sector') is a project funded by EIT RawMaterials. Our primary goal is to generate new entrepreneurial ideas in the raw materials sector, and to encourage engineering students graduating in raw materials-related programmes to start their own businesses. Additionally, it was also part of LIMBRA's mission to engage in wider society learning, and so make efforts to increase the general public's awareness about issues that are closely related to raw materials and natural resources: climate change, critical raw materials, and sustainable living.

The LIMBRA team is made up of four universities from the Visegrad countries (University of Miskolc, as leader, and AGH Krakow – University of Science and Technology, Technical University of Kosice, and Technical University of Ostrava as partners), and the Bilbao-based Tecnalia, one of Europe's leading centres of applied research and business incubation. Over the past three years our team has started several initiatives to achieve the LIMBRA goals: we have developed study materials to enhance the soft and business skills of engineering students; we have held summer schools where our study materials were deployed; we held real-life problem solving events; our expanded team conducted a comprehensive market research in order to detect market niches and business ideas in the raw materials sector; we developed materials and provided a platform for speeches directed at the wider public in order to increase awareness about such topics as energy decoupling, the role of critical raw materials, sustainability, and green growth; and we started a mentoring programme within which 20 business ideas connected to raw materials have been developed.

The conference titled Entrepreneurship in the Raw Materials Sector held on 24th November 2021 served as a summary and conclusion of our activities. Given the diversity of the LIMBRA initiatives, the conference also embraced a wide variety of topics. Some papers address macroeconomic issues such as green growth; several papers concentrate on the raw materials markets, and some of them raise specific business problems that can lead to the generation of new business ideas; a couple of papers deal with issues related to entrepreneurship training, and mentoring; and a good number of papers investigate topics related to entrepreneurship. Many of the papers are based on experience coming from LIMBRA activities (our real-life problem-solving events, our market research, and the entrepreneurship mentoring programme), and many others serve as good additions to our team's achievements.

Once again, we express our gratitude to EIT RawMaterials for the generous funding the LIMBRA team received during the 2019 – 2021 period. This proceeding offers a good summary of our approach, and our results: identify the critical trends in the macroeconomic environment; learn about the specifics of the raw materials markets; develop new business ideas, and rely on your local ecosystem for extra knowledge, mentoring, and help; and finally, "Become a stay-at-home entrepreneur" who contributes to the development of the community.

Miskolc, 28 November 2021
Zoltán Bartha, Project Manager

Technical program committee

- *Dr. Katalin Lipták, Vice Dean, Associate Professor, Faculty of Economics, University of Miskolc*
- *Dr. Zoltán Bartha, Associate Professor, Faculty of Economics, University of Miskolc*
- *Dr. Tekla Szép, Associate Professor, Faculty of Economics, University of Miskolc*
- *Dr. Dóra Szendi, Assistant Professor, Faculty of Economics, University of Miskolc*

The conference was carried out in the project entitled 'LIMBRA Decreasing the negative outcomes of brain drain in the raw material sector - EIT RawMaterials Project.'

Sponsors

Supported by

Entrepreneurship in the Raw Materials Sector – Bartha et al. (Eds)

Top OECD performers in green growth—an FOI model analysis

Z. Bartha
University of Miskolc, Miskolc, Hungary

ABSTRACT: With rising concerns about climate change, the issue of green growth have been growing in importance. The aim of this study is to establish a measurement method for green growth, and to identify the best performing countries in this field. The Future, Outside, and Inside (FOI) development model was used to measure the performance of the 38 OECD countries. Based on their 2019-20 scores, the countries that are top performers in green growth are the members of the so called Welfare-participatory cluster (Austria, Denmark, Finland, Germany, Ireland, Israel, New Zealand, Norway, Sweden), and two outliers (Iceland, and Luxembourg).

1 INTRODUCTION

As the topic of human-induced climate change came more and more to the forefront of public debate, the area that is often summarized as green growth, energy transition or (energy and/or growth) decoupling became one of the main research problems in economics. A ProQuest database search for content published in 2021 provides 589,822 hits for green growth (14% of the all-time value), 372,172 ones for energy transition (15%), and 19,408 ones for decoupling (10,5%). These abstractions refer to very similar concepts. Green growth is defined as "fostering economic growth and development, while ensuring that natural assets continue to provide the resources and environmental services on which our well-being relies" (OECD 2011, p. 9); energy transition refers to the transition from fossil fuels to renewable energy (Quitzow et al. 2019); while according to the OECD "decoupling occurs when the growth rate of an environmental pressure is less than that of its economic driving force (e.g. GDP)" (OECD 2002, p. 4). The big question is, whether green growth is happening, if the transition is happening quickly enough, and what are the policies that can facilitate the process.

This paper focuses on the OECD countries, uses the FOI model (Bartha & Gubik 2014) to evaluate their performance in the three main pillars of development (Future, Outside, and Inside potential), and investigates how green growth fits into the development model of the OECD countries. This study aims to answer two main questions: Is there a green growth pattern emerging among the OECD countries; and Which OECD countries perform the best in green growth? The contribution of this study is the following:

1. By measuring the Future, Outside and Inside potential of the OECD countries, and conducting a cluster analysis based on the FOI indices, it shows the different development paths these countries are on.
2. By investigating the variables correlated with the FOI indices, and conducting a factor analysis among them, it identifies a Green growth factor of the Future potential.
3. Finally, by comparing the average Green growth factor scores of the different OECD clusters, it identifies the group of countries that have done the best so far at achieving sustainable development.

DOI: 10.1201/9781003259954-1

The rest of the study is structured as follows: section 2 provides a short literature review of the empirical results on the topic of green growth; section 3 introduces the FOI model, and the method and sources of calculating the FOI indices; section 4 presents the results of the calculations and offers a discussion of the results; section 5 concludes the study.

2 LITERATURE REVIEW

Although the literature on green growth is very rich, most of the studies focus on either individual countries, or certain sectors/industries of selected countries. In this review I focus on studies conducted on macroeconomic indicators of the OECD countries.

Szita (2014) in an early study calculates a Greening index for the 34 OECD members. Based on the data available for the early 2010s, she finds that the following countries can be considered as green: Austria, Denmark, Norway, Sweden, Switzerland, Japan, and Iceland.

Chakraborty & Mazzanti (2021) test 33 countries that are now all members of the OECD for the 1971-2015 period. They use methodologies that consider cross-sectional dependence and find that there is a significant positive relationship between per capita economic growth and per capita renewable electricity consumption. Higher per capita growth rates seem to go together with higher rates of renewable energy consumption, but the authors could not detect any Granger causality between the two variables (despite trying many specifications).

Gavurova et al. (2021) include all current 38 OECD members in their analysis. They select 15 indicators related to green growth, calculate an average for period 1 (2000-2009), and period 2 (2010-2019) and compare them. The authors find that overall, there is an improvement from period 1 to period 2. A cluster analysis is also conducted, splitting the countries into 6 (period 1), and 7 (period 2) clusters according to the indicators. The countries' cluster placement more or less corresponds to their development level.

Wang et al. (2019) conduct a dynamic panel regression analysis based on the data of the industrial sector of 24 OECD countries for the 2004 and 2010 period to test the impact of environmental regulation policy on green productivity growth. They find an inverted U-shaped relationship, so environmental regulation seems to hurt productivity growth after a certain stringency level. After decomposing the productivity growth, the catching-up effect is found to be the primary source of green productivity growth, which partially explains why some of lesser developed countries (the Czech Republic, Korea, Poland, and the Slovak Republic) of the OECD have the highest green total factor productivity growth. The other group of countries doing well in green productivity growth consists of Finland, Sweden, and France.

Shen et al. (2017) also measure green productivity growth, using a sample of 30 OECD countries over the period of 1970 – 2011. Their results show that green productivity has grown faster than the traditional Total Factor Productivity (TFP) would suggest, because carbon emission drops in periods of downturn. Improvements in technical and structural efficiency contribute to green growth from 1971 – 2000, which is in line with the results of Wang et al. (2019) who also found technical efficiency as the main driver, but for the remainder of the period technological progress seems to have the strongest impact. Shen et al. only provide data for three groups of countries (OECD Americas, OECD Asia-Oceania, and OECD Europe); out of these three groups OECD Europe has the lowest trend in carbon emissions, but this is also the region that grows the slowest over the inspected period.

Huang et al. (2021) take a slightly different approach and focus on the so called 3E trilemma (achieving energy security, economic development, and environmental protection at the same time). The authors set up a complex measurement method based on several indicators and use a sample of 34 OECD countries over the 2000 to 2015 period to test the relationship among the three pillars of the trilemma. Huang et al. could not detect a significant relationship between energy security and decoupling, but they find a group of five countries that have done well both in energy security and in decoupling economic growth from carbon emission. Australia, Switzerland, Germany, Denmark, and Sweden are the five members of this group.

Ates & Derinkuyu (2021) incorporate a number of indicators in their analysis, measuring the economic, social, and environmental aspects of the OECD countries. The authors create a single indicator by synthetizing the different variables using multivariate I-distance approach, and find that Sweden, Luxemburg, Norway, and Denmark are the top performers in green growth.

3 DATA AND METHODS

3.1 *Data and sources*

My analysis included a sample of 38 OECD countries and incorporated a total of 95 variables measuring the level of socio-economic development. The latest available data was used, which means that most of the values belong either to 2020 or 2019.

The data was obtained from the following sources:

1. OECD.Stat: https://stats.oecd.org/
2. WEF Global Competitiveness Report (Schwab 2019)
3. IMF World Economic Outlook Database, April 2021 Edition: https://www.imf.org/en/Pub lications/WEO/weo-database/2021/April
4. World Bank Doing Business database: https://www.doingbusiness.org/en/doingbusiness
5. Solability Sustainable Intelligence: https://solability.com/
6. WHO the Global Health Observatory: https://www.who.int/data/gho/data/indicators
7. Global Footprint Network: https://www.footprintnetwork.org/
8. Trading Economics: https://tradingeconomics.com/
9. ETS TOEFL results: https://www.ets.org/

3.2 *Method: The FOI model*

This study uses the FOI model to evaluate the development paths taken by the OECD countries and then identifies a Green growth factor that is correlated with the Future potential, the first of the three pillars of FOI. A detailed description of the method is available in Bartha & Gubik (2014), here only a short summary is provided.

The FOI model is developed on the assumption that three main dimensions determine the development path of economies. The future potential considers the long-term competitiveness of the economy; the outside potential determines the current world market position of the economy; while the inside potential summarizes factors that are crucial for the current well-being of the community. The FOI model assigns several variables to each of the three potentials and following some transformations (all variables are recoded to a 1-7 scale using a minmax method) they can be used to calculate the F, O, and I indices. Table 1 shows all the variables used for the calculation of the three indices.

Once the FOI indices are obtained SPSS is used to derive clusters of OECD countries and factors of the F, O, and I potentials. The hierarchical cluster analysis generates clusters of the 38 countries according to their F, O, and I indices and these clusters can be interpreted as different development strategies or paths. During the factor analysis I select a large number of variables that are correlated with one of the three indices and generate 2 factors for each index. These factors can then be used to provide a more sophisticated description of the OECD clusters. Green growth is one of the factors being connected to the F index.

4 RESULTS AND DISCUSSION

The F, O, and I indices of the OECD countries are included in Table 2. All components were transformed to a 1-7 scale, where 1 is the worst, and 7 is the best value of the indicator. In this

Table 1. Variables used to calculate the F, O, and I indices.

Index	Variables
F-index	1. Global Sustainable Competitiveness Index (Solability, 2020)
	2. Cooperation in labour-employer relations (WEF-GCI, 2019)
	3. Flexibility of wage determination (WEF-GCI, 2019)
	4. Electricity supply quality (WEF-GCI, 2019)
	5. Total expenditure on educational institutions (OECD, 2017)
	6. Elderly (65 and above) population (OECD, 2020)
	7. Renewable energy (OECD, 2019)
	8. Life expectancy at birth (OECD, 2020) & Healthy life expectancy (WHO, 2019)
	9. Ecological Footprint (GFT, 2020)
	10. R&D expenditures & Patent applications (WEF-GCI, 2019)
	11. 15-year-old students who are not low achievers (OECD, 2018)
O-index	1. Exports+Imports/GDP*2 (OECD, 2020)
	2. Country credit rating (TE, 2020)
	3. Soundness of banks (WEF-GCI, 2019)
	4. Exchange rate stability (IMF, 2019)
	5. TOEFL iBT® Total and Section Score Means (ETS, 2019)
I-index	1. Budget transparency & Burden of government regulation (WEF-GCI, 2019)
	2. Better life index (OECD, 2018)
	3. General government revenue (IMF, 2020)
	4. Assets in pension funds and all retirement vehicles (OECD, 2020)
	5. Gross domestic product per capita & Gross domestic product percent change (IMF, 2020)
	6. Financing of SMEs (WEF-GCI, 2019)
	7. Labour market Flexibility (WEF-GCI, 2019) & Labour force (OECD, 2020)
	8. Ease of finding skilled employees (WEF-GCI, 2019)

Source: own work based on Bartha & Gubik 2014

paper I focus on the F-index, since it is correlated with many of the variables that are typically used to measure green growth.

After the indices were calculated, I checked the bivariate correlation between the index values and the 90+ variables included in my database. Initially, all variables that were correlated to the index on at least 5% significance level were included in a factor analysis using principal components as an extraction method, and varimax for rotation. Some of the variables were correlated to more than one of the indices, so as I proceeded with the iterations, I aimed at including the variables in only one of the factors. The final iteration for the variables correlated to the F-index ended up with two factors (Table 3.), with a KMO value of 0.71. The two factors explain 57.8% of the total variance, which is not great, but acceptable. I also calculated a factor score for the Green growth factor using the regression method; the score for Costa Rica and Switzerland is missing, because no data was available for these countries in at least one of the variable categories included in the factor.

The cluster analysis was the next step. Countries were sorted according to their F-, O-, and I-index values, hierarchical cluster analysis was applied and between-group linkage was used as the cluster method. I intentionally went for a high number of clusters (11), so that smaller nuances could be detected as well. Table 4 contains the different clusters that were derived, and Figure 1 shows their position along the Future, Outside, and Inside dimensions.

Table 4 also includes the Green growth factor score for the 11 different clusters. Clearly, green growth performance is very heterogeneous even among the most developed countries. Countries in the Welfare-participatory cluster, and some other outliers do relatively well, while the Market-oriented and Statist clusters perform poorly.

The difference between cluster 1 and 2 is particularly striking, as these two clusters (with the exception of three outlier countries: Luxembourg, Iceland, and Switzerland) are typically the top performers in almost all other factors. They have the best scores in both factors of the

4

Table 2. The F-, O-, and I-index of the OECD countries in 2020.

Country	F-index	O-index	I-index
Australia	3.80	5.34	4.63
Austria	4.42	5.08	3.92
Belgium	3.82	4.87	3.59
Canada	4.00	4.93	4.64
Chile	3.65	3.90	3.78
Colombia	3.17	2.68	3.12
Costa Rica	3.31	3.65	1.96
Czech Republic	3.75	4.18	3.25
Denmark	4.92	5.01	4.71
Estonia	4.16	4.73	3.61
Finland	4.63	5.07	4.95
France	4.16	4.30	3.53
Germany	4.36	4.70	4.49
Greece	3.29	2.86	1.94
Hungary	3.08	4.40	2.61
Iceland	5.34	4.23	4.96
Ireland	4.27	4.60	4.95
Israel	4.52	4.59	4.10
Italy	3.54	3.53	2.66
Japan	4.67	3.72	4.11
Korea	4.30	4.28	3.77
Latvia	3.51	4.21	3.40
Lithuania	3.63	4.34	3.62
Luxembourg	3.80	6.11	4.61
Mexico	3.04	4.12	3.26
Netherlands	4.27	5.27	5.33
New Zealand	4.54	5.08	4.78
Norway	4.70	4.87	4.86
Poland	3.69	4.00	3.12
Portugal	3.93	3.67	3.14
Slovak Republic	3.40	4.76	2.92
Slovenia	3.99	4.49	3.20
Spain	3.17	4.02	3.14
Sweden	4.93	4.93	4.56
Switzerland	5.19	5.39	5.65
Turkey	3.14	3.16	3.07
United Kingdom	3.85	5.33	4.66
United States	3.89	5.39	5.30

Source: own calculations

Inside potential (Human capital and Governance), as well as in the only clearly distinguishable factor of the Outside potential (FDI readiness).

In fact, Cluster 1 (Market-oriented) and Cluster 2 (Welfare-participatory) are very similar to each other in almost every aspects of the FDI model (see Figure 1.). Their Outside and Inside potentials are similar (with the Market-oriented countries having a slightly higher average in the O-index, and the Welfare-participatory countries a slight edge in the I-index), and they are top performers in Future potential (where the Welfare-participatory cluster has a considerable, 0.6-point edge).

When looking for differences, we can check the FDI readiness factor (variables correlated with the O-index), where Cluster 1 has a score of 0.83, while Cluster 2 only scores 0.53, but both of these values are way higher than the factor score of any other multi-country cluster, and they are at the same level as Luxembourg (0.73, very close to Cluster 1's average), and Switzerland (0.54, almost identical to Cluster 2's average).

Table 3. The two factors of the future potential (rotated components matrix).

Factor	Variable	Component 1	Component 2
Government quality	Efficiency of legal framework in settling disputes	0.921	0.21
	Property rights	0.902	0.29
	Government ensuring policy stability	0.833	0.299
	Strength of auditing and accounting standards	0.83	0.155
	Share of population with tertiary education	0.787	0.022
	Patent applications per million pop.	0.762	-0.159
	Incidence of corruption	0.756	0.312
	R&D expenditures	0.746	-0.109
	Life expectancy at birth	0.638	0.363
	Contracting with Government	-0.518	0.19
	Total expenditure on educational institutions	0.442	0.167
Green growth	Production-based CO_2 productivity	0.02	0.713
	Emissions priced above EUR 30 per ton of CO_2	0.109	0.707
	Renewable energy	0.072	0.685
	Population connected to public sewerage	0.068	0.595

Extraction Method: Principal Component Analysis.
Rotation Method: Varimax with Kaiser Normalization.
a Rotation converged in 3 iterations.

Source: own calculations

Table 4. Clusters according to their FOI-indices.

Nr.	Name	GG fac. score	Members
1	Market-oriented	-0.47	Australia, Canada, Netherlands, United Kingdom, United States
2	Welfare-participatory	0.60	Austria, Denmark, Finland, Germany, Ireland, Israel, New Zealand, Norway, Sweden
3	Statist 1 (welfare)	-0.52	Belgium, Estonia, France, Korea, Slovenia
4	Statist 2 (protectionist)	-0.04	Chile, Czech Republic, Italy, Latvia, Lithuania, Mexico, Poland, Portugal, Spain
5	Laggard 1 (rising)	-0.49	Colombia, Turkey
6	Laggard 2 (falling)	0.18	Costa Rica, Greece
7	Statist 3 (open)	-0.65	Hungary, Slovak Republic
8	Iceland	2.34	Iceland
9	Japan	-1.45	Japan
10	Luxembourg	1.08	Luxembourg
11	Switzerland	n/a	Switzerland

Source: own calculations

Based on all the FOI-related calculations, the Market-oriented and the Welfare-participatory countries have the best indicator values within the OECD (again, three, similarly well-performing outliers need to be mentioned here: Iceland, Luxembourg, and Switzerland). They have the highest factor score in Human capital development and Governance (the Market-oriented group having a slight, 0.1-point edge); they also have the highest factor score in FDI readiness (the Market-oriented group leading by about 0.3); and they have the highest F-index as well (although the lead of the Welfare-participatory group is considerable in this area, and the Market-oriented cluster is overtaken by the Statist 1 group as well). So, the only clear difference among the top performers comes from the Green growth factor: the Welfare-participatory countries are on the top of the list (if we disregard Iceland and Luxembourg),

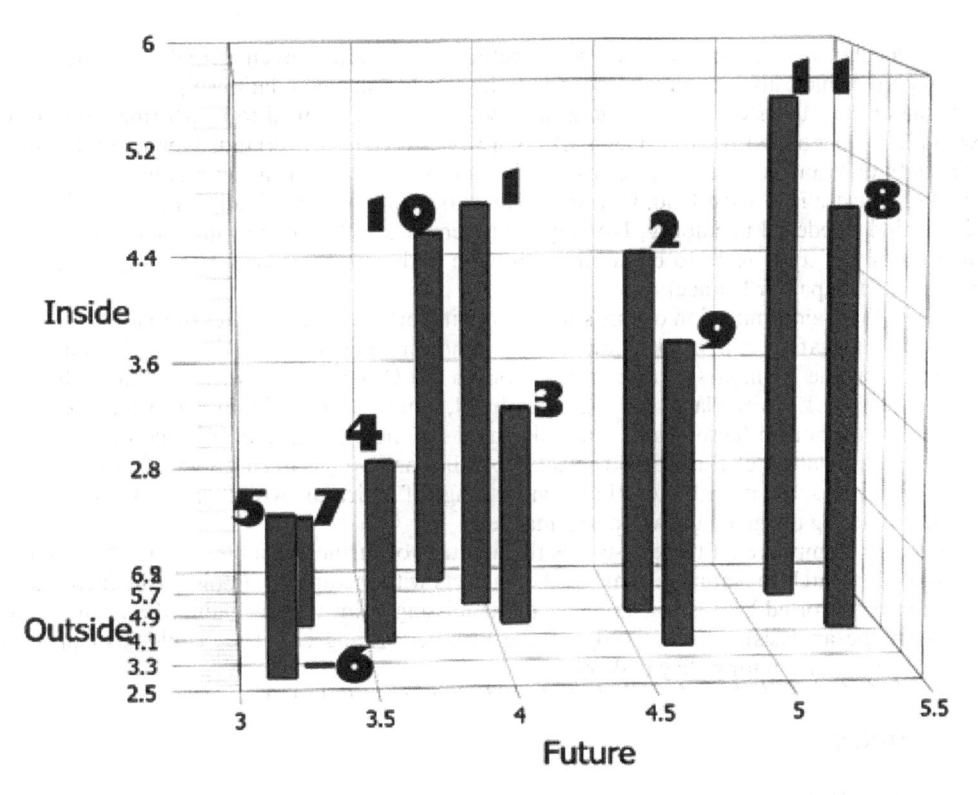

Figure 1.   Clusters based the FOI model – an 11-cluster solution.
Source: own calculations

while the Market-oriented countries are very close to the bottom of the list, with most of the Statist groups members lining up between them.

5   CONCLUSION

In this study I calculated the 2020 FOI indices for the 38 OECD member countries. The cluster analysis conducted with these indices resulted in 11 clusters. Four of these clusters are single-country outlier ones, while the majority of the countries can be found in Cluster 1 (Market-oriented model), Cluster 2 (Welfare-participatory model), and Clusters 3-4 (Statist model). The Market-oriented and the Welfare-participatory clusters are the best performing ones in all aspects measured by the FOI model. The only significant difference between the two can be detected in the Green growth performance, where Cluster 2 countries do really well, while Cluster 1 members score quite low. The countries that I found to do well in green growth are the following:

- members of the Welfare-participatory cluster: Austria, Denmark, Finland, Germany, Ireland, Israel, New Zealand, Norway, Sweden;
- outlier countries: Iceland, and Luxembourg.

According to their Green growth factor score, Norway (2.6), Iceland (2.3), and Luxembourg (1.1) are the top three countries in green growth within the OECD. No factor score was calculated for Switzerland, because at least one data point was missing from the Swiss dataset, but it is likely that they would also be close to the top of this list.

One obvious conclusion that can be drawn from this analysis is that countries with stronger welfare and statist roots have been doing better so far in green growth. This could be the result of their experience in regulating the economy. Wang et al. (2019) has found that stricter environmental regulation tends to go together with better green growth performance, although they have also found evidence for an inverted U-shaped relationship.

Some of the studies cited in the literature review have also named top performer countries. Szita (2014) mentioned Austria, Denmark, Norway, Sweden, Switzerland, Japan, and Iceland; the study of Wang et al. (2019) points to Finland, Sweden, and France; Huang et al. (2021) highlight Australia, Switzerland, Germany, Denmark, and Sweden; finally, Ates & Derinkuyu (2021) find Sweden, Luxemburg, Norway, and Denmark to be the best in green growth. The findings of this study seem to be in line with these (although there are some exceptions, such as Australia, Japan or France).

One of the major limitation of this study is that it works with aggregates of macro statistics, and the aggregation can mask some of the important details. The United Kingdom, for example, has the 7th highest Green factor score in the OECD, but it was still put in the low scoring Cluster 1. Switzerland, on the other hand, would have probably got a high score in green growth, but no factor value was calculated for them because of a single missing data point and the nature of the method selected. Additionally, the Green growth factor is made up of 4 variables, but it is obvious that a wider range of indicators would probably do a better job at evaluating the green growth performance.

One way to improve on these results is the addition of further variables to the analysis and additional research to complete some of the datasets with missing data points (the factor analysis can be distorted by missing data, since one missing point can disqualify the whole country from the analysis). A case study of the well-performing countries could also provide valuable information for policy makers.

REFERENCES

Ates, S. A., & Derinkuyu, K. 2021. 'Green Growth and OECD Countries: Measurement of Country Performances through Distance-Based Analysis (DBA)'. *Environment, Development and Sustainability* 23 (10): 15062–73. https://doi.org/10.1007/s10668-021-01285-4.

Bartha, Z. & S. Gubik, A. 2014. 'Characteristics of the Large Corporation-Based, Bureaucratic Model among OECD Countries - an FOI Model Analysis'. *Danube* 5 (1): 1–20. https://doi.org/10.2478/danb-2014-0001.

Chakraborty, S. K. & Mazzanti, M. 2021. 'Renewable Electricity and Economic Growth Relationship in the Long Run: Panel Data Econometric Evidence from the OECD'. *Structural Change and Economic Dynamics* 59 (December): 330–41. https://doi.org/10.1016/j.strueco.2021.08.006.

Gavurova, B., Megyesiova, S. & Hudak, M. 2021. 'Green Growth in the OECD Countries: A Multivariate Analytical Approach'. *Energies* 14 (20): 6719. https://doi.org/10.3390/en14206719.

Huang, S-W., Chung, Y-F. & Wu, T-S. 2021. 'Analyzing the Relationship between Energy Security Performance and Decoupling of Economic Growth from CO2 Emissions for OECD Countries'. *Renewable and Sustainable Energy Reviews* 152 (December): 111633. https://doi.org/10.1016/j.rser.2021.111633.

OECD. 2011. *Towards Green Growth*. OECD Green Growth Studies. OECD. https://doi.org/10.1787/9789264111318-en.

Quitzow, R., Thielges, S., Goldthau, A., Helgenberger, S. & Mbungu, G. 2019. 'Advancing a Global Transition to Clean Energy – the Role of International Cooperation'. *Economics* 13 (1): 20190048. https://doi.org/10.5018/economics-ejournal.ja.2019-48.

Schwab, K. 2019. *The Global Competitiveness Report 2019*. Geneva, Switzerland: World Economic Forum. https://www3.weforum.org/docs/WEF_TheGlobalCompetitivenessReport2019.pdf.

Shen, Z., Boussemart, J-P. & Leleu, H. 2017. 'Aggregate Green Productivity Growth in OECD's Countries'. *International Journal of Production Economics* 189 (July): 30–39. https://doi.org/10.1016/j.ijpe.2017.04.007.

Szita, K. 2014. 'Green Growth in the OECD: State of the Art'. *Theory, Methodology, Practice* 10 (2): 59–65.

Wang, Y., Sun, X. & Guo, X. 2019. 'Environmental Regulation and Green Productivity Growth: Empirical Evidence on the Porter Hypothesis from OECD Industrial Sectors'. *Energy Policy* 132 (September): 611–19. https://doi.org/10.1016/j.enpol.2019.06.016.

Entrepreneurship in the Raw Materials Sector – Bartha et al. (Eds)

A comprehensive indicator set for measuring the sustainable energy performance in the European Union

T. Szép
University of Miskolc, Miskolc, Hungary

T. Pálvölgyi & É. Kármán-Tamus
Budapest University of Technology and Economics, Budapest, Hungary

ABSTRACT: Clean energy transition is the key for sustainable energy. In spite of the positive tendencies, the Covid-19 has also raised many issues and highlighted the importance of the topic. The Sustainable Development Goal 7 and 13 may serve as a basis to achieve affordable and clean energy and to combat global climate change. Meeting these objectives needs well-designed energy and environmental policy with a strong holistic approach. This study aims to build a comprehensive indicator set for measuring the sustainable energy performance of the European Union Member States. To determine the indicator set we follow rigorous steps, the methodology of which is described in detail. Finally, we present the list of eight selected indicators, from which a composite indicator can be built. Additionally, the overall structure of the dataset is analyzed through correlation analysis, stationarity and normality tests. Standardization is carried out to make the variables comparable with different units. Respecting the main dimensions of the theory of sustainable development, we also determine the weighting factors and we put them up for discussion.

1 INTRODUCTION

Humanity faces many challenges in the next decades. To solve these issues takes a long time, significant changes cannot be expected from a year to another. Following a holistic approach, a priority rank of these global problems is crucially important. Smalley R. (Texas Archival Resource Online, 2021) in 2003 provided a potential full list in order of importance: 1) Energy, 2) Water, 3) Food, 4) Environment, 5) Poverty, 6) Terrorism & War, 7) Disease, 8) Education, 9) Democracy, 10) Population. It highlights the importance of energy. According to Smalley R. the clean, reliable and affordable energy is the key to the other problems. Taking into consideration the latest news about potential European and global energy shortages, here we make an additional note referring to energy security. Following the 4A concept we may not neglect the availability, accessibility, affordability, and acceptability of energy (Finszter & Sabjanics, 2018).

The global energy use is in transition, but the scope and the time requirements of that is uncertain and needs further analysis. The topic of global energy dilemma is a more and more frequently mentioned issue, which focuses on the future availability of fossil fuels (energy security) and the impact of the exploitation on the environment and planetary ecosystem (climate change, biodiversity loss, air pollution and other challenges) and furthermore it seeks for possible solutions. The main question is whether sufficient energy is available for economic development, but without increasing the emission of GHG (or in line with Paris Agreement to reduce it) and managing the transition to a low-carbon energy system and low-carbon economy.

DOI: 10.1201/9781003259954-2

We should concentrate not only on energy transition but we should raise the attention to the importance of the sustainable energy transition. It becomes clear that the global energy security, economic geography of globalization, the economics of climate change and climate policy are closely related. A new energy paradigm or a new energy model may be able to give answers. The core issue of the latter one is how we can form the energy policy considering all the three components of the energy trilemma (1. energy security, 2. environmental sustainability, 3. energy equity).

The main purpose of this article is to determine an indicator set to measure the sustainable energy performance of the European Union Member States between 2007 and 2019 and to present the process of that. Finding the right indicators is not easy. After a deep and detailed literature review we selected more than two dozen data. However, the applied tests revealed many statistical problems regarding missing values, multicollinearity, normal distribution of variables and stationarity. Based on the test results the indicators were revised and tests were calculated again. Considering the problem of different scales and units of measures standardization was carried out to make the indicator set ready for compiling the composite indicator.

This study can be considered as a first part of a more extended research work. Our main goal is to create a new composite indicator, called sustainable energy performance index. It allows us to measure the progress of the member states of the European Union regarding green energy transition and to classify countries. We organize the examined countries into clusters. The different country groups need various policy answers and can be a good basis for future collaborations.

2 THEORETICAL BACKGROUND

Following the basic definition, sustainable energy is energy that meets the needs of the present generations without compromising the ability of future generations to meet their own needs (Hollaway, 2013). Systemic changes are needed; two main dimensions can be interpreted. Sustainable energy can be achieved through a higher share of renewable energy sources in final energy consumption and/or improved energy efficiency and energy savings. Monitoring the progress of national energy policies and energy systems can provide useful feedback to policy makers and may contribute to accomplishing the goals.

For the monitoring we compile an index, which belongs to the type of composite indicators. They aim to compare country performance regarding a specific economic area. The method is widely-used, corruption perceptions index (Transparency International, 2021), world competitiveness ranking (IMD, 2021) or smart city index (Giffinger & Pichler-Milanovic, 2007) are good examples. One of their main advantages is the easy interpretation and their ability to concentrate many individual indicators and dimensions into one index. Providing a holistic approach and showing the bigger picture, the composite indicators are quite useful for benchmarking different countries (OECD et al., 2008). However, determining the indicator set and weights is a critical issue, many times the data availability or political interests have a great influence on them, which should be avoided.

For the indicator selection the starting point were the Sustainable Development Goals. On 21 October 2015 the UN General Assembly adopted 'Transforming our world: the 2030 Agenda for Sustainable Development' (hereinafter Agenda 2030) document (UN, 2015), in which a new framework was dedicated to sustainable development (coordinated by the UN). The Agenda 2030 determines the Sustainable Development Goals (hereinafter SDGs), that can be considered as a continuation of the Millennium Development Goals. The 17 global goals "aim to end poverty, protect the planet and ensure prosperity for everyone by 2030" (Sightsavers, 2017) and they came into effect on 1 January 2016 (UN, 2015). They are built on the environmental, social and economic pillar of sustainability following a holistic approach. During the data selection we followed the list of the sustainable development indicators in the Eurostat (2021). They represent the progress of the European Union regarding the Sustainable Development Goals, with special regard to the 7th and 13th Goals (SDG7 Affordable and Clean Energy, and SDG13 Climate Action).

3 DATA AND METHODS

First, criteria were defined to select the indicators. These are the 1) coverage and significance, 2) availability and reliability, 3) representativeness and 4) comparability. The indicators should reflect on not only the long-term energy and climate goals of the European Union but they have to be connected to the UN Sustainable Development Goals too. Reliable data sources are preferred. To fulfill this requirement, we used the Eurostat, as a primary data source. The indicators have to represent the social, economic and environmental dimensions of sustainable development. The indicators should be available for all European Union Member States for multiple years (long time series are preferred). It ensures that the calculations can be repeated.

Considering these criteria, the following indicators were selected from the Eurostat (2021) (Table 1). The sample period is from 2007 to 2019.

The social dimension is represented by three main indicators, i.e. residential electricity consumption, energy (electricity and gas) prices and energy poverty. In our point of view this latter is important, because it helps to catch the deprivation, social inclusion and energy justice. The

Table 1.   List of initial data.

	Abbreviation	Derived indicator	Source indicators
Social and human pillar	S1	Residential electricity consumption per capita [MWh/capita] – climate corrected	Electricity consumption in the household sector [GWh]
			Population [capita] HDD (heating degree days) Degree-days of reference (average of HDD during the period of 1980-2004) Share of heating in the residential electricity consumption [%]
	S2	Electricity price [€(PPP)/kWh] (Band-DC (Medium): annual consumption between 2 500 and 5 000 kWh)	
	S3	Natural gas price [€(PPP)/GJ] (Band D2: 20 GJ < Consumption < 200 GJ)	
	S4	Percentage of population affected by energy poverty [%]	
Economic pillar	E1	Final energy consumption (productive sectors) per GDP [GJ/million EUR]	Final energy consumption - industry sector [GJ] Final energy consumption - transport sector [GJ] Final energy consumption - other sectors - commercial and public services [GJ] Final energy consumption – agriculture [GJ] GDP [current prices, million EUR, PPS]
	E2	Energy import dependency (%)	

(Continued)

Table 1. (*Continued*)

	Abbreviation	Derived indicator	Source indicators
Environmental and natural resources pillar	N1	Share of fossil fuels in gross inland energy consumption (%)	Gross inland energy consumption [TJ] Gross inland consumption of fossil fuels [TJ]
	N2	Share of renewable energy coming from naturally replenished resources in gross inland consumption (%)	Hydro gross inland consumption [TJ] Geothermal gross inland consumption [TJ] Wind gross inland consumption [TJ] Solar thermal gross inland consumption [TJ] Solar photovoltaic gross inland consumption [TJ] Tide, wave, ocean gross inland consumption [TJ] Ambient heat (heat pumps) gross inland consumption [TJ] Gross available energy [TJ]
	N3	Greenhouse gas emission per capita (tons per capita)	CO_2 equivalent emission [thousand tons] Population [capita]
	N4	CO_2 equivalent emission per GDP [ton CO_2 equivalent/million EUR, PPS]	CO_2 equivalent emission [thousand tons] GDP [current prices, million EUR, PPS]

European Union has started to pay high attention to these issues in the last few years emphasizing that the technological energy transition has to contribute to the strengthening of democracy and public participation (this concept is called energy democracy). The prices are also significant, because it affects the energy expenditures to overall household income and finally the well-being. Electricity consumption is crucially important due to the electrification, growing e-mobility, changing habits. This indicator is also core element of the European energy and environmental policies; however, it has controversial impacts on sustainable energy transition. On the one hand, the higher number may indicate more electric and electronic appliances, but probably they are more efficient. On the other hand, it represents a higher quality energy source and it may substantially contribute to minimize the air emissions.

The economic pillar is represented by the energy intensity of the productive sectors and by the energy dependency. In case of the previous one, the focus is on the economic sectors which create added value and it serves as a marker of overall energy productivity of the economies. The energy import dependency highlights the importance of security issues, especially during the current energy shortages worldwide (even in Europe).

The key for the clean energy transition is the shift from the fossil fuel consumption toward the renewables. However, the share of renewable energy coming from naturally replenished resources may represent better the clean energy sources than the traditional biomass. The other important aspect of the environmental pillar is the emission per capita and the emission intensity of the economy, recognizing the clear link between climate change and the greenhouse gases.

In selected data the 'per capita' approach is preferred (in case of emission per capita and energy use per capita). We follow O'Neill et al. (2018) and Bithas and Kalimeris (2013) who argue this approach highlights that the at the end of the supply chain we can find human beings and it represents a world where the resources are distributed equally.

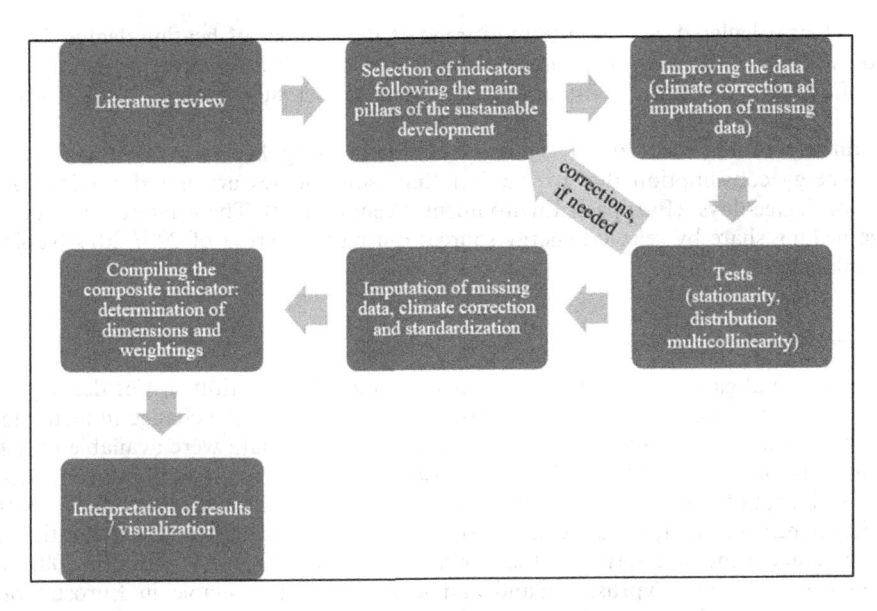

Figure 1.   Research model.

Building the sustainable energy performance index the main steps suggested by OECD, European Union, and Joint Research Centre - European Commission (2008) are followed. After the solid theoretical background, we put a strong emphasis on the selection of indicators including the imputation of missing data. The overall structure of the dataset was analyzed through correlation analysis, stationarity and normality tests. Standardization was carried out to make comparable the variables with different units. Respecting the main dimensions of the theory of sustainable development the weighting factors was determined and the composite indicator was calculated. Hereinafter these main steps (Figure 1) are described in detail.

3.1   Climate correction

The S1 indicators are climate corrected, so the heating degree days are used to normalise the residential electricity consumption.

In making these calculations, the following formula was applied (similarly to Enerdata and Eurostat):

$$E = E_{wc} * 1/(1 - K * (1 - DD/DD_n))\qquad(1)$$

and

$$K = k * a\qquad(2)$$

where
E = climate-corrected energy indicator;
E_{wc} = energy indicator;
K = corrected heating share for normal year;

k = heating share for normal year;
a = share of heating dependent on degree days (i.e. 90%);
DD = heating degree days; and
DD_n = average number of heating degree days for the 25-year period of 1980–2004.

The DD_n is calculated as a long-term average of the number of heating degree days over a period of time in the past. The number of years taken into account depends on the data source; Eurostat takes into consideration 25 years (i.e. 1980–2004) (ODYSSEE-MURE, 2021).

Introduction of a is necessary. The climate correction is applied only to 90% of the space heating energy consumption due to the fact that 'some losses are not dependent on the number of degree-days' (European Environment Agency, 2012). The k reference value is the average heating share by selected energy sources during the period of 2007-2019 (subject to data availability).

3.2 Imputation of missing data

There were several gaps in the raw data set that needed to be substituted. For dealing with it case deletion and single imputation were also applied. Because of the change in methodology within the source database regarding energy prices, consistent data were available only from 2007 onwards for SET2 and SET3. For this reason, 2007 was chosen as the starting year for the time series data for all SET indicators. In cases where there was only one value missing for a specific country and year, it was replaced with the average derived from the quantities of the next three years in the time series for that country (S2 – Italy 2007, S4 – Croatia 2007-2009). Regarding S3, data for Cyprus, Finland and Malta weren't available in Eurostat or the national statistical institutes' databases. For these countries, the time series were replaced with the EU average values for each year to avoid change in statistical parameters. In addition, natural gas price data was also missing for Greece from 2007 to 2011. The missing values were calculated using a harmonized index of consumer prices for gas in Greece obtained from FRED (2021), fuel price obtained from the Heat Roadmap Europe strategy (Duić et al., 2017) and auxiliary data from Eurostat.

3.3 Stationary analysis

The analysis requires that the variables should be stationary. A time series is said to be stationary if both its mean and its variance (amplitude) remain constant through time (Maddala, 2004; Wadud et al., 2007). Most time series (the levels of the time series) are not stationary, but the first differences will be. "If the first differences of the series are stationarity we say that the series are integrated of order 1 or I(1)." (Ramanathan, 2003, p. 492). One of the most popular stationarity tests was developed by D.A. Dickey and W.A. Fuller and it is called the augmented Dickey-Fuller test:

$$\Delta Y_t \alpha + \lambda Y_{t-1} + \sum_{j=1}^{\rho} \theta_i \Delta Y_{t-j} + u_t \tag{3}$$

where Y_t is the economic variable in time period t, $\Delta Y_{t-1} = Y_{t-1} - Y_{t-2}$ and u_t is the residual term.

The null hypothesis is that $\lambda = 0$ (or $\rho = 1$); if we reject it, we can state that the series is stationary. We utilized the DF-GLS and the KPSS test worked out by Kwiatkowski to confirm the stationarity. According to Adkins, these tests have significantly greater power than the previous version of the ADF test. "Consequently, it is not unusual for this test to reject the null hypothesis of non-stationarity when the usual augmented Dickey-Fuller test does not." (Adkins, 2014, p. 288)

3.4 *Standardization*

Standardization of the values is necessary in order to ensure the comparability of the indicators with different units of measurement and scaling. A method to do so is z-transformation, which converts all indicator values to standardized values with a mean of zero and a standard deviation of one. Its advantage is that it takes the heterogeneity of the units into account within the group and provides metric information. In addition, this transformation significantly increases the indicator's sensitivity to changes that occur. The method is widely used when data have different scaling/units of measurement and the aim is the comparability or the aggregation of individual components. The method is based on a linear transformation of the data. The STD value for indicator i is calculated as follows (IMD, 2017, p. 8; Nagy et al., 2021, p. 36).

$$(STD \ value)_i = \frac{x - \bar{x}}{S} \qquad (4)$$

where x is the original value, $\bar{x}$ is the average value of all the economies and S is the standard deviation.

The standard deviation is calculated using the following formula (IMD, 2017, p. 7):

$$S = \sqrt{\frac{\sum^{(x-\bar{x})^2}}{N}} \qquad (5)$$

where x is the original value, $\bar{x}$ is the average value of all the economies, N is the number of economies.

The main advantages of this method are:

- it allows aggregation of different sets of data (like kg, %, m^2) while retaining the original relationships,
- it does not cause data loss or distortion.

4 RESULTS

After the climate correction and the imputation of the missing data we built up a solid indicator set. As a next step the stationary analysis was carried out. First, the results of N3 and N4 show some problems. According to the ADF test the series is integrated, however the ADF-GLS test and the KPSS test (p-value has to be above 0.1) do not indicate such a problem in these cases.

Table 2. Analysis of the stationarity with augmented Dickey-Fuller, DF-GLS, and KPSS tests.

Variable	ADF test H_0: the series is integrated H_1: the series is (trend) stationary	ADF-GLS test H_0: the series is integrated H_1: the series is (trend) stationary	KPSS test H_0: the series is (trend) stationary H_1: the series is integrated	Stationarity
S1	I(1) Logit test: t(139) = -13.0491 [0.0000]	I(1) Logit test: t(139) = -7.1024 [0.0000]	I(0) test = 0.120252, p-value > .10	I(1)
S2	I(0) Logit test: t(139) = -4.50775 [0.0000]	I(0) Logit test: t(139) = -7.22272 [0.0000]	I(1) test = 0.135801, p-value > .10	I(0)
S3	I(0) Logit test: t(139) = -1.67907 [0.0477]	I(0) Logit test: t(139) = -4.37707 [0.0000]	I(1) test = 0.216118, p-value > .10	I(0)
S4	I(0) Logit test: t(139) = -2.86663 [0.0024]	I(0) Logit test: t(139) = -3.60441 [0.0002]	I(0) test = 0.129682, p-value > .10	I(0)

(Continued)

Table 2. *(Continued)*

Variable	ADF test H$_0$: the series is integrated H$_1$: the series is (trend) stationary	ADF-GLS test H$_0$: the series is integrated H$_1$: the series is (trend) stationary	KPSS test H$_0$: the series is (trend) stationary H$_1$: the series is integrated	Stationarity
E1	I(1) Logit test: t(139) = -14.3463 [0.0000]	I(0) Logit test: t(139) = -3.24549 [0.0007]	I(1) test = 0.129091, p-value > .10	I(1)
E2	I(0) Logit test: t(139) = -9.77277 [0.0000]	I(1) Logit test: t(139) = -12.3599 [0.0000]	I(1) test = 0.137348, p-value > .10	I(1)
N1	I(1)Logit test: t(139) = -12.0452 [0.0000]	I(0) Logit test: t(139) = -1.98281 [0.0247]	I(1) test = 0.13553, p-value > .10	I(1)
N2	I(1) Logit test: t(139) = -12.3047 [0.0000]	I(0) Logit test: t(139) = -2.68673 [0.0040]	I(1) test = 0.189084, p-value > .10	I(1)
N3	-	I(1) Logit test: t(139) = -3.43729 [0.0004]	I(1) test = 0.175102, p-value > .10	I(1)
N4	-	I(1) Logit test: t(139) = -4.08727 [0.0000]	I(1) test = 0.165817, p-value > .10	I(1)

Where: I(0) – zero order integrated time series; I(1) – first order integrated time series; the value in [] is level of significance

The normality and multicollinearity tests confirm the problem around N3 and N4. Additionally, we compile a heat map (Figure 2) for a final check. It clearly shows that the correlation between N3, N4 and other indicators is moderate.

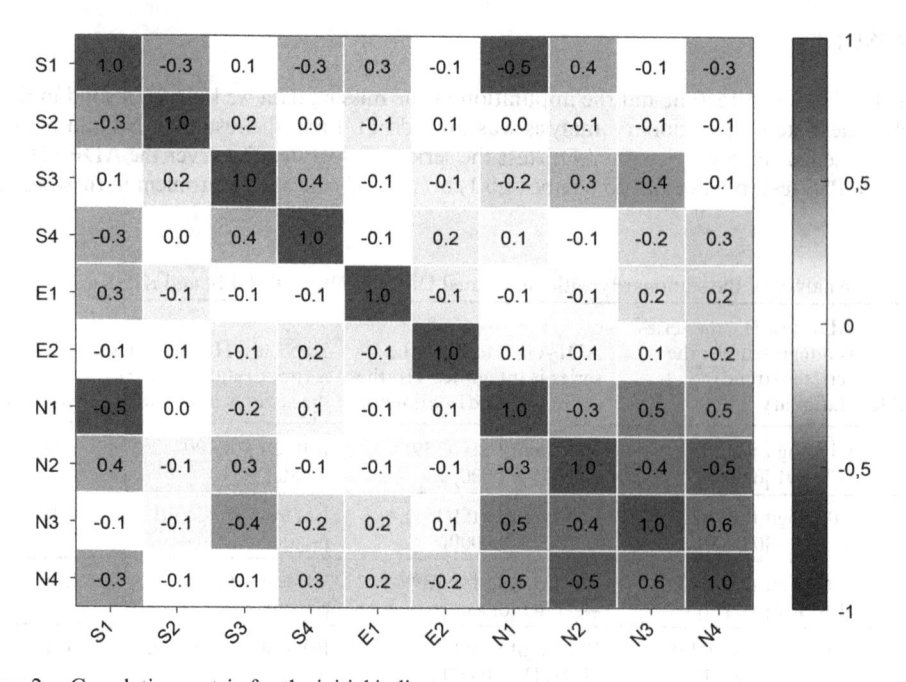

Figure 2. Correlation matrix for the initial indicator set.

Based on these results the N3 and N4 are left and the final indicator set is presented by Table 3.

Table 3.   Indicator set.

Pillars	Abbreviation	Indicator
Social and human pillar	*SET1*	Climate corrected electricity consumption per capita in the household sector [MWh per capita] – climate corrected
	SET2	Electricity price [EUR, PPP/kWh] (Band-DC (Medium): annual consumption between 2 500 and 5 000 kWh)
	SET3	Natural gas price [EUR, PPP/GJ] (Band D2: 20 GJ < Consumption < 200 GJ)
	SET4	Percentage of population affected by energy poverty [%]
Economic pillar	*SET5*	Final energy consumption (productive sectors) per GDP [GJ/million EUR]
	SET6	Energy import dependency [%]
Environmental and natural resources pillar	*SET7*	Share of fossil fuels in gross inland energy consumption (%)
	SET8	Share of renewable energy coming from naturally replenished resources in gross inland consumption (%)

The correlation matrix (Figure 3) is compiled again, and does not show any serious problem in the final indicator set. Finally, the indicators were standardized to meet the comparability requirement.

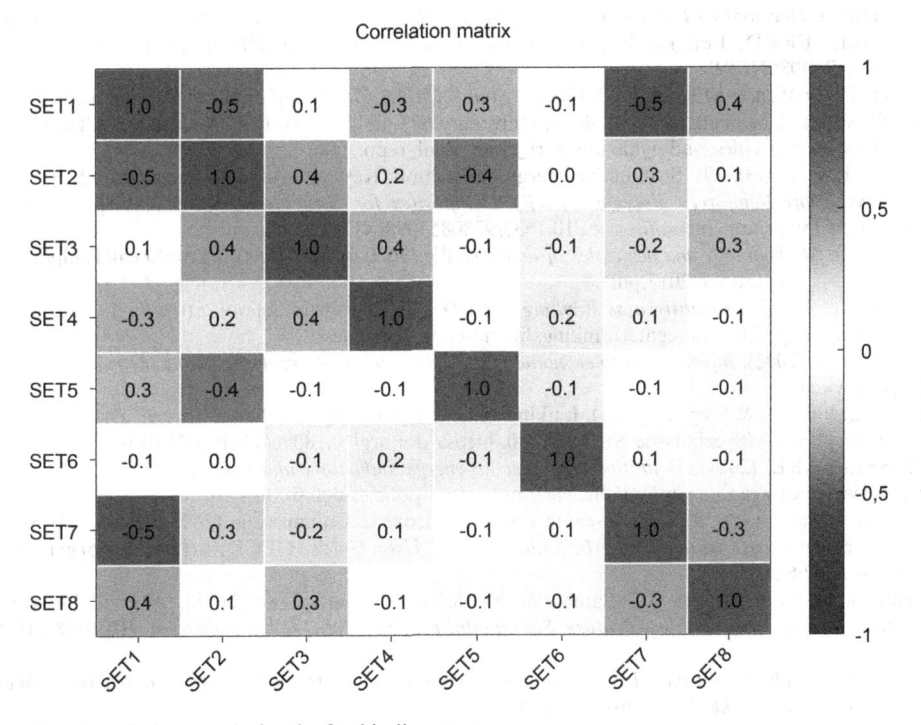

Figure 3.   Correlation matrix for the final indicator set.

5 CONCLUSION

In this paper we showed the procedure of building an indicator set. We followed the main pillars of the theory of sustainable development, such as its social, economic and environmental dimensions. The SDG7 and SDG13 were the starting point for the indicator selection. Our main aim was to collect data that are eligible to develop new indicators to measure the clean energy transition. The basic principles were the coverage and significance, availability and reliability, representativeness and comparability. The initial indicator set met these requirements. However, we had to cope with the problem of missing values and climate distortion. To avoid that, we carried out the imputation of missing data and we did the climate correction. As a result of the statistical tests (normality diagnostics, stationarity and multicollinearity) some indicators dropped out. The tests were done again without indicating any problems. Finally, an indicator list was created and we can move to the next step of the research to calculate the composite index (sustainable energy transition index).

REFERENCES

Adkins, L. C. (2014). *Using gretl for Principles of Econometrics, 4th Edition Version 1.041*. Oklahoma State University. http://www.learneconometrics.com/gretl/using_gretl_for_POE4.pdf

Bithas, K., & Kalimeris, P. (2013). Re-estimating the decoupling effect: Is there an actual transition towards a less energy-intensive economy? *Energy, 51*, 78–84. https://doi.org/10.1016/j.energy.2012.11.033

Duić, N., Štefanić, N., Lulić, Z., Krajačić, G., Pukšec, T., & Novosel, T. (2017). *Heat Roadmap Europe. EU28 fuel prices for 2015, 2030 and 2050. Deliverable 6.1: Future fuel price review*. (Ref. Ares(2017) 5872522-30/11/201;HeatRoadmapEU, p. 40). https://heatroadmap.eu/wp-content/uploads/2020/01/HRE4_D6.1-Future-fuel-price-review.pdf

European Environment Agency. (2012). *Influence of climate on household energy consumption per dwelling* [Figure]. https://www.eea.europa.eu/data-and-maps/figures/influence-of-climate-on-households-2

Eurostat. (2021). *Database—Eurostat*. https://ec.europa.eu/eurostat/data/database

Finszter, G., & Sabjanics, I. (2018). *Security challenges in the 21st century*. Dialóg Campus.

FRED. (2021). *Harmonized Index of Consumer Prices: Gas for Greece*. FRED, Federal Reserve Bank of St. Louis; FRED, Federal Reserve Bank of St. Louis. https://fred.stlouisfed.org/series/CP0452GRM086NEST

Giffinger, R., & Pichler-Milanovic, N. (2007). *Smart Cities: Ranking of European Medium-Sized Cities* (p. 28). Vienna University of Technology, University of Ljubljana and Delft University of Technology. http://www.smart-cities.eu/download/smart_cities_final_report.pdf

Hollaway, L. C. (2013). 19 - Sustainable energy production: Key material requirements. In J. Bai (Ed.), *Advanced Fibre-Reinforced Polymer (FRP) Composites for Structural Applications* (pp. 705–736). Woodhead Publishing. https://doi.org/10.1533/9780857098641.4.705

IMD. (2017). *Methodology and principles of analysis*. file:///C:/Users/szept/AppData/Local/Temp/methodology-and-principles-wcc-2017.pdf

IMD. (2021). *World Competitiveness Rankings—IMD*. IMD Business School. https://www.imd.org/centers/world-competitiveness-center/rankings/world-competitiveness/

Maddala, G. S. (2004). *Introduction to econometric (in Hungarian: Bevezetés az ökonometriába)*. Nemzeti Tankönyvkiadó.

Nagy, Z., Szendi, D., & Szép, T. (2021). Linking smart city concepts to urban resilience. *Theory, Methodology, Practice, 17* (SpecialIssue Nr. 1), 31–40. https://doi.org/10.18096/TMP.2021.01.04

ODYSSEE-MURE. (2021). *Definitions for specific energy indicators and policies | ODYSSEE-MURE*. https://www.odyssee-mure.eu/faq/efficiency-indicators-policies-definitions/

OECD, European Union, & Joint Research Centre - European Commission. (2008). *Handbook on Constructing Composite Indicators: Methodology and User Guide*. OECD. https://doi.org/10.1787/9789264043466-en

O'Neill, D. W., Fanning, A. L., Lamb, W. F., & Steinberger, J. K. (2018). A good life for all within planetary boundaries. *Nature Sustainability, 1*(2), 88–95. https://doi.org/10.1038/s41893-018-0021-4

Ramanathan, R. (2003). *Introduction to econometric with applications (in Hungarian: Bevezetés az ökonometriába alkalmazásokkal)*. Publisher Panem.

Sightsavers. (2017, September 25). Global Goals | Policy and advocacy. *Sightsavers*. https://www.sightsa vers.org/policy-and-advocacy/global-goals/

Texas Archival Resource Online, R. E. (2021). *Guide to the Richard Smalley papers, 1943-2007, bulk 1990-2005 MS 490*. Rice University Fondren. https://legacy.lib.utexas.edu/taro/ricewrc/00058/rice-00058.html

Transparency International. (2021). *2020—CPI*. Transparency.Org.https://www.transparency.org/en/cpi/2020

UN. (2015). *Transforming our world: The 2030 Agenda for Sustainable Development*. https://documents-dds-ny.un.org/doc/UNDOC/GEN/N15/291/89/PDF/N1529189.pdf?OpenElement.

Wadud, Z., Graham, D. J., & Noland, R. B. (2007). A cointegration analysis of gasoline demand in the United States. *Applied Economics*, *41*(26), 3327–3336.

Challenges for universities in the aspect of the growing importance of the sustainable development and circular economy

M. Sukiennik

AGH University of Science and Technology, Krakow, Poland

ABSTRACT: The article discusses issues related to the tasks faced by universities in the aspect of broadly understood environmental education. The terms that have become a permanent element in the dictionaries of everyday life, both scientific and public institutions, enterprises, and more and more often the wider society (mainly thanks to the mass media) are the following: clean production, sustainable development, circular economy, CSR, ESG, zero strategy waste, etc. Their functioning in life should be consolidated and developed, and universities are assigned a special role in this respect. The publication also indicates the results of surveys showing how awareness of the trained students in the field of the raw materials industry and sustainable development is increasing.

1 INTRODUCTION

1.1 *Circular Economy as one of the key trends in the world*

One of the more essential concepts that evaluate the actions of actors is the ESG criterion. ESG is derived from the names: Environment, Social, Governance, and is an essential indicator of how socially responsible entities are. With corporate social responsibility now a reality, the need to integrate it into organisational culture seems to be a mere formality. The new reality of business manifests itself in many levels of actors. The requirements and desire to move towards Industry 4.0, ESG standards, the European Green Deal, and what took the whole world by surprise, the SARS epidemic - COV19 are forcing changes in management processes and the organisation of companies in every industry (Sukiennik, Kaputsta & Bąk, 2020).

Nowadays, there is much talk in the EU member states, but not also around the world, about the European Commission introducing the European Green Deal (European Commission, 2019). It is a kind of European roadmap that provides directions and guidelines for European countries to become climate-neutral by 2050. The European Green Deal involves, among other things, the provision of clean, affordable and secure energy, the mobilisation of the industry for a transparent Circular Economy and the pursuit of a zero non-toxic environment. The decarbonisation and climate-resilient future scenarios put forward by the European Green Deal seem feasible, as many analyses and projections confirm an increase in the share of renewables in energy production to two-thirds within thirty years (Bloomberg 2020).

Clean production, sustainable development, Circular Economy, CSR, ESG, zero waste, etc., are terms that have become part of the everyday vocabulary of scientific and public institutions, companies and, increasingly, the general public (mainly, due to the mass media). Circular Economy is a term that enters into economic life through legislation (formal and informal), but it is also a concept that is widely communicated as an idea of perfect economic life.

The crucial aspects of the Circular Economy are defined as the following postulates (Sukiennik et al. 2021):

DOI: 10.1201/9781003259954-3

1. Maximum extraction with minimum wastage. Industrial reuse and recycling, i.e. moving towards the complete closure of material cycles,
2. The introduction of the assessments of the Circular Economy in the value chain, which includes both suppliers and customers of a specific product and is the basis for creating cyclicality and new business models, which should be based on cooperation and responsibility between actors.
3. Seeking a solution that contributes to economic development while minimising environmental impact. The action requires policy support and continuous promotion of new economic and environmental methods.
4. The Circular Economy linked to innovation and new environmentally friendly technologies.

The Circular Economy is the future of world economies. It is slowly entering the activities of economic entities, sometimes step by step, sometimes immediately holistically in every area of their functioning. However, for this philosophy to be fully and successfully implemented in management structures, two factors are needed:

1. The conviction and implemented thinking of both management and staff that such a philosophy is needed and must be applied,
2. Raise awareness and convince the public that they can and should require economic operators to act according to this philosophy.

In my opinion, in order to achieve this, a special role for universities (but also for the whole education system) is needed, which will be explained in the following chapters.

1.2 *Tasks and objectives of higher education institutions*

The role of universities in the social and economic life of any country is of vital importance. The defined missions and objectives enshrined in the statutes are generally consistent and similar to each other, regardless of the adopted direction of the university's scientific activity. The new challenges for higher education related to the development of the knowledge economy have been overlaid with changes resulting from the massification of higher education and changes in young people's attitudes, values, and aspirations. In the case of Poland, according to the relevant ministry, there was a nearly fivefold increase in the number of students between 1990 and 2005 (MNiSW, 2021).The system change allowed for the creation of non-public schools alongside public universities. The range of courses on offer has also expanded rapidly, with new courses and specialisations being created (and still being created). After Poland opened up politically and economically to Western countries, especially the countries of the European Union, there has been a marked increase in contacts between academic staff and students through international programmes such as Erasmus. In contacts, these changes have shaped the educational market and the competition between schools,

Knowledge and education are increasingly becoming instrumental values in societies, so their importance is undeniable. For years, the Polish tradition and practice of academic education served to socialise the intelligentsia into a social category. The changes that have taken place in the last twenty-five years have meant that not only has the relationship between education and the Economy - and especially the labour market - changed and the number of university graduates increased, but also the expectations of employers and graduates have changed. These changes have caused that in the centre of students' interests, which are connected with the motives for undertaking studies, there is now professional work, which gives rise not only to different expectations towards universities than before but above all to the loss by universities to employers of the role of the "significant other". The above also results from the massification of higher education has meant that the selection functions of higher education have been severely curtailed. (Górski, 2018)

Decarbonisation, green deal, sustainability, CSR, CO_2 emissions, ecology - these terms have been significantly influencing the functioning of the raw materials industry over the last few years, but also the industry as a whole, and finally, noticeably, everyone's life. CSR, i.e., corporate social responsibility, is a trend that strongly correlates industrial activity and caring for people, society. The genesis of social responsibility, according to J.J. McMillan, lies in people's lack of interest in caring for others. So now this role is taken over by organisations, but also by universities. The increasing prevalence of the phenomenon is precisely due to strong economic development, the growth of enterprises, institutions, etc. Along with the progress of civilisation and the Economy, the idea of social responsibility has been developing.

The vision of complete, even comprehensive responsibility of the organisation for its actions seems to be gaining ground. Universities play an essential role in implementing and disseminating the idea of Corporate Social Responsibility, and by introducing these issues to the study programme, they raise the awareness of future social and economic leaders. An important role is also played by the constantly growing number of consultants, legal regulations or international activities promoting socially responsible business and the practice of social reporting.

The aim of the article is to show that universities have a kind of social license and social expectations regarding the creation and implementation of trends in social and economic life. The example of a technical university (AGH UST, Kraków) shows that the implementation of international programs increases awareness and knowledge of contemporary environmental trends, including circular economy and sustainable development.

2 ENVIRONMENTAL EDUCATION

Education is a system of learning, acquiring attitudes, skills and knowledge. Formal and informal education can be provided. Formal education is education provided in educational establishments such as kindergartens, schools, and universities and delivered through professional training according to the core curriculum (...) Non-formal education, on the other hand, lasts throughout the life of a person, starts at birth. Its first source is the family and immediate environment. Informal education is provided by institutions, organisations, foundations, non-governmental and governmental associations through campaigns and social actions. Nowadays, the most substantial source of informal education is the media (Buchcic 2009).

Ecological education is also defined as a psychological and pedagogical process of influencing people in order to shape their ecological awareness (Dobrzańska et al. 2008).

The above definitions of environmental education are close to what can be called sustainable development education, or more "timely" - Circular Economy education. When looking at history, several milestones in the field of environmental education can be identified. Figure 1 shows the key moments, crucial in this respect, in the world.

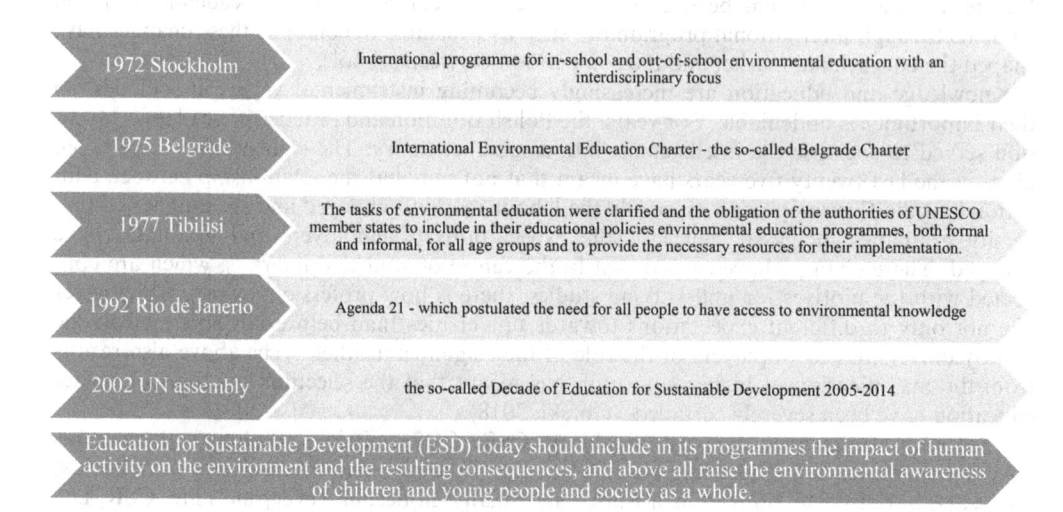

Figure 1. The key moment of environmental education.

After 2002, when the UN Assembly defined the so-called Decade of Education for Sustainable Development, there are no longer critical moments in the world related to strengthening the importance of this type of education. However, this does not mean that its role is not emphasised - on the contrary, it has become an immanent feature of every educational system in the world.

The relevance of considering the importance of environmental education is undeniable. It seems that it is possible to identify a few universal statements that are valid for any country, regardless of its level of development or technological advancement.

Environmental education is a very complex process and should be carried out with the active participation of the whole community. This process implies the involvement of all actors in countries, from educational actors to the organs of government, to economic actors in public awareness and education. Obviously, it is required to adopt the appropriate tools to the level of the learner.

Education should be based on the continuous acquisition of knowledge in various fields of science and life, encompassing all knowledge about the environment and the social and economic development of the country and the world. This ties in firmly with the idea of sustainability and CSR or ESG, which is dynamically entering economic life.

The paramount goal should be to educate future generations in a climate of respect for the environment and demonstrate a thorough understanding of sustainable development

Education for sustainable development must be an integral part of general education, which (suitably adapted to the age of the children) should already begin at pre-school age. However, it should not be presented as an "unpleasant obligation" (e.g. the need to separate waste) but as a principle of social life. Unfortunately, this requires a mental change, which is not an easy thing to do.

Education for sustainable development should also be cultivated in the area of adult development as part of the concept of lifelong learning. This kind of education is where a significant role can be played by universities, which already shape adult people, but also society at large (through their prestige and the esteem they hold).

3 CHALLENGES FOR UNIVERSITIES IN THE ASPECT OF THE GROWING IMPORTANCE OF THE CIRCULAR ECONOMY

The challenges faced by universities can be divided into many categories. Their primary task is higher education and research.

It has also long been known that universities are institutions with a high level of trust from the public. Academic staff are treated with respect, both by society and by institutions and market players. In addition to a certain sense of the importance of their work, academics even have an obligation to society to deepen and then pass on knowledge, thereby shaping the level of society. This ethical and moral duty is definitely of great importance. In addition, an unwritten rule is placed before universities to shape and support (or negate) social attitudes. Figure 2 presents the interactions of the crucial areas.

Global trends (in the case of sustainable development or Circular Economy, we can even talk about megatrends) influence broadly-understood law. Whether global, organisational, international, national, or local law is enacted according to legislation and affects a broad audience. This right should be and is respected and adhered to by universities. Moreover, it is taught and interpreted at these universities. The universities teach how to implement and apply the regulations in professional and everyday life. The audience for this university education is divided into two parts. The first group is students, the primary target group of universities. During the didactic process, whether

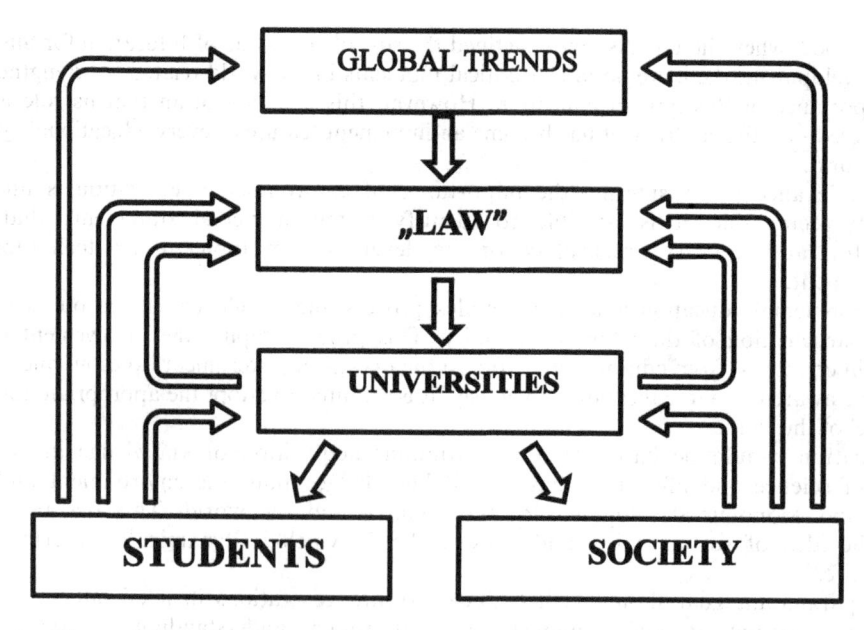

Figure 2. The crucial areas of interactions between global trends and universities.

formal during classes or informal, through participation in academic life (study circles, events, celebrations or traditions maintained), students observe, learn about, and implement the trends translated through the law into their world. The second group that universities reach out to is the wider society. Here, direct contact, and thus the message, is somewhat more difficult, but the current world offers opportunities to reach out to the public. Open access research articles, open lectures, universities of the third age, organised Researchers' Nights, open days, and community outreach activities are tools with which universities can, and should, shape global trends, including environmental education.

The pattern also works the other way round - students, through their attitudes, beliefs or actions, can influence their home universities in terms of modification or change of the content taught. Similarly, society and social pressures can cause universities to change their operations. The stronger force is in the university and legal relationship. This relationship has existed for a long time - scientific centres are opinion leaders, their reputation guarantees the correctness and reliability of legal provisions. Another pathway is law and trends - here again, there can be coupling - established law can change or establish trends that will have a broad reach.

It is also worth noting that both students, society and universities can influence the law separately, but also trends. According to the assumption of the synergy effect, if all these actors shared common goals and objectives, they would have tremendous clout, both in relation to legislation and emerging trends.

Another important point according to which universities should orient themselves is to act according to the Deming cycle principle (Figure 3). According to the concept, combining change with the Deming cycle, continuous improvement occurs in several logically consecutive stages. These are planning, executing, checking and acting (also understood as improving). Plan - Do - Check - Act, hence the cycle is also called the PDCA cycle).

The Deming cycle is currently the primary form of shaping activities related to introducing changes, innovations or increasing the effectiveness of the operation. Therefore, the Deming cycle should be used in cases of transformations or changes in the organisational culture of business entities.

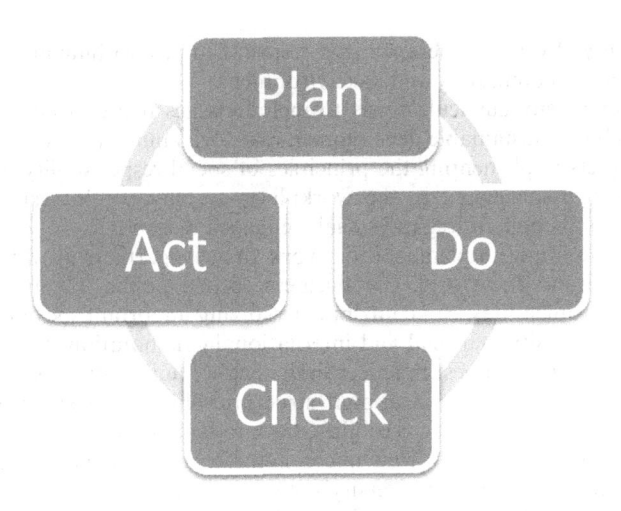

Figure 3. The PDCA cycle.

4 THE AGH UNIVERSITY OF SCIENCE AND TECHNOLOGY IS AN EXAMPLE OF A SOCIALLY RESPONSIBLE UNIVERSITY

The AGH University of Science and Technology in Kraków is a university that primarily educates engineers in many different fields, but also humanists (as befits a university). According to the Deming cycle, it is in continuous improvement change. The university is changing to meet the demands of the world and the expectations of students.

The history of the AGH University of Science and Technology in Krakow dates back to 1912, when a group of outstanding engineers and mining activists, led by Jan Zarański, initiated the process of applying for a consent to establish a school of higher education that would educate mining engineers in Krakow. The endeavours were successful, and in 1913 the Ministry of Public Work in Vienna appointed the Organizing Committee of the Mining Academy, chaired by Professor Józef Morozewicz. By force of a Supreme Order issued by Emperor Francis Joseph on 31st May 1913, the establishment of the Mining Academy in Krakow was approved. The outbreak of World War I prevented the Academy from beginning its activity in 1914. When Poland regained its independence in 1918, the Organising Committee recommenced its work, and on 8th April 1919, the Council of Ministers passed a resolution to establish and open the Mining Academy in Krakow. The first professors were nominated by Józef Piłsudski, Chief of State, on 1st May 1919. On 20th October 1919, Marshal Józef Piłsudski, Head of State, inaugurated the Mining Academy in the main hall of the Jagiellonian University. (www.agh.edu.p)]

The AGH University of Science and Technology is a technical university, however, which cares a great deal about implementing the basic principles of sustainable development and raising awareness and implementing its fundamental principles in everyday life. Proof of this fact is the University's Declaration of Social Responsibility, to which nearly 100 Polish universities are its signatories.

It defines four major university functions with regard to cultivation of academic values, implementation of projects and research programmes pivotal for support of social responsibility initiatives, work organisation and fostering the collaboration with stakeholders. University's social responsibility principlesSignatories of the University Social Responsibility Declaration undertake to (University social responsibility report of AGH UST):

1. Cultivate academic values, such as those outlined in the "Code of Ethics for Researchers", especially diligence, objectivity, freedom, accountability, and transparency.
2. Shape the social and civic attitudes of future elites that promote community building, creativity, openness, and communication, as well as social sensitivity and a culture of work.

3. Promote equality, diversity, tolerance, and respect and protect human rights in relation to the entire academic community and its environment.
4. Broaden the university curricula so as to include issues related to ethics and corporate social responsibility, sustainable development and social innovations.
5. Carry out projects implementing the principles of social responsibility, in particular concerning diversity management in the workplace, employee volunteering, promotion of ethics, intersectoral cooperation and socially engaged marketing.
6. Undertake research and implementation work that, in partnership with other academic centers from around the world, the business sector, public administration and non-governmental organizations, can contribute to solving important social problems.
7. Develop inter-university, national and international collaborations that enable the adaptation and enhancement of best practices in the field of university's social responsibility.
8. Maintain the university's organizational structure while establishing a foundation for management based on social responsibility, both in strategic documents and the resulting activities that contribute to the academic community's comprehensive development and effective implementation of the university's mission.
9. Ensure transparency of the activities of the university through, among other things, results measurement, promotion and dissemination of accomplishments, and indication of the of person or team to coordinate these activities.
10. Conduct operations in a way that minimizes the negative impact of activities carried out by the academic community and its stakeholders on the natural environment in all its dimensions.
11. Get engaged in a continuous stakeholder dialogue on the priorities of the university's social responsibility policy and disclose its results.

Adhere to the principles of ethics and responsibility in the process of teaching and research for the purpose of providing optimal conditions for stakeholders to benefit from the knowledge, intellectual capital and achievements of the university.

Thus the importance of the university mission is emphasised, demonstrating its commitment to promotion of social and civic attitudes among the future elite, supporting the development of the community and social sensitivity. The document emphasises the need to spread the idea of tolerance, equality and diversity and to incorporate the principles of respect and protection of human rights with regard to the entire academic community. Much attention is given to fostering the partnership between the university and business, enabling the development of research projects, which in turn, will lead to improvement of social and economic conditions.

In addition, all scientific research projects carried out in 2019-2020 have been categorised and assigned to the Sustainable Development Goals. Figure 4 presents the results of these analyses.

Sustainable Development Goals

1. End poverty in all its forms everywhere
2. End hunger, achieve food security and improved nutrition and promote sustainable agriculture
3. Ensure healthy lives and promote well-being for all at all ages
4. Ensure inclusive and equitable quality education and promote lifelong learning opportunities for all
5. Achieve gender equality and empower all women and girls
6. Ensure availability and sustainable management of water and sanitation for all
7. Ensure access to affordable, reliable, sustainable and modern energy for all
8. Promote sustained, inclusive and sustainable economic growth, full and productive employment and decent work for all
9. Build resilient infrastructure, promote inclusive and sustainable industrialization and foster innovation
10. Reduce inequality within and among countries
11. Make cities and human settlements inclusive, safe, resilient and sustainable
12. Ensure sustainable consumption and production patterns

13. Take urgent action to combat climate change and its impacts
14. Conserve and sustainably use the oceans, seas and marine reso-urces for sustainable development
15. Protect, restore and promote sustainable use of terrestrial eco-systems, sustainably manage forests, combat desertification, and halt and reverse land degradation and halt biodiversity loss
16. Promote peaceful and inclusive societies for sustainable deve-lopment, provide access to justice for all and build effective, ac-countable and inclusive institutions at all levels
17. Strengthen the means of implementation and revitalize the global partnership for sustain-able development

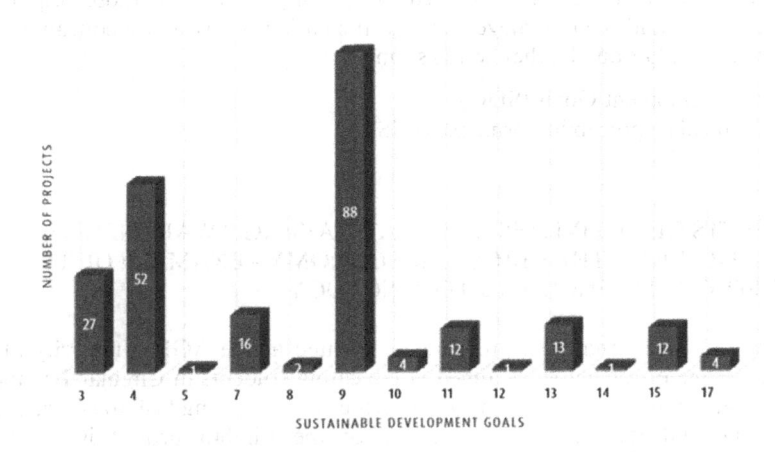

Figure 4. AGH-UST projects with sustainable development goals.

Nearly 40% of initiated projects are aligned with Goal 9 "Build resilient infrastructure, promote inclusive and sustainable industrialisation and foster innovation", which is a natural consequence of the fact that AGH UST is a technical university actively involved in practical implementations of projects, mostly in industrial plants. A large number of projects are aligned with Goal 4 "Ensure inclusive and equitable quality education and promote lifelong learning opportunities for all". Projects in the area of education are aimed to improve the quality of teaching, to create new courses and trainings addressed to employees, to support development of innovative syllabuses in compliance with the Polish Qualifications Framework. The first and foremost mission of the university is to provide education, hence the projects aimed at improvement of skills and competence of both internal and external stakeholders should be regarded as top priority. Elimination of un equal opportunities and providing access to education are of major importance too, hence 12% projects pursued at the AGH UST are aligned with Goal 3 "Ensure healthy lives and promote well-being for all, at all ages" (University social responsibility report of AGH UST):.

AGH UST has also launched numerous initiatives to meet the objectives of sustainable development and to promote environment protection and circular economy principles. As an environmentally-aware part of the ecosystem, the AGH UST is committed to engaging internal and external stakeholders in a range of activities for the climate. The strategic areas are defined which are of key importance in the context of climate changes and with an eye to build the society aware of their responsibility for future generations.

The areas that were studied were (University social responsibility report of AGH UST)::

1. Costs of waste treatment and waste disposal
2. Investment grants brought into operation in 2019 and 2020
3. Cost of preventive measures against environmental damage and of environmental protec-tion management

4. Total consumption of Energy from renewable sorces, fuel types
5. Reduction of Energy consumption as a direct effect of programmes aimed at environmental protection and Energy efficiency improvment
6. Environmental protecion expenditures
7. Greenhouse gas emissions
8. Number of usend reamsa of paper
9. Water consumption and the amount o generated waste

The described activities, apart from their value for the stakeholders, contribute to promoting socially responsible attitudes and good practices at the local, regional, national and international levels and foster strategic partnerships for the development of a sustainable future. These practices were identified and described by the originators and those responsible for their implementation, and then organized around thematic priority areas: educational, social, and environmental. Additionally, they were assigned to:

- Sustainable Development Goals (SDG);
- University's social responsibility principles (USR).

5 THE EFFECTS OF ACTIVITIES AIMED AT RAISING AWARENESS OF THE GROWING ROLE OF THE CIRCULAR ECONOMY - EXAMPLE OF THE AGH UNIVERSITY OF SCIENCE AND TECHNOLOGY

As part of the Limba international project implemented at the AGH University of Science and Technology, one of the activities aimed at educating students in Circular Economy, sustainable development and pro-environmental activities is an ongoing task to activate entrepreneurship among students. The main objective of the Limbra project is to strengthen entrepreneurship in the V4 countries in line with the recommendations of the "Green action plan for SMEs" (European Commission, 2014) in a way to meet the requirements of a Circular Economy ("Closing the loop - An EU action plan for the Circular Economy" - European Commission, 2015), and five selected AGH students are currently implementing their ideas for business entities in the raw materials industry in Poland. A list of projects is presented below (Figure 5), together with a brief description of each project. The students had a series of meetings with specialists who introduced them to the ins and outs of entrepreneurship, naturally including aspects of the Circular Economy.

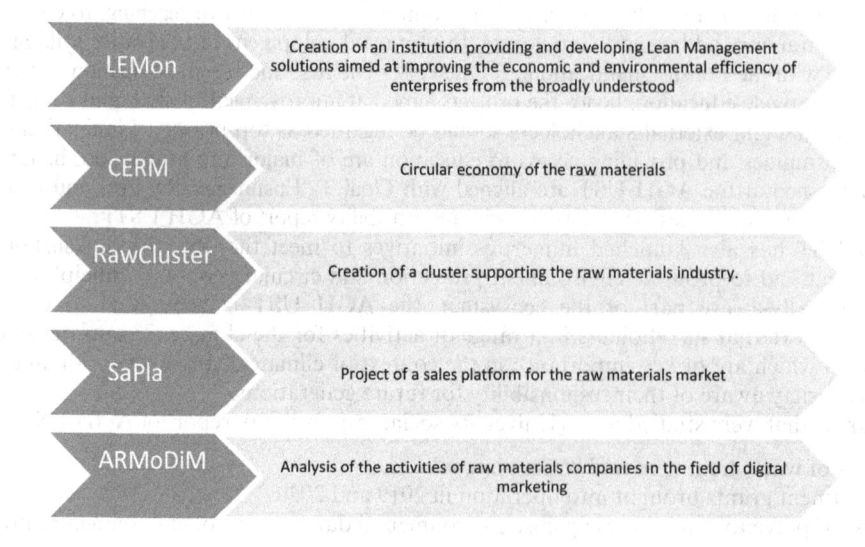

Figure 5. Students ideas for business entities in the raw materials industry.

Another activity that took place at the AGH University of Science and Technology as part of the project was summer school. The participants became acquainted with typical problems of the mining and raw materials industry in Poland and solved from the group of environmental, ecological activities. Before and after the lessons, a questionnaire (5-point scale) was administered, and one of the questions was about self-involvement in the topics of the school and absorption of knowledge and the following questions:

- How would you rate your level of knowledge about entrepreneurship in the resource industry area before summer school?
- How would you rate your level of knowledge about entrepreneurship in the raw materials industry after summer school?

Figure 6 presents the results of the responses - it is clear that the participants who described their activity as high also recorded high knowledge gain.

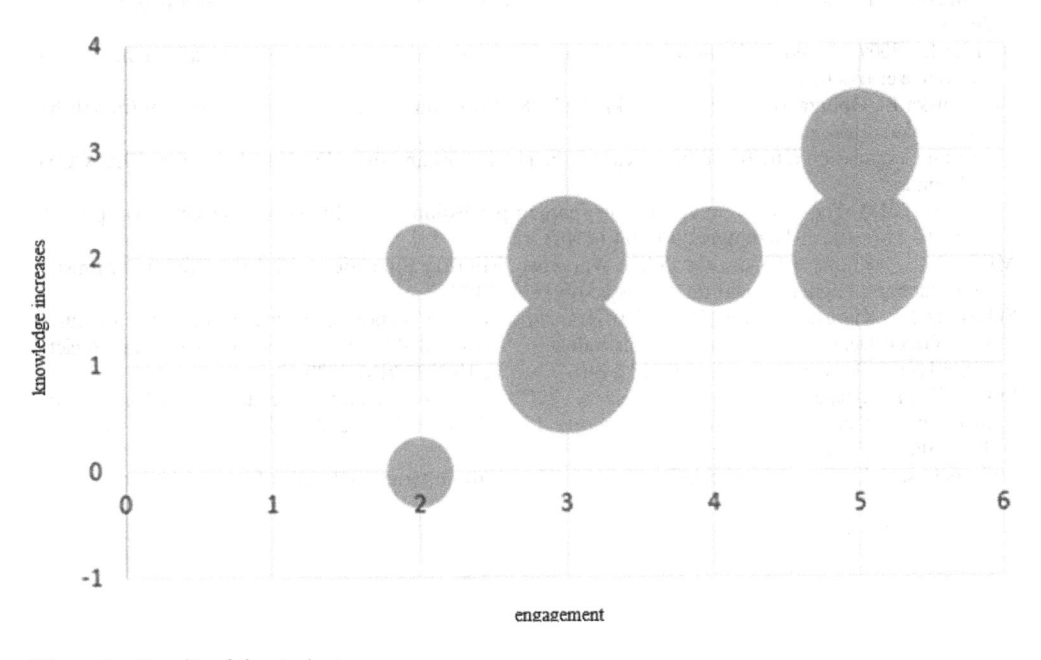

Figure 6.   Results of the students responses.

The research sample was small due to the size of the group (summer school included study for 25 students); however, even on such a small group, it can be seen that as engagement increases, knowledge increases. These results confirm the necessity of pro-environmental education at every level of education, also among adults.

6 SUMMARY

Higher education institutions operate on many levels: research, scientific and social. They are, in many cases, carriers and advocates of global trends, but they can and (and sometimes should) also shape these trends. Amongst essential universities' missions is to shape and implement pro-environmental attitudes and trends related to sustainable development. To sum up the above reflections, it can be noted that environmental education in universities should consist of:

- education aimed at introducing future graduates of all higher education institutions to environmental issues. The scope of this kind of education, its forms should be treated in a differentiated manner.
- preparing professionals for professional work in the field of environmental protection.
- organising postgraduate studies to supplement knowledge in the field of environmental protection.
- conducting informal environmental education through the organisation of open universities and lectures.
- other activities organised by universities (open activities)

REFERENCES

Bloomberg, New Energy Outlook (NEO) (2020). Available online: Bloomberg.com (accessed on 18/ 01/ 2021)

Buchcic E. (2009), Ecological education as a priority for the education of contemporary man, "Studia Ecologiae et Bioethicae" no. 7, p. 203

Dobrzańska B., Dobrzański G., Kiełczewski D. (2008). Protection of the natural environment (in polish). PWN, Warszawa

European Commission (2019). Communication on The European Green Deal, 11 December 2019, COM 640 Final

Górski P. (2018), The role of universities in shaping professionalism. Students' perspective (in polish), https://doi.org/10.25944/znmwse.2018.03.175183

MEiN, 2021. Szkolnictwo wyższe w Polsce Warszawa: Ministry Education and Science (earlier: Ministry of Science and Higher Education. (accessed on 11/ 10/2021)

Sukiennik M., Kapusta M., Bąk P., (2020). Transformation of corporate culture in the aspect of European Green Deal - Polish raw materials industry. Journal of the Polish Mineral Engineering Society ISSN 1640-4920. vol. 2 no. 2, s. 177–182, http://doi.org/10.29227/IM-2020-02-59

Sukiennik M., Zybała K., Fuksa D., Kęsek M., (2021). The role of universities in sustainable development and circular economy strategies. Energies ISSN 1996-1073. — 2021 vol. 14 iss. 17 art. no. 5365, 10.3390/en14175365

University social responsibility report of AGH UST. (2020) - internal materials of the university

Research on employee bonus systems in Polish enterprises

Magdalena Czernikiewicz & Katarzyna Styk
Faculty of Civil Engineering and Resource Management, AGH University of Science and Technology, Kraków, Poland

ABSTRACT: Nowadays, the only motivation for an employee to work efficiently is not salary. Modern companies are increasingly deciding to implement employee bonus systems. Unfortunately, it is not uncommon for these systems to not be transparent and easy for employees to interpret, which can be one source of conflict. The complexity and diversity of bonus systems in companies has become a topic of research undertaken by the Student Research Group "Management". The first step for the project team implementing the study was to review the literature and other similar studies. An original survey was then created and distributed to potential respondents.

Through the results of the survey, the project team was able to determine the effectiveness and often fairness of these employee bonus systems.

1 INTRODUCTION

Nowadays, in modern companies, employees of all levels - production workers, managers or team members - when taking a job pay attention not only to the amount of basic salary, but also to the bonuses. The amount and method of determining bonuses will affect employee motivation. A correct, efficient and transparent bonus system will have a positive impact on employee morale. However, a system that is not clear and fair can unfortunately cause conflict. Companies should therefore continually improve their employee bonus systems, streamline them in line with trends and communicate any changes to all stakeholders. If systems are not in place, you may want to consider introducing them, but first examine the needs of your employees.

The purpose of this article is to present the results of a survey conducted by the Student Research Group "Management" operating at the AGH University of Science and Technology in Krakow on employee bonus systems in Polish companies, which examined the principles of operation of the bonus system and employees' subjective evaluation of the functioning system.

This article describes briefly functioning systems of employee bonuses in Poland. Then the idea and assumptions of the research conducted by SRG "Management" were presented. Subsequently, the characteristics of the research group and the direct results of the two parts of the study, concerning the mentioned operating principles and the subjective evaluation, are presented.

2 FEW WORDS ABOUT EMPLOYEE BONUS SYSTEMS

A bonus is a component of current remuneration granted to an employee in addition to basic work, which is justified by the fulfilment of certain criteria. Bonuses belong to the so-called

DOI: 10.1201/9781003259954-4

moving remuneration, i. e. all elements of remuneration the amount of which changes in accordance with the adopted rules. Mobile pay also includes bonuses and allowances [Ciekanowski 2014, Krzemiński 2015]. The bonus itself is a component of remuneration dependent on the results obtained by an individual, a group of employees or the entire organization. However, bonus should not be treated as an element of salary, but as a motivational element for achieving additional effects or benefits for the organization [Kuc 1999]. There are many titles for awarding bonuses, and their choice depends on the management of the company, which by their introduction wants to achieve certain results. Bonus criteria should be defined as measurable effects of work, but above all they should be clear and understandable and accessible to the employee [Pawlak, Smoleń 2012; Manikowski 2021] . Such criteria include [Pawlak, Smoleń 2012]:

- labour productivity - a bonus for a certain productivity or increase in productivity,
- quality of work - work without shortages and complaints,
- savings - in cost or material,
- absenteeism levels - attendance at work,
- discipline - no tardiness,
- punctuality - completing tasks before or on time,
- Reliability - no interruptions or stoppages,
- meeting health and safety guidelines - no accidents, etc.

To use the employee bonus system as a motivational factor, the company must tailor the system to its own needs. Many different bonus systems can be found, but the general division is shown in Figure 1.

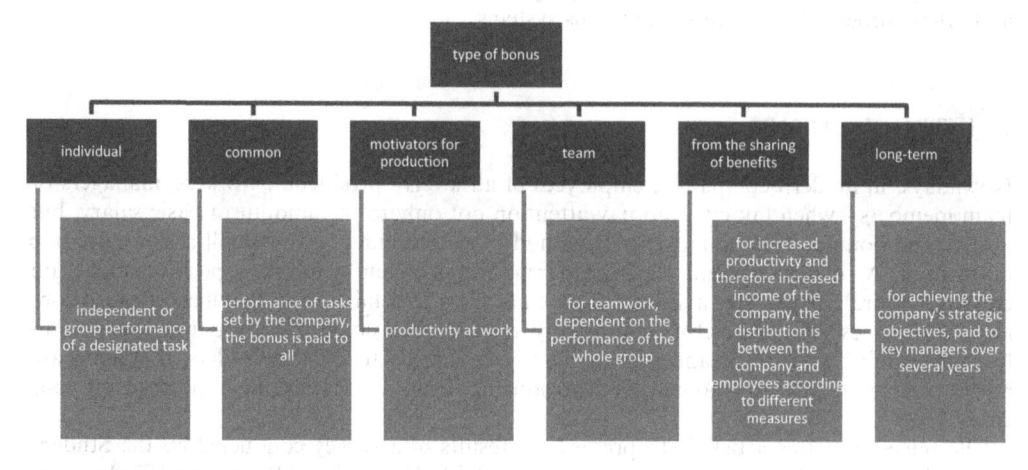

Figure 1.   Type of bonus.
Source: own work based on [Gick, Tarczyńska 1999]

Bonuses can be awarded in a variety of ways, it can be a percentage of base salary or a variable amount or a combination of both. The frequency of payment of bonuses, which may be monthly, quarterly, semi-annually or annually, is also not standardized.

3   SURVEY ON BONUS SYSTEMS

As mentioned in the introduction, the students who are part of a project group called "SMAT Analysis" operating within the framework of the Student's Research Group "Management" functioning at the Faculty of Civil Engineering and Resource Management of the AGH University of Science and Technology in Kraków conducted a study on the principles of functioning and subjective assessment of beneficiaries of employee bonus systems operating in companies. The following subsections present the detailed design of the study and the results and conclusions of the study.

3.1 Premise of the study

The main objective of the survey was to find out the rules of employee bonuses in Polish enterprises and to examine the opinions of final beneficiaries. The research group, to which the study was addressed, became the employees of companies operating in Poland, the study was not narrowed down to any industry or smaller territorial area. The qualitative study took the form of an online survey that was shared on LinkedIn and via email. The survey had a total of 37 survey questions, but the number of questions to be answered by each respondent varied due to the use of conditional questions. The questions varied in nature: single-choice questions, multiple-choice questions, open-ended questions and a scale.

3.2 Characteristics of the study group

A total of 173 people participated in the survey. The respondents were asked about the industry they work in, their responses are shown in Figure 2. Due to the occurrence of 44 responses from the category "Other", the authors of the study decided to create categories, marked with *, and group the individual responses to them. The largest group are employees of the Automotive industry - 32 people, followed by between 10 and 20 respondents from heavy industry, FMCG, broadly understood manufacturing and the furniture industry. Other industries showed less than 10 respondents.

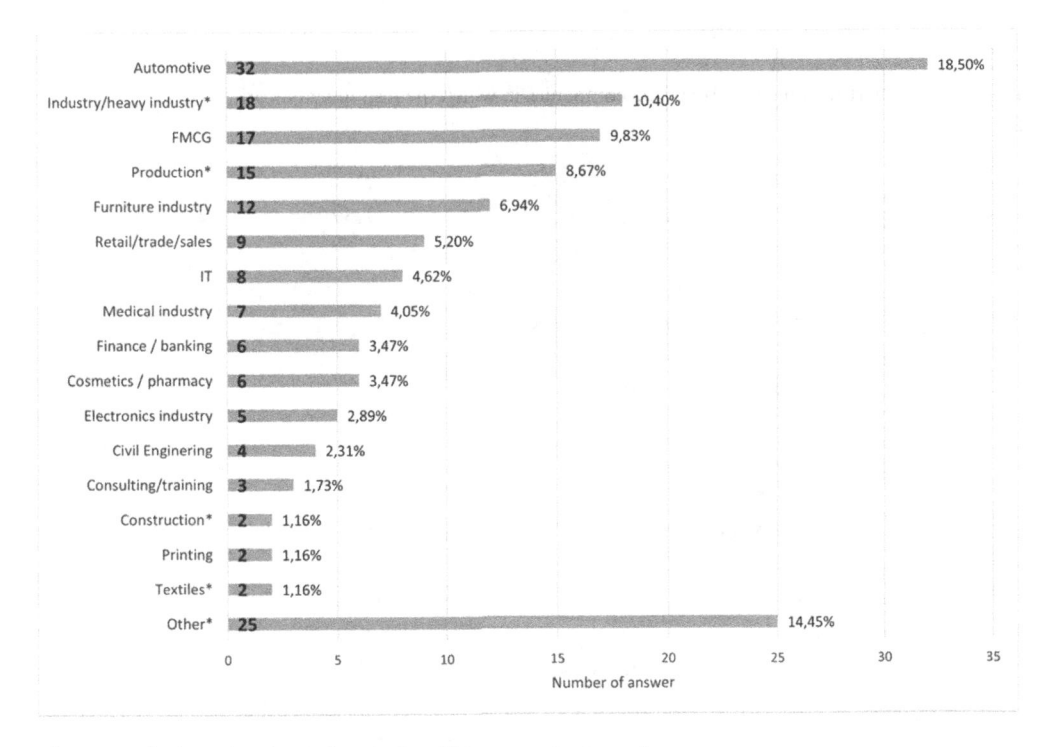

Figure 2.   A chart showing industries in which respondents work.
Source: own work

The majority, almost 50%, of those taking part in the survey work in a large company, i. e. with more than 250 employees. Detailed survey results are shown in Figure 3.

In the next question the respondents answered the question about the department in the company they work in. The most common answer given by the respondents was engineering/

quality department, accounting for 21. 39% of the responses or 37 respondents. It should also be noted that 17 people representing the company's Board of Directors participated in the survey. Detailed responses are shown in Figure 4.

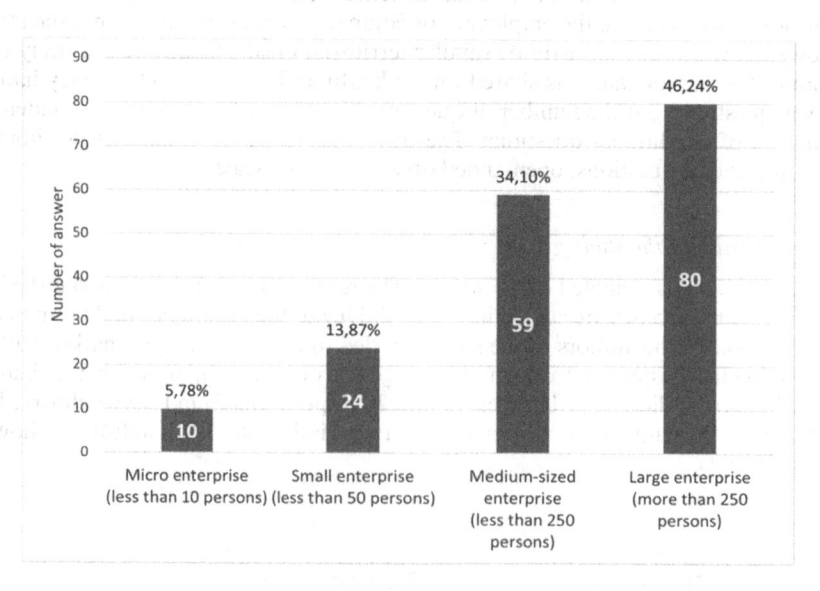

Figure 3.   A chart showing the size of the companies in which the respondents work.
Source: own work

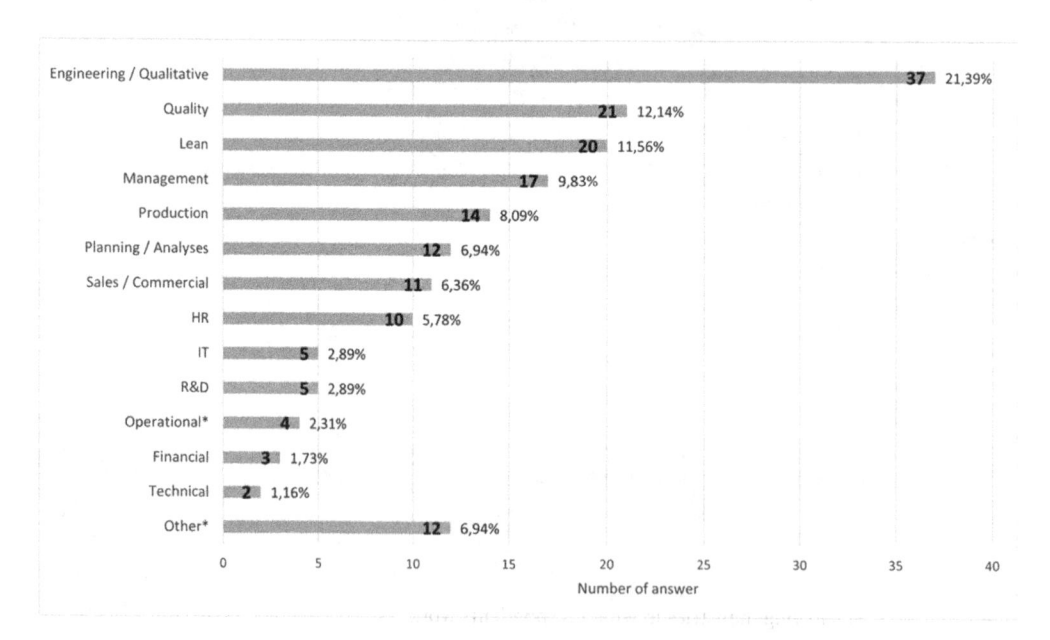

Figure 4.   A chart showing the answers of the respondents about the different departments in the company.
Source: own work

The respondents were also asked about their position in the company. The variety of results is shown in Figure 5. More than 40% of the respondents were managers, although production workers (~ 17%) or directors (~ 13%) also participated in the survey.

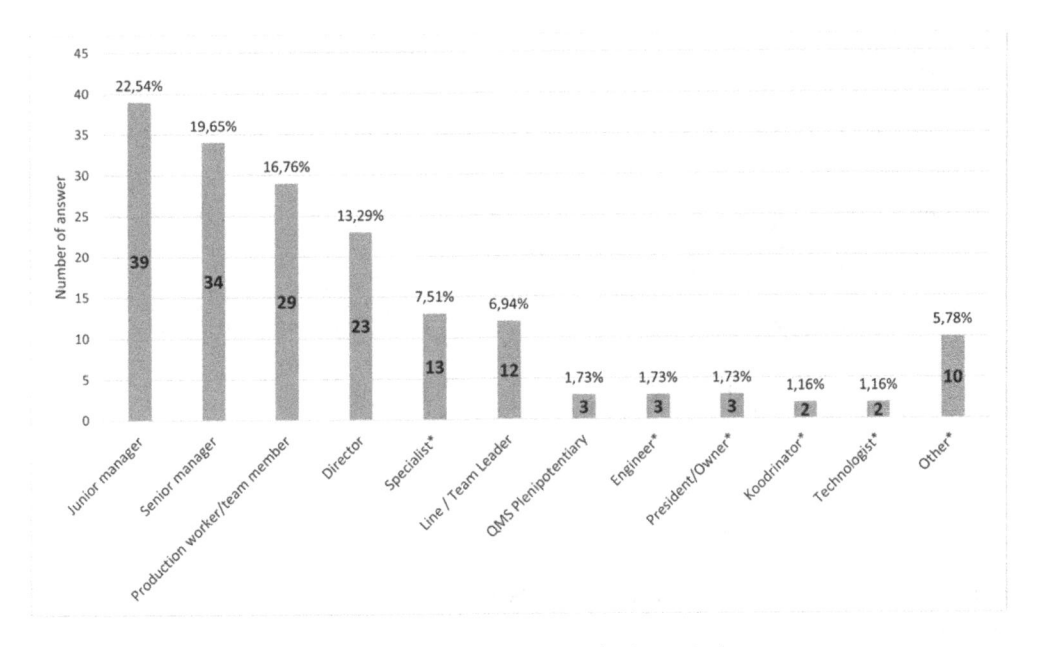

Figure 5. A chart showing the positions of the respondents in the workplace.
Source: own work.

3.3 *Operation of the bonus system*

The first question asked the respondents to estimate how many of their workplaces have a bonus system. A considerable part - 68. 21% or 118 respondents - have such a system, while 16. 76% or 29 respondents have a partial system. The others answered that the bonus system does not exist.

When the respondents were asked whether there were plans to launch a bonus system in their company, only 9 people answered in the affirmative. The same group was asked if this system had worked before, 6 people answered in the affirmative. Another question was then asked about the reason for suspending the system, then the most common answer was the ineffectiveness of the system, i. e. lack of benefits and too little revenue for the company.

Subsequent questions asked to all respondents allowed for a more detailed insight into the bonus systems in place at their workplaces.

The majority of the respondents (85. 03%), i. e. 142 persons, confirmed that only cash bonuses are used in their company. Other respondents, when asked about the form of bonus in their company, mentioned, among others, vouchers, training, trips, material rewards such as cinema tickets, flowers, fitness cards. Responses also included medical care do-overs, health cards, and promotions.

In the next question, about financial allowances, respondents were given the option of multiple responses. The most frequent answer indicated 108 times was a discretionary bonus, followed by a regulatory bonus given twice as often by about 35% of respondents. Detailed responses are shown in Figure 6.

Another question concerning the types of bonuses awarded in the company was also asked with the possibility of giving several answers. A large part of the respondents - 93 (over 58%), indicated an individual bonus, i. e. independent or group performance of a designated task. Other survey results are shown in Figure 7.

In the next question about additional criteria for awarding bonuses, the respondents most often indicated the completion of additional tasks (answer given by about 35% of the

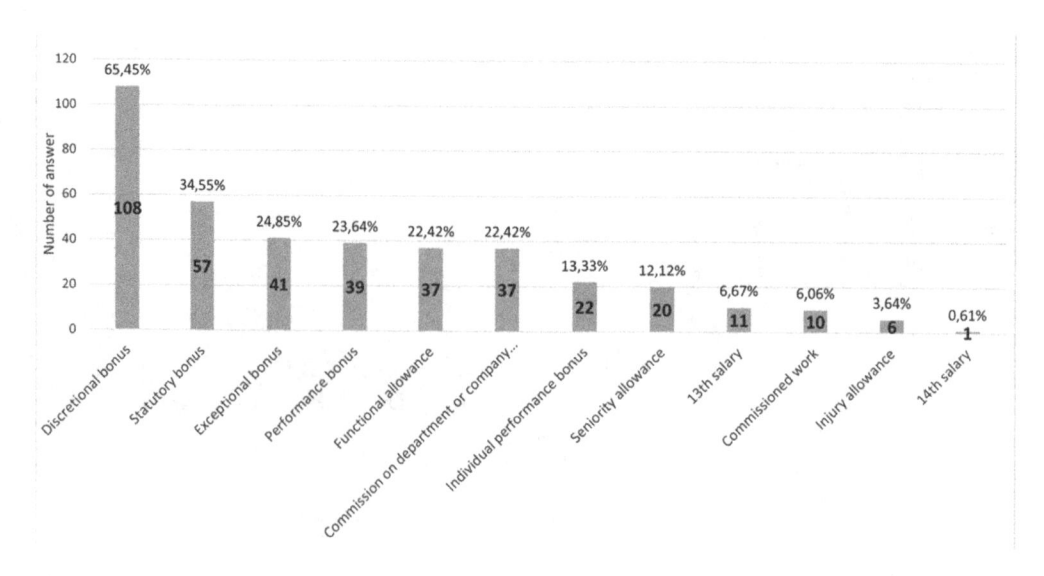

Figure 6. A chart showing answers about financial bonus.
Source: own work

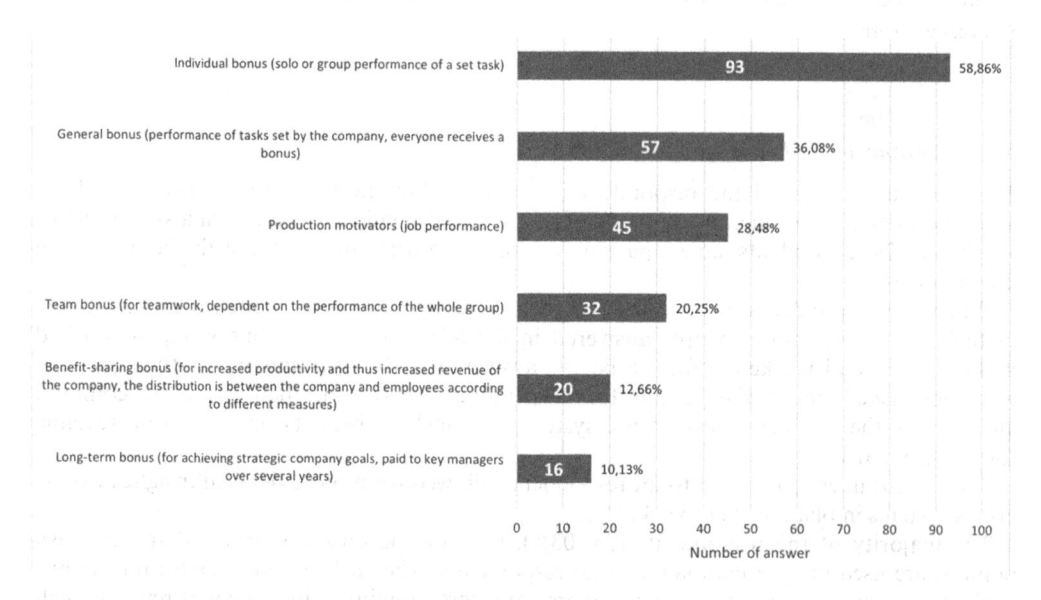

Figure 7. A chart showing answers about giving a bonus.
Source: own work

respondents) as well as the criterion of absenteeism (29% of the respondents) and implementation of job improvements (22% of the respondents). The remaining responses are shown in Figure 8.

For the majority, 58. 18% of the respondents, bonus systems (types of bonuses) do not differ depending on the department in the company.

The majority of respondents - 82% - indicated that depending on seniority, the types/rates of bonuses for employees do not vary. When asked on what principles differences in bonuses related to seniority are built, the remaining part indicated, among others, that the principles have not

36

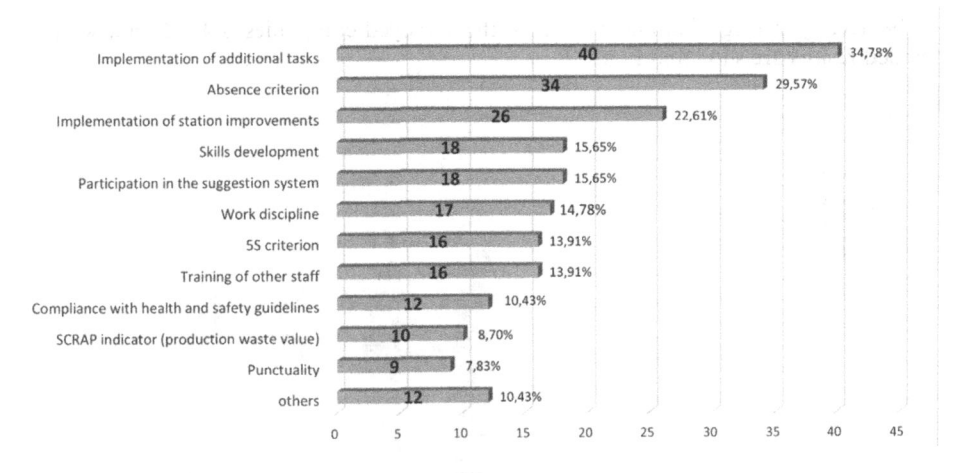

Figure 8. A chart showing answers about additional criteria additional criteria for awarding bonuses. Source: own work

been defined, it is the manager's knowledge, greater seniority means a greater opportunity to receive a bonus or leave, bonuses increase in proportion to years of work or by a jump, bonuses occur only after working a certain number of years, they differ in relation to position, are awarded based on the manager's evaluation or individually reported by the employee.

More than half of the respondents (55. 97%) answered that the company reduces bonuses due to employee absenteeism. Most of these respondents (58. 43%) answered that the amount of the bonus depends on the reason for absence, with sick leave being the most common reason (47 responses).

The amount of bonus for the majority of respondents, i. e. 47. 44% is a variable amount rate, a percentage of basic salary was indicated by 39. 10%, the remaining part of respondents indicated a combination of percentage and amount rate. When asked what is the percentage of basic salary awarded as a bonus, the most frequent answer (26. 67%) was 10%, followed by 20% indicated by 9 respondents, 5, 15 and 30% were indicated 6-7 times. The most frequent answer to the question how much is the quota rate was the amount of 500 PLN indicated 14 times, the next amount was 1000 PLN indicated 11 times.

To the open question about on what principle the bonus for employees is calculated in the surveyed companies, the participants answered in percentages (10, 25, 30 %, etc.) and the formulas enabling its calculation were given.

For 51. 5% of survey participants, bonuses are awarded monthly, for 25% annually.

The overriding condition for awarding bonuses indicated by 48. 67% of respondents was the supervisor's evaluation.

In the majority of respondents (71. 61%) there are rewarded tasks, and their implementation is measured most often in percentage terms (45. 45% of responses).

For 32, 26% of the respondents bonus rules are not clearly defined and 47. 10% are unable to calculate the approximate amount of their bonus themselves.

3.4 *Evaluation of bonus schemes*

More than half (60%) of the respondents are not satisfied with the current bonus system, most of them (more than 60%) do not feel motivated for additional activity/effort with the current system.

In the majority of the surveyed companies - 80. 59% - no surveys or research are conducted on the current bonus system in place at the workplace.

The average rating of bonus systems in the surveyed companies is 4. 72 on a scale of 1-10, detailed results are shown in Figure 9.

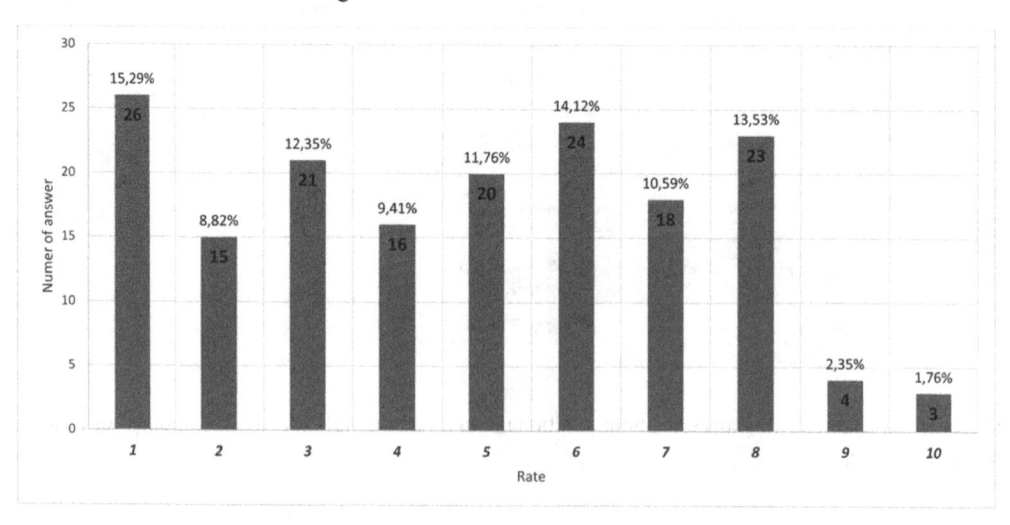

Figure 9. A chart showing answers to the question on evaluation of the bonus system.
Source: own work

According to the survey participants, the bonus criteria that should change is the type of bonus criteria indicated 107 times (68. 15%). The amount of the bonus was indicated by 78 respondents (49. 68%), a similar number of 70 votes (44. 59%) was collected by the bonus calculation system.

A vast majority of respondents (90. 06%) indicated that after changing the bonus system in the company, the productivity of employees could be improved.

4 SUMMARY

The paper presents the results of a study on bonus systems in companies and the evaluation of their beneficiaries. The project team looked at existing surveys so that they could develop a comprehensive set of questions for their survey.

173 people from various industries and departments and positions participated in the survey. A significant number of the surveyed have bonus systems in their company, most often only monetary ones. Most of the respondents who do not have bonus systems are not planning to launch them and some of those who previously had such systems in place had them suspended most often due to their ineffectiveness.

The respondents indicated individual bonuses as the most common type of bonuses, and the main criterion for awarding bonuses was performance and productivity indicated by over 56% of the respondents, and as an additional criterion, the performance of additional tasks was indicated most often.

In the majority of respondents, bonus systems do not differ depending on the department and length of service. However, for 55.97% of the respondents, the amount of the bonus is affected by the employee's absenteeism, which for 41.57% does not depend on the reason for the absence.

Among the respondents, the bonus is most often set as a variable amount, most often 500 or 1000 PLN. As a percentage of bonus from base salary, the most common response was 10%. From the survey, we can also observe that bonuses are most often awarded every month and the overriding condition for award is the supervisor's evaluation.

Bonus tasks, most often measured by percentage, are not popular with respondents. For 32.26% of the respondents, the bonus rules are not clearly defined and only 52.90% can calculate their bonus amount.

About 60% of respondents are not satisfied with their bonus systems, and a similar number do not feel motivated by the system. In most of the respondents, there is no research on the system currently used. On average, employees rate their company's bonus system 4.72 out of 10. For a large part of the respondents, the type of bonus criteria should be improved, and a change in the bonus system should, according to 90.08% of the respondents, improve employee productivity.

The survey made it possible to examine remuneration systems in Polish enterprises. On this basis, it can be concluded that in the majority of companies in Poland there are systems of employee suggestions, although the employees mostly indicate their ineffectiveness, that is, the lack of fulfillment of the basic motivational task. Most companies use cash bonuses awarded individually or as part of a universal bonus. Criteria are always used to award bonuses, and they vary depending on the department in which the employee is employed.

The study was conducted as part of the AGH Rector's Grant competition. The authors conducted the study in cooperation with a consulting company, then a free webinar was prepared for dissemination and discussion. The results of the study are published as a publicly available report.

REFERENCES

Ciekanowski Z., 2014. Płacowe narzędzia motywowania w organizacji. Zeszyty Naukowe Uniwersytetu Przyrodniczo-Humanistycznego w Siedlcach Seria: Administracja i Zarządzanie, no. 100: 215–223

Gick A., Tarczyńska M., 1999. Motywowanie pracowników. Warszawa: Polskie Wydawnictwo Ekonomiczne.

Krzemiński M., 2015. Analiza efektywności systemu oceniania pracowników. Promotor.

Kuc B. 1999. Zarządzanie doskonałe. Warszawa: Oskar-Master of Biznes, page. 201.

Manikowski R., 2021. Projektowanie systemów premiowych: Wydanie: 2. Wolters Kluwer.

Pawlak Z., Smoleń A., 2012. Zasady budowy współczesnych systemów wynagradzania w przedsiębiorstwach. Rocznik Naukowy Wydziału Zarządzania w Ciechanowie 1-4 (VI): 85–112.

Entrepreneurship in the Raw Materials Sector – Bartha et al. (Eds)
© 2022 Copyright the Author(s), ISBN: 978-1-032-19596-4
Open Access: www.taylorfrancis.com, CC BY-NC-ND 4.0 license

Mentoring as a tool supporting the development of student entrepreneurship in the raw materials industry

A. Napieraj

AGH University of Science and Technology, Krakow, Poland

ABSTRACT: Mentoring is often recognized as a useful tool of human resource development. The essence of mentoring is the support that the mentor gives the mentee, based on the relationship between the entities involved in this process, in order to develop the mentee's potential. The article presents the possibilities of using mentoring as a tool for the development of entrepreneurship among students. The considerations are based on the experience gained from the LIMBRA project's mentoring program, which aims to prepare a startups for the raw materials industry.

1 INTRODUCTION

Although many associate coaching and mentoring with modern fields of science and human development, their roots go back to ancient times. Even then, psychological mechanisms responsible for our development were recognized and close emotional contacts shaping and building human wisdom were appreciated. So it is a form of education that responds to a deep need for authority and support. We all need a dialogue with someone with more experience and wisdom.

Each of us has had situations, events and experiences in our lives, during which we felt the presence of a person in a special way. Certainly, these circumstances were of exceptional importance. They could be about making an important life decision, they could result in significant changes or otherwise affect our lives. We are then not always sure about the steps to be taken. Usually, we look for someone who will give us some advice, show us the direction, dispel doubts or simply support us on the way to the new. The features of such a special person are primarily the so-called life wisdom combined with the will to truly engage in our affairs. Who is he and where can you meet such a person? Of course - around us. Such a person can be someone from our family, acquaintances, friends, or even a complete stranger who appears on our way at the moment when we need it very much. This person is someone who is a life teacher. We call her a mentor (Coaching School, 2021).

In conclusion, people at different times and in different cultures, since the dawn of the centuries, have really missed relationships that deeply support them. In these relationships, knowledge, life experience and close emotional contacts have built and still build our wisdom in life.

2 CHARACTERISTICS OF MENTORING

2.1 *The genesis of mentoring*

The etymology of the word "mentor" comes from the Greek language and simply means "thinker". The mythical hero named Mentor was a friend of Odysseus, who, on entering the

DOI: 10.1201/9781003259954-5

Trojan War, entrusted him with looking after his son Telemach. The relationship between Mentor and Telemach plays an indirect role in the Homeric epic, but gains importance in 1699, when François Fénelon's study entitled "Les Adventyres de Telemarque" is published. The pedagogical aim of this study was to present the master-student relationship and to emphasize how, with the help of older, experienced people, young people can develop their abilities and talents. This new meaning of the term "mentor" spread in the 18th century and gained real popularity around 1970.

It should be noted that conceptually, the term "mentor" also refers to:

- the Hindu sampradaya tradition of succession of teachers and students who pass on religious knowledge to successive generations;
- medieval craft guilds, the activity of which was based on apprenticing apprentices to guild masters;
- humanistic psychology that is optimistic about the potential of human nature and proclaims the possibility of continuous personal development (Rogers, 2003); and
- American social movements in the second half of the 20th century that promoted equality in the workplace and the need for superiors to recognize the contribution of women and ethnic minorities (Walker Laird, 2006);
- the traditional master-apprentice relationship. Mentoring has been accompanying humanity since the dawn of time, which is confirmed by the literary sources preserved to this day from long before our era, in which its nature and essence can be found. It is used in new areas, but the essence of the action has not changed for centuries.

2.2 Definition of mentoring

There are different definitions and approaches to mentoring, so it is difficult to choose one. In the specialist literature, we find several definitions, which are summarized in Table 1. It is easy to notice that they contain common parts that, when combined, define mentoring well. Thus, mentoring is a process carried out in the mentor-mentee relationship, where the mentor supports the development of the mentee, has knowledge and experience greater than the mentee and is able to share his knowledge and experience. The subject of work during mentoring can be very wide, you can work not only on the development of knowledge, but also skills (Mentoring Handbook, 2021).

Although many associate coaching and mentoring with modern fields of science and human development, their roots go back to ancient times. Even then, psychological mechanisms responsible for our development were recognized and close emotional contacts shaping and building human wisdom were appreciated. So it is a form of education that responds to a deep need for authority and support. We all need a dialogue.

Table 1. Definitions of mentoring.

Definition	Author/Source
Helping one person make significant changes in knowledge, work or thinking.	Megginson & Clutterbuck, 2010; after: Meginnson i in.,2010
A confidential relationship between two people in which experiments, exchange of experiences and learning can take place, and skills, knowledge and intuition are developed.	Mumford;1993; after: Megginson i in., 2010
Helping people become what they want to become.	E. Parsloe & M. Wray, 1992; after: Meginnson i in., 2010

Mentoring is mainly based on the benefits of the mentee, so its goals are related in particular to the development and learning of a less experienced person (Figure 1).

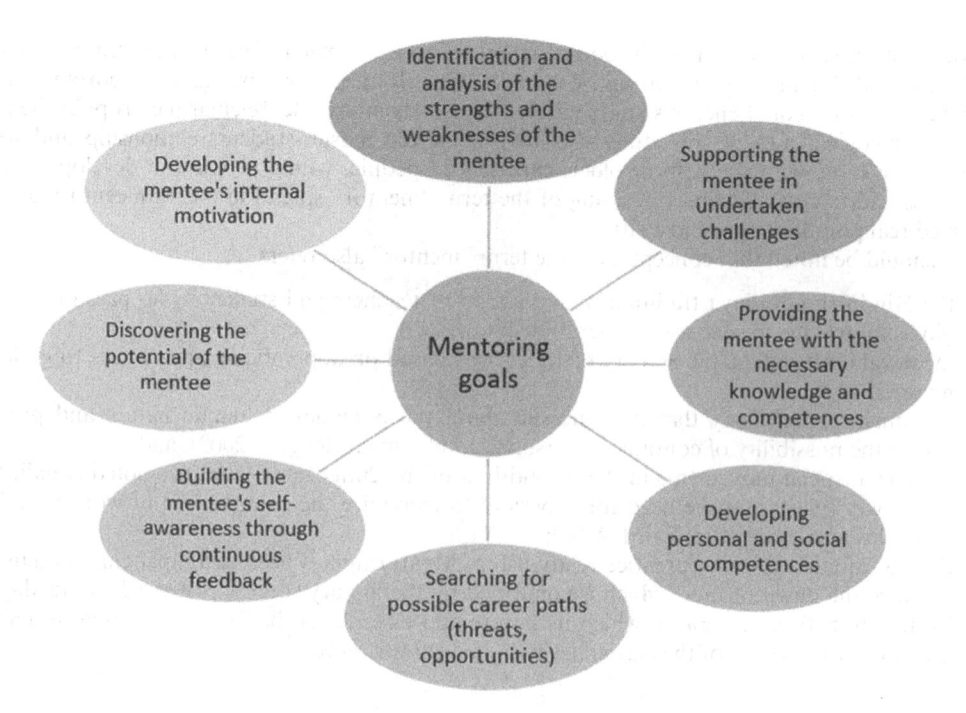

Figure 1.　Mentoring goals.
Source: (Mentoring Handbook, 2021)

Mentoring is successfully used in business, where it takes the form of effective training and employee adaptation. It consists in caring for a mentor during the development of competences and the implementation of the trainee's professional path. Mentoring is giving advice not only on specific tasks, but also on shaping your professional path and personal development. It is a partnership relationship that remains only at the professional level. Moreover, this process is a long-term relationship between a person with a greater baggage of experience and a person with less competences or shorter work experience. Contrary to coaching, it is conducted over a longer period of time (1-3 years) (Rosen, 2011).

Mentoring is a form of development that benefits both parties involved. The mentor improves his interpersonal skills, and his mentee develops self-awareness and strives to use his own potential. Moreover, mentoring is less costly as it relies on the company's internal resources, that is, its employees (Redakcja, 2021).

All of the above-mentioned features of mentoring mean that it can also be successfully used in academic and civic environments.

There are basic types of mentoring:

- Individual mentoring - these are dedicated, specialized mentoring programs that are created according to the individual needs of the mentees.
- Group mentoring - consisting in counseling, sharing experience and supporting a group of mentees by a group of mentors, mentors in this mentoring formula have contact with many mentees.

2.3　Who is a mentor?

In Homer's "Iliad", the Mentor's job was to raise, teach and improve skills of Odysseus' son . The mentor is a good guardian who can be entrusted with the most important people, issues or things. He also becomes the incarnation of the guardian deity - the guide.

Currently, a mentor is an expert in a given field, industry or company, but also becomes a tutor, a teacher and a guide. A mentor is a knowledgeable leader who is an authority for the mentee. By assumption, he has very high competences. He advises the mentee thanks to previously developed methods and focuses on his professional development. A mentor is primarily a source of unsaved (informal) knowledge, authority and role model. A coherent person, internally orderly, acting according to how he speaks and thinks, a person who is willing to talk to and who is eagerly asked for his opinion (Mentoring Vademecum, 2001).

A good mentor does not directly offer his experience and knowledge according to the known pattern: "if I were in your place, I would …" Although the mentor's knowledge would not be valuable, this approach is ineffective as a method of development of the other person and additionally carries a high risk of error. No mentor is able to be "in the place" of his mentee.

A mentor is a person who acts as a friend and trusted advisor, but the entire relationship is on a professional level. Mentors and students meet and communicate with each other on a regular, but not on fully formal ground. They trust each other, understand and empathize. Confidentiality is very important to them. In order for mentoring to be effective, it is necessary to remember about the principles by which it operates (Figure 2).

The mentor uses his knowledge, experience and intuition to support the process of searching and reflection of the mentee with the help of often difficult questions concerning basic matters, just like a coach. David Clutterbuck bluntly refers to such questions as BDQ (bloody difficult questions). These questions often lead the client to see his situation or problem from a completely new perspective (Czekaj, 2007)(Parsloe, Leedham, 2018).

Mentoring, based on continuous support, provides an opportunity for learning and development, not only for the "learner" but also for the "trainer". The first one, thanks to working with a mentor, gets to know his strengths, develops self-awareness and strives to realize his own potential. The second one, on the other hand, improves interpersonal skills (Neale, Spencer-Arnell, Wilson, 2016).

Generation Y is the generation of Facebook and other social networks. Therefore, the mentee can teach a mentor how to use the Internet, and above all social media, at work. He also has invaluable knowledge about his peers, which may be helpful, for example, when the company introduces new products to the market, but also when hiring new employees. Reverse mentoring does not have to mean cooperation between a very young, inexperienced person and a much older employee in a high position. Reverse relationships fulfill their role equally well among the representatives of the X generation.

3 MENTORING IN THE MATRIX OF EDUCATIONAL INTERACTIONS

Based on the concept of Gestalt's psychology, the matrix of educational interactions (Karwala, 2007) was created, which clearly illustrates the methods used in adult education and business and allows for finding a place for mentoring in the structure of educational and developmental interactions (Figure 3) .

The first axis of the learning methodology consists of two dimensions, freedom of interaction, which we understand as methodological freedom in the transfer of knowledge, skills and experiences by the teacher and the same freedom in acquiring new skills, experiences and learning by the student, as well as directivity, which is arbitrariness and repeatability in choosing a method of learning, acquiring skills and experience.

The second axis deals with procedures and algorithms, and the course of the learning process. It is made up of such dimensions as the finished figure and the figure closing. The finished figure is the confirmed learning algorithm. The teacher's task is to master the method and, in accordance with its principles, apply it to the student, imparting specific skills to him in accordance with the expected results. Closing the figure is the free discovery of subjective development strategies and finding personal solutions by the student. The teacher only accompanies the change and gives feedback on individual activities.

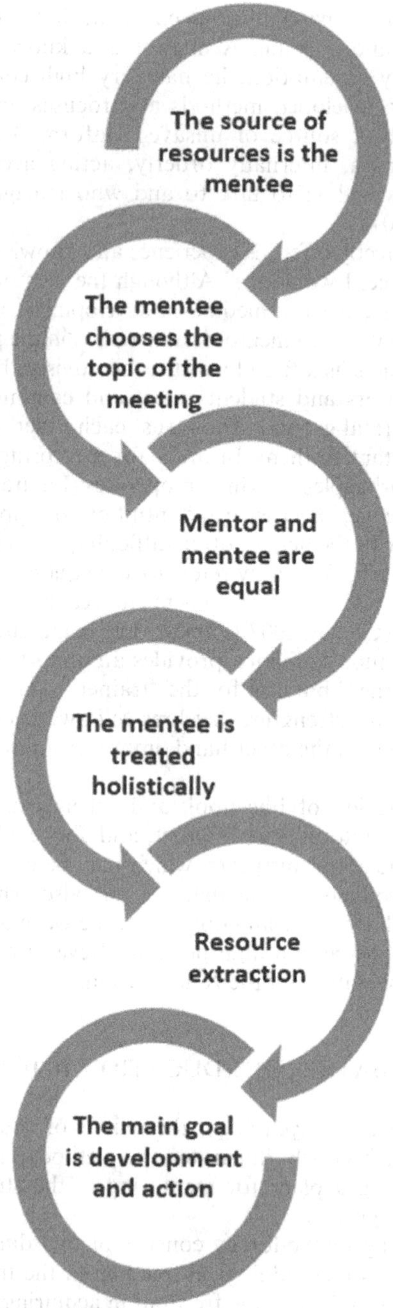

The source of
resources is the
mentee

The mentee
chooses the
topic of the
meeting

Mentor and
mentee are
equal

The mentee is
treated
holistically

Resource
extraction

The main goal
is development
and action

Figure 2.   Principles of effective mentoring.
Source: (Pietrzycka, 2021)

Mentoring is created from the combination of ready-made figures and directives. It is understood here as the application of ready-made algorithms and procedures along with a strictly defined learning method. The closest to this pattern is sports training, in which both exercise models and methods are clearly defined and assigned to the respective sports disciplines. (M. Bennewicz, 2011).

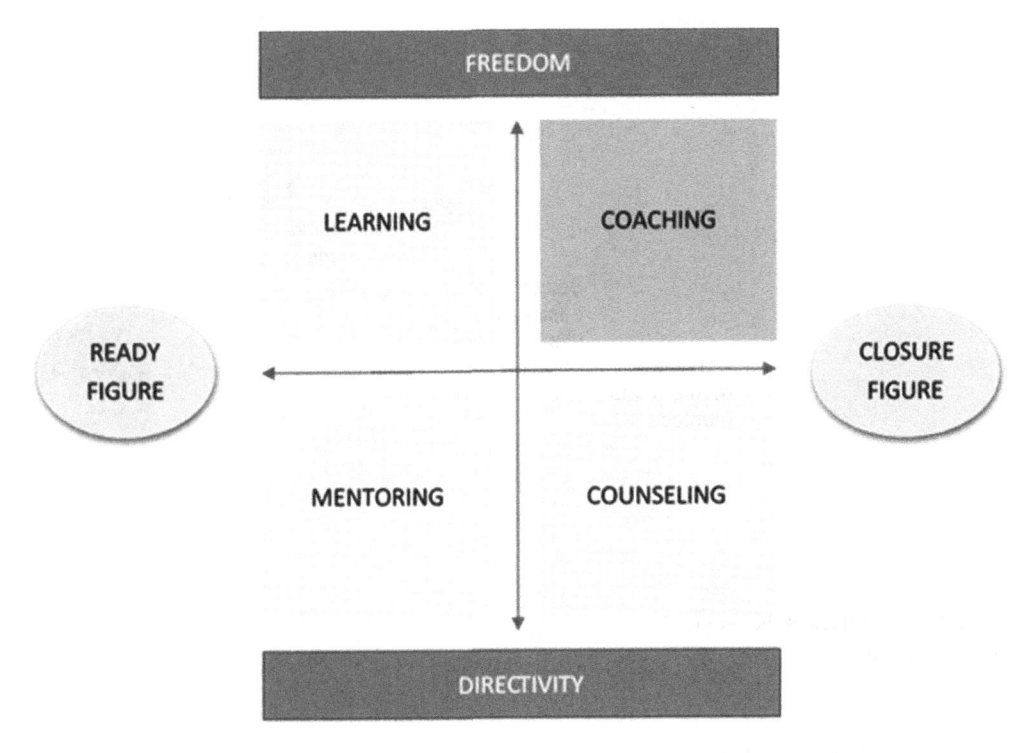

Figure 3. Educational impact matrix.

Source: (M. Bennewicz, 2011)

4 LIMBRA MENTORING PROGRAM

As part of the Limbra project, a mentoring program was launched, involving the best students in four partner countries to support them in their entrepreneurial development. The next stages of activities undertaken in the program are presented in Figure 4.

The five best students from each of the partners (VŠB – Technical University of Ostrava, AGH University of Science and Technology, Technical University of Kosice, University of Miskolc) were recruited to the program. In this article, students from AGH University of Science and Technology in Krakow, Poland will be analyzed. In the second stage, a mentor was assigned to each participant.

In the next stage, the final topics to be implemented under the program were approved. Their list with acronyms is presented in Table 2. Currently, students are working hard with mentors to prepare startups. We know that this work is well advanced.

Each student starting the mentoring program completed an evaluation questionnaire that covered five basic areas: Area 1 called Market Analysis Study, Area 2 Customer Segmentation, Area 3 IPR protection, Area 4 Business Model, Area 5 Implementation Plan.

Students assessed their level of knowledge on a scale from 1 to 10. The results of these assessments are presented in Figures 5 to 10.

In Area 1 - Market Analysis Study, the average grade of our students ranges from 4,2 to 5,6. In this area we have six questions:

1. Market Segmentation: Who are the users of our research? Conducting market segmentation studies we're generally asking survey questions aimed at capturing needs, values, attitudes, behaviors and demographics.
2. Product Testing: How will our client use our technology? A detailed understanding of how your research meets (or doesn't meet) your customer's needs is crucial both to product development and marketing.

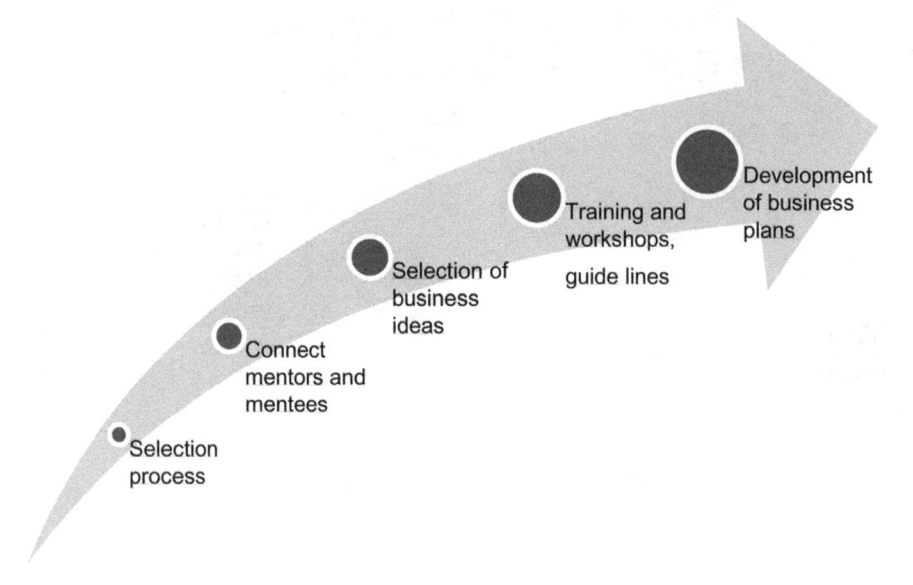

Figure 4.   Main steps of the program.
Source: own study

Table 2.   List of topics covered.

Project #	Project Acronym	Short Project Description
1	LEMon	Creation of an institution providing and developing Lean Management solutions aimed at improving the economic and environmental efficiency of enterprises from the broadly understood mineral resources industry
2	CERM	Circular economy of the raw materials
3	RawCluster	Creation of a cluster supporting the raw materials industry.
4	SaPla	Project of a sales platform for the raw materials market
5	ARMoDiM	Analysis of the activities of raw materials companies in the field of digital marketing

Source: own study

3. Advertising Testing: How much do you know about reaching your target audience? Tests of your advertising campaigns can save you valuable time and resources. By taking potential campaigns directly to your audience and gauging their response you can focus on creating truly impactful advertising.
4. Satisfaction and Loyalty Analysis: How likely are your colleagues to continue working on your project? And your collaborators? This type of research is aimed at identifying key drivers of satisfaction and measuring the likelihood of customers to continue using a company's products and services.
5. Brand Awareness and Reach: How well is your research known by those you plan to commercialise it to? By conducting regular, well-designed brand awareness surveys you can keep tabs on how effective your marketing campaigns really are.
6. Pricing Research: Surveys that ask customers to choose between different products with unique features and price points can help you identify what features are most valuable to your audience and what they'd be willing to pay for them.

Detailed results are shown in Figure 5.

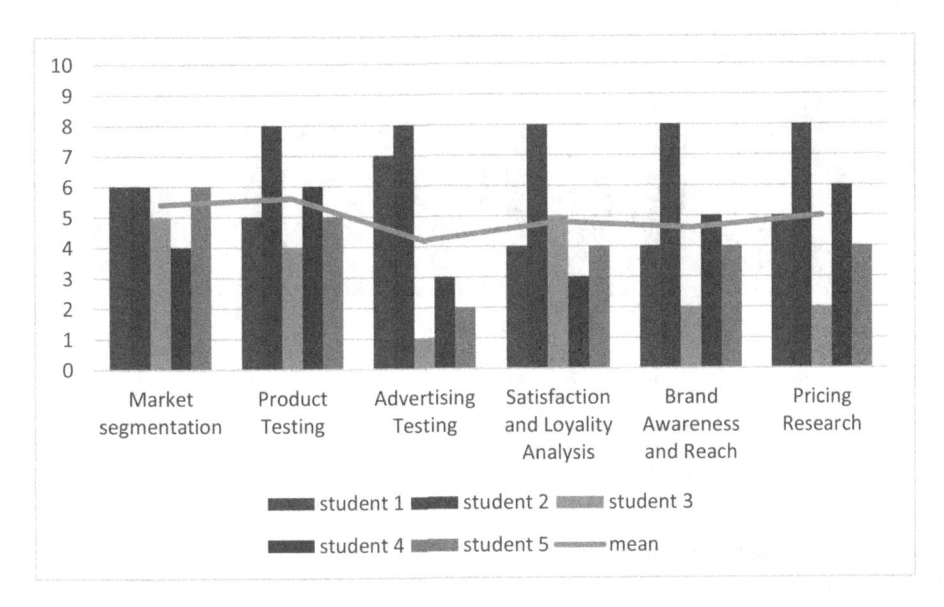

Figure 5. Area 1 market analysis study.
Source: own study

In Area 2 - Customer Segmentation, the average grade of our students ranges from 4,8 to 6,4. In this area we have five questions:

1. Geographic Customer Segmentation: When the customers are segregated based on their location, it is termed as Geographic customer segmentation. The customer segments, in this case, can be country, region or city or even specific homes in particular towns.
2. Demographic Customer Segmentation: When the market is segmented based on certain characteristics of the audience it is called as demographic segmentation. These characteristics may include but not limited to ethnicity, gender, age, religion, marital status, education, occupation, income etc.
3. Behavioral Customer Segmentation: Based on the decision making in the behavior of the customers which include but is not limited to lifestyle, purchases consumption and other various factors, behavioral customer segmentation is carried out.
4. Psychographic Customer Segmentation: When the psychological aspects of the customer and his behavior are taken into consideration it is known as psychographic customer segmentation. various factors are taken into consideration while dividing the customers according to the psychographics like their values our lifestyle opinions and interests and other relevant factors.
5. Smart customer segmentation: customers are divided according to various categories and mix and match all the types of available customer segment combinations. For example, customers are segmented according to age gender and their preference which is nothing but a combination of demographic and psychographic or behavioural segmentation. smart segmentation helps to target the audience more effectively and helps to minimize the unnecessary expenses incurred to target the nonaudiences.

Detailed results are shown in Figure 6.

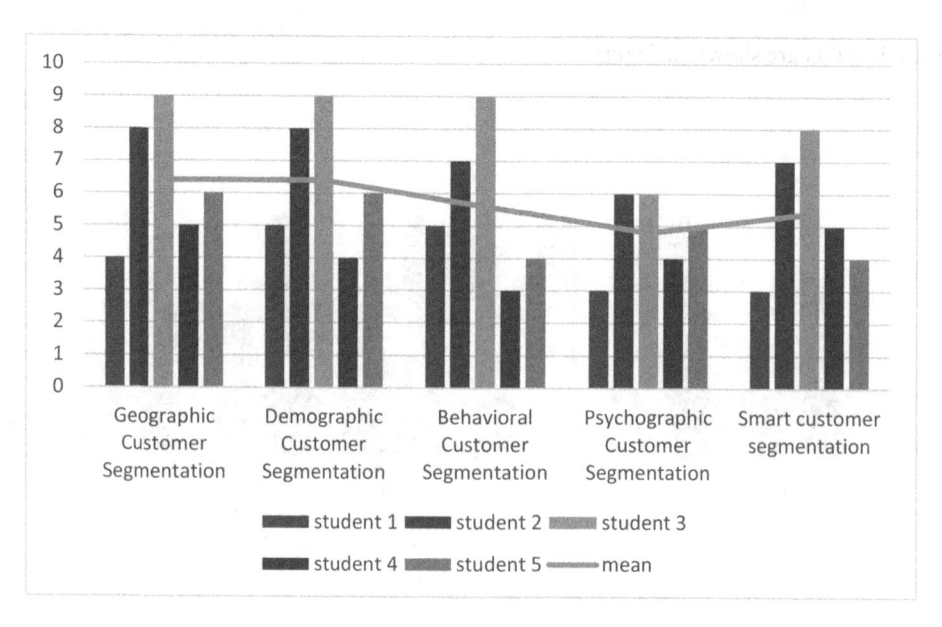

Figure 6.　Area 2 Customer Segmentation.
Source: own study

In Area 3 - IPR protection, the average grade of our students ranges from 3 to 6. In this area we have five questions:

1. Basic concepts: What are Intellectual Property Rights? Should I protect the IP that comes out of my research?
2. The differences between Industrial Property and Copyright: When should we apply one or the other?
3. Types of IPR protection: Do you know the difference between patents, trademarks, utility models, industrial designs...?
4. Protecting your IP: How to know whether your IP can be protected (e.g. patent searches)
5. The process of IP protection: Do you know how to protect your IP (where to go, forms to fill in, geographical considerations, costs...)?

Detailed results are shown in Figure 7.

In Area 4 Business Model, the average grade of our students ranges from 3 to 6. In this area we have three questions:

1. General concepts: How much do you know about aspects you need to keep in mind when presenting your business model?
2. About your research project: Do you know how you'll monetise the results of your research? Do you have a proposition about customer segments, value propositions, channels, customer relationships, revenue streams, key activities, key resources, key partnerships, cost structure...?
3. Tools: Do you know about tools to illustrate, explain and follow-up on your business model (e.g. Business Model Canvas)?

Detailed results are shown in Figure 8.

In Area 5 - Implementation Plan, the average grade of our students ranges from 3 to 3,8. In this area we have three questions:

1. Roadmap: Have you established short, mid and long-term goals for the project?
2. Tool: Do you have a tool to establish a roadmap for your business plan?

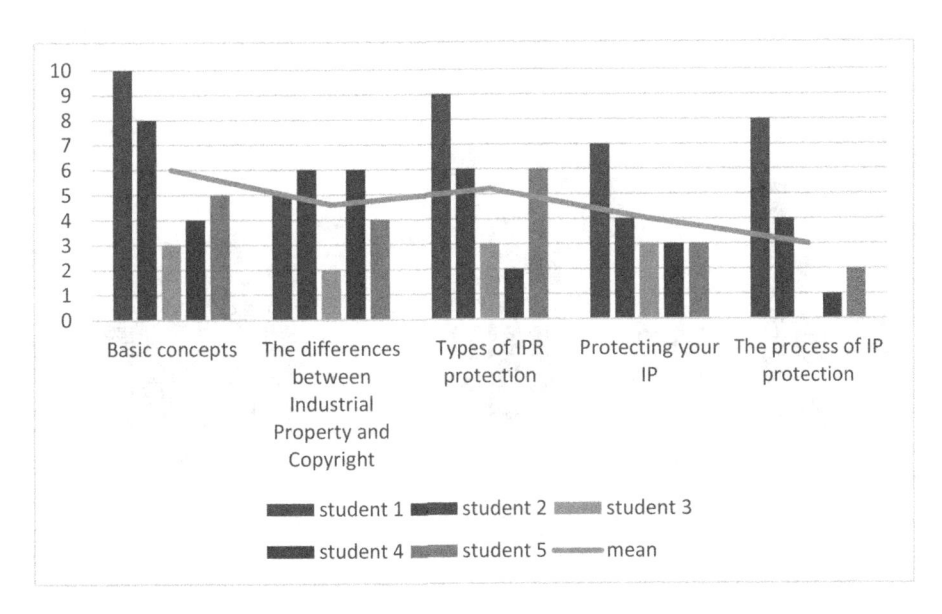

Figure 7.   Area 3 IPR protection.
Source: own study

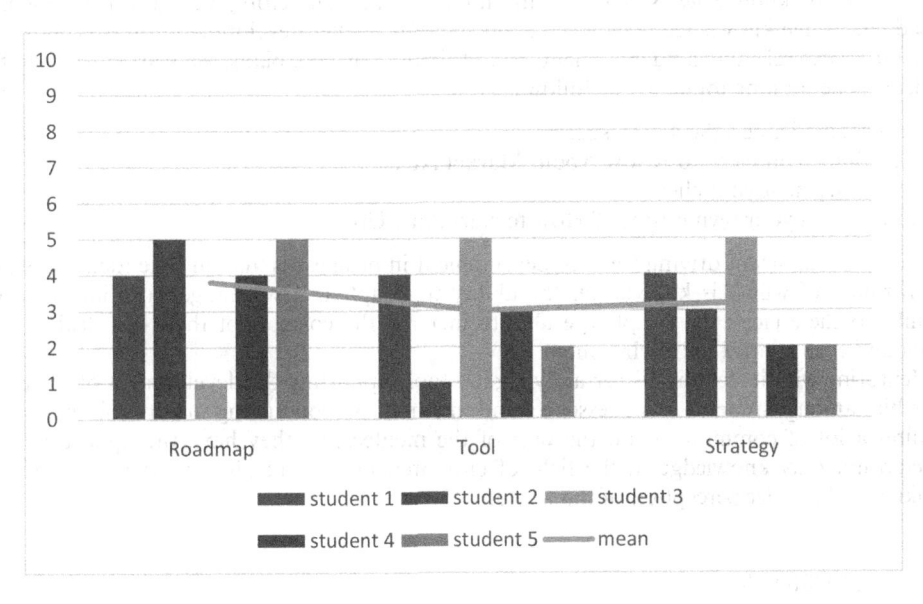

Figure 8.   Area 4 business model.
Source: own study

3. Strategy: How strong is your business strategy? Do you have a revision plan? Do you have a set of hypotheses that you will test over time? Are you ready to modify your strategy in accordance with the results of your tests?

Detailed results are shown in Figure 9.

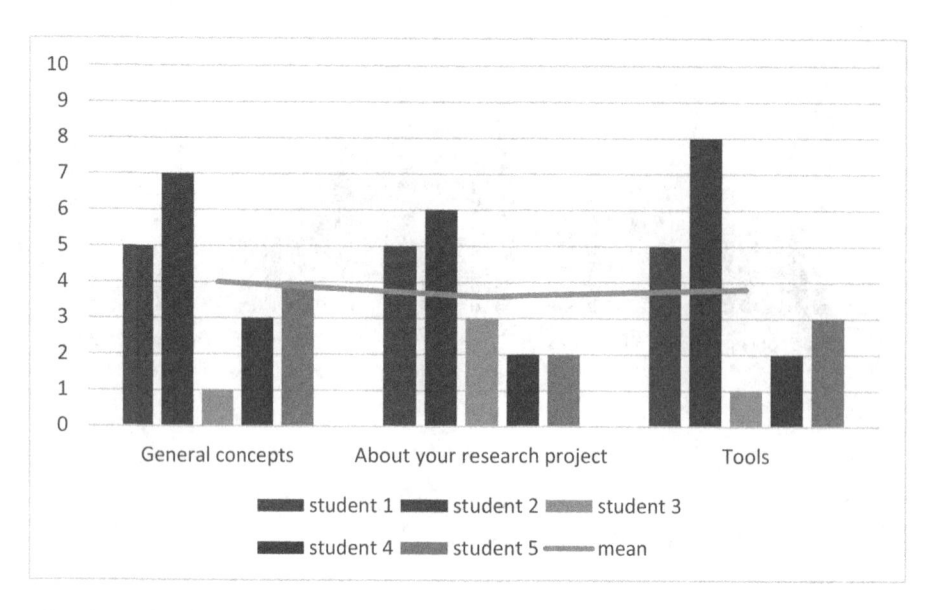

Figure 9.   Area 5 implementation plan.
Source: own study

The level of knowledge is halfway around the scale. Therefore, the group of students already has some knowledge, which is a good start for further development towards entrepreneurship. After selecting students, mentors and finally business plans, we started training for students. The training topics are as follows:

- Business modeling - the key to success
- Everything You Need to Know About Market Analysis
- How to segment your clients
- How to start your own business? How to start Start Up?

The most important driving force of development in business is human potential, the greatest attribute of which is knowledge, the ability to adapt to new changes and imagination. Thanks to these elements, people are able to increase the comfort of their life, deal with it better and even control the environment.

Mentoring with its features is certainly a good tool supporting the development of entrepreneurship among students. The essence and method of conducting mentoring programs requires a lot of commitment on the part of the mentees, so they have the opportunity to develop not only knowledge in the field of entrepreneurship but also creativity, innovative thinking and a wider perception of the world.

5   CONCLUSIONS

Mentoring programs similar to the one implemented under Limbra were established at various universities. One can cite here Universität Basel or ETH Zürich - Fachhochschule Nordwestschweiz (http://www.fhnw.ch), University of St. Gallen (http://www.mentoring.unisg.ch), or Collegium Invisible, operating at the University of Warsaw.

The quality of higher education is considered to be the main factor determining the competitive advantage of a school. The quality of education includes the value of curricula (range of courses, foreign languages), adequacy of education to market requirements, teaching skills of the staff and their scientific potential, IT and library facilities or methods of knowledge verification (internships and other programs)(Karwala, 2007).

Raising the quality of education requires bottom-up and top-down initiatives, including a change of strategy and approach - orientation towards success. Each student is committed to success, and the school's goal is to support them in this process. One of the essential elements of quality management in a university is to create appropriate conditions allowing each student to discover their potential, develop competences and achieve success.

Mentoring programs certainly create added value through collaboration between students and an experienced group of experts (professors) willing to share their experience and knowledge, provide support and expertise. The student (mentee), thanks to the acquired expertise in the field and industry of interest to him, is able to more consciously create a career path, strengthen the network of contacts, and formulate and verify expectations for his future job. All this will enable an easier and, above all, more conscious start in your professional life. What's more, the student's motivation and his view of the issues included in educational programs proposed by universities increases. He will be able to select knowledge from the angle of its usefulness in career development. The mentoring system is supposed to stimulate the curiosity of the mentee, and consequently to encourage action and learning.

It also works the other way around. The inquisitiveness of students has a motivating effect on the staff, which means that they approach students more individually. In the context of the development of entrepreneurial skills of students, as well as management of the quality of education in a modern university, it is necessary to answer the question whether it is not worth reevaluating the educational path chosen by the university and putting emphasis on programs that would enable the creation of leaders and entrepreneurial units.

Mentoring is an opportunity that some universities are still discovering while looking for new ideas and ways to implement and run it effectively.

REFERENCES

Bennewicz, M. 2011. *Coaching i mentoring w praktyce*, G+J Gruner + Jahr Polska, Warszawa.

Clutterbuck, D. 2002. *Każdy potrzebuje mentora*, Warszawa

Czekaj, J. 2007. *Metody organizacji i zarządzania*, Wydawnictwo AE w Krakowie, Kraków,

Karwala, S. 2007. *Model mentoringu we współczesnej szkole wyższej*, Nowy Sącz

Parsloe, E., Wray, M. 2011. *Trener i mentor, udział coachingu i mentoringu w doskonaleniu procesu uczenia się*, ABC Wolters Kluwer business, Warszawa.

Rosen, K. 2011. *Coaching sprzedawców, przemiana zwykłych sprzedawców w mistrzów sprzedaży*, Oficyna Wolters Kluwer Polska, Warszawa.

*Google:*Google Ngram. *[data: 2021-10-6]*.

Rogers, C. 2003. *Client Centred Therapy: Its Current Practice, Implications and Theory*, Robinson,

Walker Laird, P. 2006. *Pull: Networking and Success since Benjamin Franklin*, Cambridge: Harvard University Press

Neale, S. Spencer-Arnell, L. Wilson, L. 2016, *Emotional intelligence coaching*, Wolters Kluwer

Parsloe, E. Leedham M. 2018. *Coaching and Mentoring Practical Techniques for Developing Learning and Performance*. Wydawnictwo Naukowe PWN

Pietrzycka, A. 2021. *Mentoring - co to jest i na czym polega?* www.rekruter .pl. data: 21. 20.2021

Mentoring Handbook, 2021. https://forum-mentorow.pl/edukacja, data: 16.10.2021

Coaching School, 2021. https://szkolacoachingu.edu.pl/baza-wiedzy/dla-biznesu/geneza-mentoringu, data: 20.10.2021.

Redakcja, 2021. https://www.karierawfinansach.pl/baza-wiedzy/slownik-pojec/mentoring-co-oznacza-pojecie-mentoring, data: 21.10.2021

Mentoring Vademecum, 2021. https://forum-mentorow.pl/edukacja/, data: 21.10.21

Entrepreneurship in the Raw Materials Sector – Bartha et al. (Eds)

Entrepreneurial opportunities in the waste management sector in Hungary

A.S. Gubik, Á. Horváth, M. Kis-Orloczki & K. Lipták
University of Miskolc, Miskolc, Hungary

ABSTRACT: The objective of the article is to examine whether the area of the Hungarian waste management sector could be an attractive entrepreneurial target for young people participating in raw material-related education. Our research based on desk research and interviews with stakeholders and students provide a complex picture of the entrepreneurial opportunities inherent in waste management. According to our results intention of students to be entrepreneurs is low among students in the technical field. Career opportunities for students need to be addressed more intensively, and students need to be made aware of them so that they can think in time and prepare according to their plans. In order to be able to turn their business ideas into well-developed business plans, they also need economic/business/entrepreneurial knowledge or peers who can perform these tasks in the planned business. The institutional framework for this needs to be created within the university, which also requires stronger communication and collaboration between faculties. Our work contributes to the entrepreneurial intention literature. It shows how important the sectoral characteristics are in the formation of the decision and the success of the activity, in addition to the students' intention.

1 INTRODUCTION

The role of entrepreneurship in economic growth has become accepted in recent decades. (Carree & Thurik, 2010; Hope, 2016). Besides the economic role the social significance of becoming an entrepreneur is unquestionable. The role of entrepreneurship in preventing the migration of young workers is also important for regions where it is more difficult to provide an employment perspective for young people.

The decision to start a business is very complex, one of the defining elements of which is the entrepreneurial opportunity and the recognition and exploitation of these opportunities by the individual. We agree with Shane and Venkataraman (2000) that although recognition of entrepreneurial opportunities is rather subjective, the opportunities themselves are objective phenomena even if it is not known to everyone at all times.

Entrepreneurial opportunities are influenced by a number of factors, such as the general macroeconomic environment and economic policy, but we also started from the premise that entrepreneurial opportunities are basically determined by sectoral characteristics.

Each sector creates very different opportunities for young entrepreneurs, this article deals only with the examination of entrepreneurial opportunities in the waste management sector. However, it is necessary to examine not only the business opportunities in the waste sector, but also whether students are able to recognize these opportunities, identify the competencies, attitudes and intention that are the basic conditions for starting their own business.

DOI: 10.1201/9781003259954-6

The article seeks to answer the question of what entrepreneurial opportunities the waste management sector offers for young people participating in raw material-related education. As well as whether young people studying in the sector recognize these opportunities and have entrepreneurial plans.

To determine the significance of the sector, we used the statistics of the CSO, OPTEN and Eurostat and performed several analyses. Our sectoral analysis was complemented by an analysis of the macro environment (PESTEL), which verified the existence of important elements of the entrepreneurial ecosystem as well as expert interviews that also shed light on a number of hidden insider aspects. Finally, students were asked what entrepreneurial opportunities they see in the sector, whether they have entrepreneurial intention, ideas, whether they have already taken steps to start their own business.

The structure of the article is as follows: in the first step, we present the specifics of the waste management sector based on statistical data and PESTEL analysis, and then we present the results of the semi-structured expert and student interviews. Finally, we summarize our main findings.

2 LITERATURE REVIEW

Businesses cannot be created without entrepreneurial opportunities. Opportunities and opportunity recognition therefore are critical issues for entrepreneurship.

In the context of opportunities, authors dealing with the topic have quite different viewpoints. Following Kirzner who defines entrepreneurship as recognizing opportunities (Kirzner, 1973), many authors see the recognition of opportunities as a key factor of entrepreneurial activity (Stevenson, & Jarillo, 1990). Others emphasise that opportunities should not be explored but created. Drucker (1985) sees innovation as a specific tool of entrepreneurs, by which they exploit change as an opportunity. According to Zahra (2008) it is a circular process where discovery enriches creation which, in turn, fosters the discovery of new opportunities.

There are also different views in the literature regarding to whether opportunities are objective or subjective in their nature. The authors also emphasize that the discovery of the opportunity is a necessary but not a sufficient condition of the business, a decision on the use of the opportunity is also needed. We agree with Shane and Venkataraman (2000), and consider opportunities objective but consider their recognition to be subjective. To clarify the concept of opportunity, Davidsson (2015) recommends to separate 3 dimensions of it: External Enablers, New Venture Ideas and Opportunity Confidence. The first covers aggregate-level circumstances, the second stands for "imagined future ventures" last is about the individuals' subjective evaluation. In this way, he separates objective circumstances from subjective perception and evaluation.

A number of works address the importance of individual differences (individual nexus) in opportunity recognition. A group of authors highlights the role of information, knowledge and experience (Shane, 2000; Grégoire & Shepherd, 2012, Gruber et al., 2012), the ability to recognize seemingly unrelated patterns and the relationship between them (Baron & Ensley, 2006), the role of entrepreneurial intention (Grégoire & Shepherd, 2012), and other personal characteristics such as self-efficacy (Krueger & Dickson, 1994), education etc.

We consider it critical whether an individual shows intention to start his or her own business, that is, whether he or she wants to take advantage of the opportunity he discovered. From this aspect, the formation of intention, as an important factor in the opportunity recognition, should also be the focus of attention. The academic literature frequently investigates issues related to how entrepreneurial intention develop in individuals, what its components are, and how it can be influenced. The role of education on entrepreneurship has been proven in many cases (Nowiński et al. 2017, Maresch et al. 2016, von Graevenitz et al. 2010, Egerová et. al. 2017, Kolstad & Wiig, 2015, Gubik 2013; Szerb & Lukovszki, 2013, Ling & Venesaar, 2015), also the social environment and culture (Autio & Wennberg, 2010, Thomas & Mueller, 2000; Thurik & Dejardin, 2012, Shane et al. 1991; Zhao et al. 2012) and personal characteristics (Meager et al. 2003, Gauthier et al., 2018) are decisive.

The waste policy aims of European Union to protect the environment and human health and help the EU's transition to a circular economy. Waste management occupies a special place in the Hungarian system of public service provision. In 2012, a new law was adopted, under which the provision of public waste management services was transferred to the state from 1 January 2013. The primary objective of waste management policy is to minimise the negative impacts of waste generation and management on human health and the environment, while reducing the use of resources, in line with the EU's targets and commitments up to 2030. One of the fundamental problems of waste management in Hungary is that the person who collects, sorts and pre-treats the waste is not the same as the person who then sells it on the market. As a consequence, the waste product chain already contains a major economic depreciation in the waste product.

3 RESEARCH METHODOLOGY

In our research, we sought to answer whether the conditions for successful entrepreneurship in the waste sector are met, what challenges and difficulties the actors in the sector face, and finally, whether entry into the sector can be attractive for potential entrepreneurs. The conditions for a successful business are an innovative idea and the recognition of business opportunities creating a marketable product or service, for which there is solvent demand.

The favorable development of the profitability prospects and the existence of a supportive, business-friendly environment are essential for the long-term operation of the company. To be successful, both the role of the entrepreneurial aptitude and the entrepreneurial knowledge should not be underestimated. We examined the existence of these key success factors based on industrial and environmental analysis on the one hand, and demographic and economic data of companies operating in the waste sector on the other. In parallel, we conducted expert and student interviews, focusing on the attractiveness of the sector for potential start-ups.

Our research can be divided into four parts:

- sectoral analysis
- PESTEL analysis
- expert interviews
- student interviews.

We conducted semi-structured interviews among ten experts in the sector. Table 1 shows the main characteristics of the interviewed stakeholders. During the selection of the interviewees, we aimed to represent different areas of the sector so that their experiences would cover the waste management sector as widely as possible.

Table 1. The main characteristics of the stakeholders.

	Interviewee position	Main activity of the company	Number of employees
1	manager	Treatment and disposal of non-hazardous waste	4
2	EMS leader	Quarrying of stone, plaster and chalk	160
3	colleague	Activities of other membership organisations n.e.c.	4
4	research field leader	Other research and experimental development on natural sciences and engineering	223
5	manager	Treatment and disposal of non-hazardous waste	282
6	editor in chief	Engineering activities and related technical consultancy	0
7	researcher	Other research and experimental development on natural sciences and engineering	210
8	university professor	Higher education	
9	university professor	Higher education	
10	university professor	Higher education	

Source: own elaboration

In parallel, we also conducted interviews with seven students in the waste management sector. In selecting the interviewees, we tried to represent all levels of training, so students who are currently in PhD programs were also included in the interviews. Table 2 gives a brief overview of the participants.

Table 2. Main characteristics of the respondents.

	Education	Current studies	Work experience	Entrepreneurial experience/ background	What stage is he or she in
1	Faculty of Earth Science and Engineering BSc	Faculty of Economics MSc	technical preparation department engineer	family entrepreneurial background (husband, husband's parents)	brainstorming
2	Faculty of Earth Science and Engineering MSc, Faculty of Economics MSc	PhD	project manager	former own business	brainstorming
3	Faculty of Earth Science and Engineering MSc	PhD	student work, research assistant	-	brainstorming
4	Faculty of Natural Sciences MSc		Production Manager	family entrepreneurial background (parents)	brainstorming
5	Faculty of Earth Science and Engineering BSc	Faculty of Earth Science and Engineering MSc	research/engineering field	-	brainstorming
6	Faculty of Earth Science and Engineering MSc	PhD	participation in university projects	-	brainstorming
7	Faculty of Earth Science and Engineering BSc	Faculty of Earth Science and Engineering MSc	trainee in design	-	brainstorming

Source: own elaboration

The interviews took about 40-60 minutes. The interviews were recorded and then transcripts were prepared. We then analysed the responses. Due to the low number of interviews, we did not use qualitative data analysis software.

4 RESULTS

4.1 *Identification of the business opportunities in the Hungarian waste management sector*

In the last decade, the problem of resource scarcity on the one hand and of the management of large amounts of waste on the other has gained more and more emphasis along the industrial value chains. As these problems worsen, key areas such as resource efficiency - recycling - the circular economy are receiving increasing attention. Material recycling is conceivable both within a given sector (even within a company/facility) and through collaboration between different industries. The waste management sector is seen as an intermediary in solution of above mentioned problems. Figure 1 illustrates the intermediarial role of the waste sector in facilitating the implementation of the circular economy. The collection, treatment, disposal, and possible processing of waste contribute to the production of secondary raw materials. Ultimately, the energy recovery of waste also reduces the amount of materials transported to landfills. To ensure the circulation of materials and create value for networks, expanding the functions and the role of the waste management sector is a necessary condition (Aid et al. 2017; Horváth & Bereczk 2019).

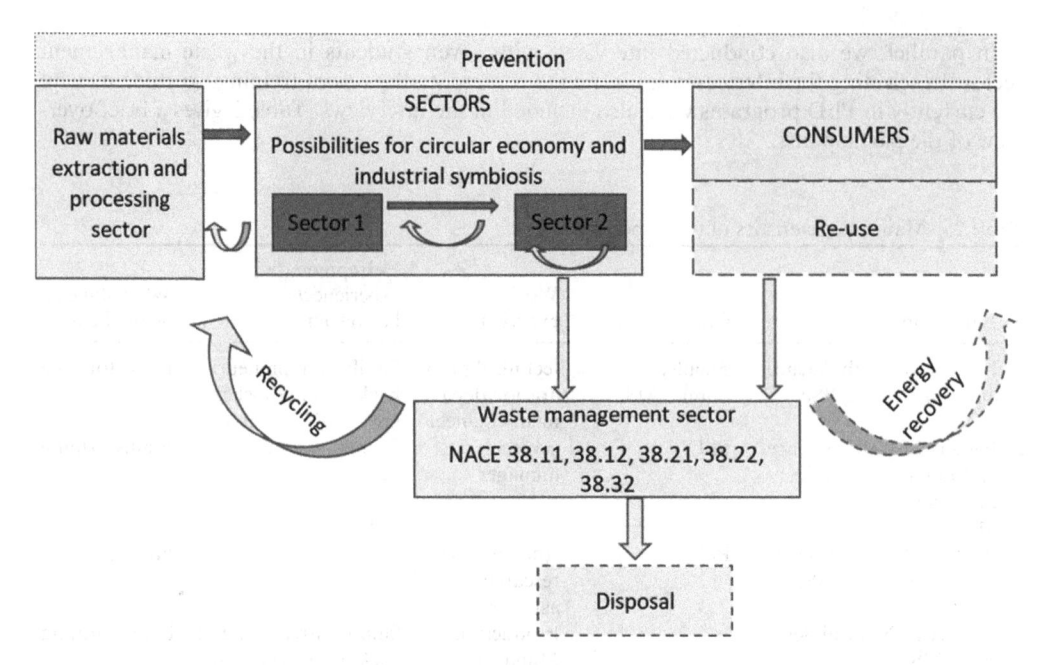

Figure 1.   Role of the waste management sector in the industry value chain.

Source: own elaboration

4.2   *Innovative ideas, business opportunities – marketable product, solvent demand*

Compliance with the principles of sustainable resource management and of environmental sustainability requires new solutions, business models and a new approach from both the companies and consumers. Therefore, we believe that a number of business opportunities can be identified in the waste sector. All areas of the waste pyramid offer many opportunities to implement innovative ideas. It is important to emphasize the performance and importance of the waste management sector cannot be judged solely on the performance of companies with a given NACE Rev 2. code. The performance of the sector is underestimated in official statistics; its real performance could be interpreted along the industry value chain as many innovations and achievements related to waste management or recycling are reported in the user sectors under other NACE Rev 2. codes.

However, the market for recycled waste as a secondary raw material is relatively narrow (due to its special nature), confidence in these raw materials is in many cases even lower, sometimes saturated (see waste paper market crisis), so finding viable demand is a key issue for companies.

4.3   *Corporate demography*

The companies of the waste management sector and their characteristics were examined on the basis of the OPTEN database.

Based on the corporate demographic data, the following conclusions can be drawn from the point of view of the examination of business opportunities:

The dominance of micro-enterprises is typical (72%). The share of micro and small enterprises together is 90.3 percent. The waste management sector employed 20,367 people in 2018, of which the SME sector accounts for 71%. Based on this, it can be said that it is a laurel for small start-ups. 76 percent of companies have 5 closed years, so there is a possibility of long-term, stable operation. Twenty-four percent of businesses operating today have been established in the past five years, most of them operate in the recycling industry. This also proves

Table 3. Business demography of the Hungarian enterprises operating in the waste management sector.

NACE Class	Activity	Number of enterprises 2019	Data available for 2018	Number of companies sur- viving 5 years	Change in number 2014-2019	Closed without a legal successor 2014-2018
38.11	Collection of non-hazardous waste	433	409	356	76	200
38.12	Collection of haz-ardous waste	43	43	38	4	16
38.21	Treatment and dis-posal of non-hazardous waste	212	190	138	71	90
38.22	Treatment and dis-posal of hazardous waste	57	54	46	10	23
38.32	Recovery of sorted materials	311	277	221	95	196
Division 38	Waste management total	1056	973	799	256	525

Source: own elaboration based on OPTEN database

Table 4. Distribution of companies by size (based on the number of employees) (2018).

NACE class	Enterprises with 0 employee	Share of micro-enterprises %	Share of small enterprises %	Share of medium-sized enterprises %	Share of large enterprises %
38.11	71	66.3	20.0	12.2	1.5
38.12	8	79.1	18.6	2.3	0.0
38.21	53	76.3	15.3	6.8	1.6
38.22	16	55.6	31.5	13.0	0.0
38.32	82	78.7	16.2	5.1	0.0
Division 38 total	230	71.7	18.6	8.7	0.9

Source: own elaboration based on OPTEN database

the existence of business opportunities. However, the number of companies closed over the past five years has been high, which in turn draws attention to the need for a careful analysis of conditions.

4.4 *Net sales revenue, profitability indicators in the sector*

We drew conclusions about the development of the net sales revenue of the sector on the basis of the data of 799 companies with 5 closed business years. The aggregated net sales revenue of these companies increased by 32% from 2014 to 2018. The largest increases were in the collection, treatment and disposal of non-hazardous waste, but there was also an increase in the recovery of sorted materials. The collection, treatment and disposal of hazardous waste accounts for a smaller share of the sector's net sales revenue, and growth was also the smallest in these areas.

In the Hungarian waste management sector in 2018 the average net sales revenue was the highest in the recovery of sorted materials class (NACE Rev 2. class 38.32).

Out of the TOP 50 companies in the waste management sector of Hungary concerning the highest net sales revenue, 24 operate in the collection of non-hazardous waste and 11 in the

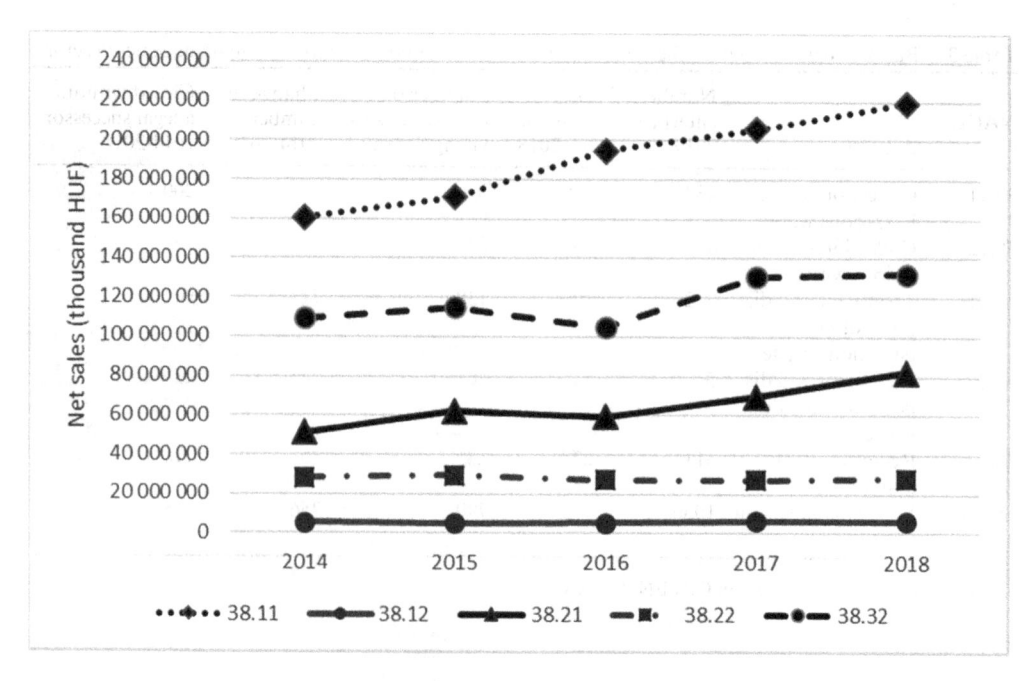

Figure 2. The development of the waste management sector's net sales for companies with 5 closed business years.
(38.11: 356 enterprises, 38.12: 38 enterprises, 38.21: 138 enterprises, 38.22: 46 enterprises, 38.32: 221 enterprises, Total 799 enterprises)
Source: own elaboration based on OPTEN database

Table 5. Net sales revenue of the SMEs in the waste management sector.

NACE Rev 2. Classes	Average net sales revenue of SMEs 2018 excluding enterprises with 0 net sales revenue	Change in net sales revenue of enterprises with 5 closed business years 2014–2018 (%)
38.11	444 404	+36,6
38.12	166 520	+13,9
38.21	539 383	+60,8
38.22	649 359	+0,08
38.32	674 890	+21

Source: own elaboration based on OPTEN database

field of Treatment and disposal of non-hazardous waste. This is not surprising, most of these companies are public service companies. It should be noted, however, that among the TOP 50 companies there are 11 operating in the field of Recovery of sorted materials. It also shows the importance of this field that half of the TOP 12 companies operate in the field of recovery.

In the first three years between 2014 and 2018, the profitability indicators for waste collection, treatment and disposal were typically better than those for the recovery of sorted materials, but in the last two years the profitability indicators of the latter sector also increased. In 2018, 64% of companies in the sector were profitable (based on data from 973 companies). The proportion of profitable companies in the field of recovery of sorted materials was lower. Profitability indicators were calculated on the basis of aggregate data from 596 profitable SMEs and the results are shown in Table 5. It can be seen that profitability varies from class to class.

Table 6. Profitability characteristics of the waste management sector of Hungary.

NACE class	Rate of profitable enterprises % (2018)	operating profit /total assets (%, 2018)	operating profit//net sales revenue (%, 2018)
38.11	69	8	7
38.12	81	14	11
38.21	62	12	10
38.22	69	2	13
38.32	54	11	6
Division 38 total	64	-	-

Source: own calculations based on OPTEN database

It can be seen that the average profitability in the sector was around 9-11 percent, so there is an opportunity to carry out high-quality, profitable activities. However, both the typically depressed price of secondary raw materials and of waste and the unpredictable change in prices have an adverse effect on the profitability outlook. Consumers' price sensitivity is increased by the lack of knowledge about secondary raw materials and the low level of trust in them. These materials are usually incorporated instead of the primary raw materials when they are much cheaper. This, in turn, has an understandable negative impact on profitability.

4.5 *Analysis of the macro environment (PESTEL)*

In the following, we review the macro-environment of the waste sector according to PESTEL, covering the most important legal, economic, social, technological, and natural environmental issues. The legal environment both helps and complicates the situation of companies operating in the waste sector. There may be a growing demand for the products and services provided by the waste sector due to the introduction of tightening environmental and climate protection regulations on manufacturing companies such as the "polluter-pays principle" and the "extended producer responsibility". With the spread of the life cycle approach, the role of secondary raw materials or more energy efficient solutions in production may increase. On one hand this can be identified as an opportunity for the waste sector. On the other hand, the waste sector is also subject to strict European Union and domestic regulations, and it is difficult for the actors in the sector to comply with the legislation. There are difficulties with the classification of secondary raw materials and waste.

The economic environment was examined by analyzing the available sources. We reviewed the European Union and domestic research project funds, structural funds and government resources available by analyzing the calls for proposals and the supported projects. We reviewed the venture capital investment opportunities provided by business angels and the low-interest government loan programs available to SMEs. There are sector-specific opportunities among the research project funds and structural funds but they are not targeted at start-ups. The opportunities that help start-up companies (start-ups or support for young people to become entrepreneurs) are not sector-specific, so there is a huge competition for resources. The low-interest, state-subsidized loan programs are available for SMEs. However, the conditions of these are not necessarily suitable for start-up companies. For example, a condition may be at least two closed business years. The opportunities offered by venture capitalists and various start-up idea competitions can provide a good foundation for start-ups. However, this is hampered by the fact that business angels expect complete business plans, credible and confident action, and sometimes risky future commitments, so in many cases young start-ups are unable or unwilling to take advantage of these opportunities.

The advanced technological environment plays an important role in the development of the sector. The demand for state-of-the-art technologies is emerging at all levels of the waste pyramid, both within the sector and at the level of related industries. Due to the stricter environmental standards greater use of secondary raw materials (waste and by-products is desirable) in production processes (recycling). Sectors that sell and use secondary raw materials need to recognize the potential of industrial symbiosis, and the waste management sector, as a kind of accelerator, is involved in the process through efficient collection, sorting and preparation. Waste collection systems, sorting, cleaning, shredding, preparation for different wastes require different technologies. Using the appropriate technology is essential at the other levels of the waste pyramid too. During energy recovery, waste incineration plants produce combined heat and power (CHP) in most cases. The modern flue gas purification technologies and processes ensure that emissions from incinerators are below the strict EU limit values. At the level of disposal construction and operation of modern landfills is a basic condition. In some cases, landfill gas (biogas) generated in landfills can be used for heat and electricity generation. In general, the technology is available in all areas of domestic waste management, but it means a high entry barrier for start-ups.

We consider the role of society in the success of businesses to be significant. The consumer behavior of the society influences the production processes, the attitude towards new initiatives, the environmental awareness is a key issue. Emphasis should be placed on shaping social attitudes, developing and organizing awareness-raising programs, while the importance of information, communication and education should increase. It offers an outstanding business opportunity for start-ups. In addition, the effect of spill over can be identified, as there are many initiatives and entrepreneurial ideas that build on the growing sensitivity of society. We have examined many good practices and initiatives in our research. Here we can mention the many auction portals and classifieds websites, which offer opportunities in reuse by linking the demand and supply side. The emergence of Re-use Centers or the growing number of re-use shops, repair shops, organized second-hand shops, donation shops and commission stores, as well as online second-hand shops should be highlighted. The key to successfully exploit the business potential of reuse is to increase public awareness.

As far as environmental factors are considered, through the recycling of waste the use of primary raw materials is reduced. The production from a secondary raw material also results in a reduction in energy consumption, CO_2 emissions and other environmental load compared to the production from a primary raw material. The recovery of waste therefore plays a key role in achieving climate protection objectives. As a result, the number of business opportunities is increasing through innovation and R&D in this field.

Now that we have reviewed the quantitative data of the waste management sector, we supplement our analysis with a qualitative assessment in the following section, based on interviews with stakeholders of the sector.

4.6 *Entrepreneurial opportunities according to the stakeholders*

First of all, it should be emphasized that the waste management sector is extremely diverse, with each level of the waste hierarchy (prevention, re-use, recycling, energy recovery and disposal) having a number of specific characteristics, while being closely interlinked. Secondly, it is very difficult to estimate the real weight of the sector, as in many cases innovations related to waste management and their results do not directly appear in the waste management sector.

As a first step, we addressed the challenges facing the sector and the business opportunities that arise from it. We focused on the opportunities that the interviewed experts see for newly graduated engineering students planning to start their own business.

In the case of Hungary, compliance with EU directives on waste recycling is a major challenge. Fluctuations in material prices and primary raw material prices are a problem, and if the price of oil falls, so will the price of energy generated from waste.

The issue of municipal solid waste versus industrial waste needs to be addressed separately when discussing waste management issues, as they are subject to different frameworks and need to be treated differently. In the case of municipal solid waste, a strong state presence can be observed (collection is mostly concentrated in the hands of state and local governments) and its framework is determined by a government regulation. In the latter, however, market solutions predominate (resulting in highly volatile prices), but the secondary raw material market is expanding rapidly and there are plenty of opportunities in the long run. For industrial waste, prevention has a huge potential. Operating costs are lower when less waste is generated, as wastes have to be treated and this treatment is costly. One of the experts in this field sees many business opportunities.

Almost all market participants have emphasized that the necessary technology is available in most areas, but it creates a high barrier to entry, even in areas that are not otherwise concentrated on the regulatory side. And where there is competition, such as in writing studies or grant applications, there are depressed prices in the market. At the same time, an engineer, if he/she has a good overview of his field and examines the environmental problems in a system, can find a possibility of use where the disposal and transformation of a waste can gain new meaning.

For students just after graduation, respondents identified a number of market niches. It was felt that the increased administrative burden due to state regulation, as well as access to grant funds and then the task of managing the funds, also created an opportunity. Environmental life cycle analyses, economic life cycle analyses and SLCA models examining social impacts are increasingly becoming an aspect that also requires the training and employment of professionals who are competent in these activities. Finally, climate protection was mentioned as a new option. At the same time, they believe that previous experience and social capital are still important, so it is very important that potential entrepreneurs in this area gain the necessary experience during their university years.

There was no consensus among respondents as to whether there is a business opportunity for young people to promote industrial symbiosis (e.g. establishing an intermediary network that connects waste donors and recipients, software development, etc.). It is mainly the professionals who see that the market is already and narrow, but those working in the academic line feel that the establishment of a nationwide network of intermediaries is a priority, without which waste recovery cannot be efficient.

The innovation culture of Hungarian companies is not yet mature, the willingness to take risks is low. They are afraid of new solutions, and recycled material made from waste will only be incorporated into production if it is much cheaper than the standard materials. Although many island-like innovations and development ideas emerge, they often die. There is a need to bring together island-like initiatives. There has already been an example of this in connection with a grant: hundreds of local governments came together and agreed relatively easily and quickly in order to gain EU funding. This could work well in the entrepreneurial sphere, whether it is fundraising or R&D.

Paradoxically, EU and state grants are not conducive to innovative ideas because participants do not take risks, they strive for mature technology. For example, in a state-funded project in which the employer of one of the respondents was also a consortium partner, the development of 16 marketable products was undertaken, with full product descriptions and patent applications. This is a big risk that companies in the market would not take on. Instead, companies prefer ready-made, workable solutions (such as those already proven in Western Europe).

As regards access to finance for young entrepreneurs, respondents see that loans are mainly available to them in the market. The Economic Development and Innovation Operational Program (GINOP) and other asset grants are not tailored to start-ups. Respondents were unaware of the existence of incubation activities in this sector, but university colleagues stressed that they were trying to help young people implement their ideas. However, this is still not enough for incubation. There are examples of the existence of venture capital, but not specifically focused on this area. There are young entrepreneurial competitions, but also not sector-specific. Funders expect a complete, elaborate business plan, so young people need business, entrepreneurial knowledge, and credible action in addition to a professional idea.

Regarding the importance of the change of attitude, all respondents agreed on the importance of the issue. At present, the Hungarian market participants are price sensitive, consumers have little knowledge of this area, they are hostile to planned projects (for example, the construction of a waste incinerator or landfill), while producing more waste. Companies prefer predictable, financially secure solutions, which delays resolving the issue of producer responsibility. At the same time, it is not possible to rely on the fact that the environmentally conscious willingness to pay will develop on its own; the changes must be initiated through pricing, ie. the change of attitude is also a regulatory and financing issue.

The tasks related to the change of attitude will also be manifested in financial resources, which at the same time may provide an opportunity for new companies to enter the market. There are a number of communication, information and education tasks that need to be pursued following a central strategy but at the local level, taking into account the diversity of the target group and generational differences. If we want to create a circular economy, we need to make market participants aware that waste has value and is not rubbish. The change of attitude has begun, but it is still in its infancy. Information to residents is important because they see that waste is taken away once a week and they do not see the path of waste, recycling or re-use opportunities. More demonstration activities would be needed, either by civilians or by state-owned companies. The marketing of this sector is particularly bad. This could be helped by young people – marketing activities could be carried out in this sector, which could also create entrepreneurial opportunities for young people.

We need to emphasize that work is now under way to prepare a waste management strategy that will determine the future focus of waste management and thus the direction of change in the sector.

4.7 Reflection of potential entrepreneurs

It should be mentioned at the beginning that the entrepreneurial intention is low in Hungary (Gubik & Farkas, 2019) and this is also true at the University of Miskolc. At the University of Miskolc, 8 percent of the surveyed students (764 students) plan to start their own business or take over the family business after graduation. This statistic is only 5 percent for engineers (3.2 percent of whom would like to found a company), which means only 15 of the 221 engineering students surveyed.[1] These data predict that it was not easy to find students with an entrepreneurial intention among engineering students.

All of the students interviewed are more or less proficient in waste management. Due to their field of training, they have some knowledge about the sector. It is a completely different question, however, whether they feel they have the basis needed to start a business. The first part of our questions focused on whether they studied subjects related to entrepreneurship. All respondents answered yes, but it should be emphasized that in the framework of university education, these are not special entrepreneurial subjects related to the skills or knowledge required to start one's own business, but basic economics and business subjects (microeconomics, macroeconomics, statistics, business economics). This became clear later when we asked them about the nature of the external help needed to start a business. The topics highlighted by the respondents: the areas of accounting, economic consulting, legal advice and other tasks related to starting a business (preparation of a business plan, market analysis) suggest that this is an area that could be strengthened. According to one of our respondents (H3), more practical examples would have been needed in teaching these subjects. Two students (H1 and H6) also mentioned that if they started a business, they would look for an accountant and a lawyer first. Student H6 also has a professional training degree National Training Registry course in business administration and thus studied all economics and business subjects; his reason for the decision of applying for this training was that once he got into a business, he would have the appropriate knowledge. He does not want to start a business right now because he does not have the confidence and he does not have enough financial capital, even though he has the knowledge to do so.

Interviewees were divided on the question of the usefulness of the business-related subjects they had taken. Two considered that these did not play a role in their entrepreneurial decision

---

1. Data are based on the GUESSS 2018 database.

(H3, H5), while the others felt that these objects were decisive, either because of their entrepreneurial ideas or from a professional point of view in general.

The majority of students have so far only dealt with starting a business at the level of brainstorming. Their plans are relatively detailed and clear, especially for those who have an entrepreneurial family background and thus have an insight into how entrepreneurial processes take place and what it means to be an entrepreneur in general. According to one of our interviewees (H2), career choice is already determined by family background – many people choose their field of training to suit the family business or based on their parents' work experience (where there is a demand for labor, what income can be earned). Of those who accidentally got into their field, several left the field, unable to prevail in the profession.

It is also important how confident the students are in their decisions. This is called self-efficacy in the literature and can be developed with special programs (Gubik & Farkas, 2019). For example, one of our respondents (H1) was not brave enough to start his own business, although he had contributed several good ideas to the family business.

One interviewee has entrepreneurial experience. She emphasized two things. One is that she would not have dared to start a business if she had not studied at the Faculty of Economics in parallel; she did not consider her technical knowledge alone to be enough to start her own business. The other is that she gained additional knowledge compared to what she studied at the university through taking part in a student research society competition. The business opportunity itself came from here. Eventually, she closed down the company and found a job at a multinational company. This was because she had few orders and did not have enough acquaintances to search for orders on her own, so for a long time she could only have been a subcontractor for a fraction of the real amount of the order. She emphasized that although she did not really need much capital to start the business, she needed a relatively predictable income; in the absence of savings, she could not bear the financial risk arising from the uncertainty of the orders. There was another interesting counter-argument on her part: as an entrepreneur, she had to focus on one thing on a long-lasting basis, which she found very tiring because she loves variety and new tasks. She sees that large companies have an advantage here, as one can also switch within a company.

The interview with her confirmed one of the lessons of the discussion with stakeholders: although there are areas where capital requirements are not high, there is still a barrier to entry due to the lack of social capital and awareness of those already in the market. This was also confirmed by H7, who said that in order for someone to start a business that is profitable in the field of waste management), large start-up capital and political connections are needed.

It is important to emphasize that entrepreneurship is more than a good business idea. You need to be able to articulate this idea in a good business plan, you need to be able to sell it to investors. The product, the service, yourself as an entrepreneur, all of these need to be advertised, the processes need to be organized, and so on. There are a number of professional tasks that require additional knowledge, to which are added the administrative tasks (starting a business, tax, accounting tasks).

The interviewed students are in the brainstorming phase; the elaboration of ideas among them is very diverse. Only the interviewee with entrepreneurial experience (H2) has a detailed business idea. They all agree that there is great business potential in waste management: "I see a business opportunity, as waste is a big problem all over the world, so its management and prevention is not only important from an environmental point of view, but also has serious business opportunities .... I see prevention as being attractive from an entrepreneurial as well as from an environmental point of view" (H3). A business idea mentioned by respondent H6 was that "it would be worthwhile to start a business that deals with waste analysis, as it is mandatory to do a quarterly waste analysis in the waste management sector. If I had to start a business as easily as possible, that would be it. Obviously this required engineering qualifications and chamber membership. Maybe that would be the least complicated, but you need the right knowledge."

H1 suggested "...especially in the part of recovery to make something new out of something used, whether jewelry or everyday objects.... or smart energy use can also be an area of interest".

Interviewee (H2), who already has entrepreneurial experience, only wants to be an entrepreneur as a second job, and in addition to waste management, she also has business plans in other areas.

The students interviewed gave very varied answers to our question about mobility[2]. The financial reasons, which we consider to be the main motivation, do not seem to appear as sharply in students' decisions as we had previously thought. Several students mentioned the importance of family as a factor against mobility (H1, H3). Other important aspects for the interviewees in general included a number of aspects related to their job expectations, such as performing challenging tasks, diversity, and the opportunity for continuous improvement. There were also some motivations mentioned that a larger firm is more likely to provide, such as working in an international environment and the opportunity to use English on a daily basis (H2).

4.8 *Findings*

A good business idea is not enough. In order to raise capital, a ready-made business plan must be put on the table, here it is important to have an economics/business background as well. Thus, not only should students be motivated to acquire well-founded, competitive knowledge related to their own profession, but they should also be able to independently identify their further training needs (business-related knowledge) and organize their own learning accordingly and/or work with those who already have those skills. Together, economic and technical qualifications can lead to more competitive solutions. The institutional framework for this needs to be created within the university, which also requires stronger communication and collaboration between faculties.

Incorporating entrepreneurial knowledge into educational materials and promoting existing programs are important tasks, but is not enough to ensure the availability of the service. It would also be an important task to arouse students' interest in the topic, as without this participation the utilization of what they have learned will not take place.

Career opportunities should be addressed consciously, and students should be made aware of them so that they can think in time and prepare according to their plans. In addition to material knowledge, their self-efficacy should also be improved. It is not enough to have the knowledge, but you also have to believe that you can be successful in the market with it.

5 CONCLUSIONS

It is important to note that the real performance and importance of the waste management sector is higher than estimations from official statistics, as many innovations and achievements related to waste management/recycling in user sectors are reported under other NACE codes.

The role of the waste sector in industrial value chains has been defined as a kind of intermediary, which, through the collection, treatment and processing of waste, contributes to the generation of secondary raw materials that can be sold to industries. In our analysis, we examined all levels of the waste hierarchy (prevention, reuse, recycling, energy recovery, landfilling) based on its potentials. The preparation of the Hungarian Waste Management Strategy is in progress. Its objectives – to increase the role of the sector in economic policy, to support the achievement of sustainability goals and the transition to a circular economy – will further increase the future potential of waste management.

Our research based on desk research and interviews provided a complex picture of the entrepreneurial opportunities inherent in waste management. The necessary technology is

---

2. "What are the most important considerations in connection with the decision to stay or leave the Northern Hungary region (or even Hungary) after completing your studies?"

available in most areas, but it also creates a high barrier to entry. Even in areas that are not otherwise concentrated on the regulatory side, smaller companies are being pushed out. At the same time, increasing administrative burdens due to strict regulatory requirements and conditions for grants for the waste sector, as well as environmental and economic life cycle analyses, SLCA models, etc. result in an expanding market for skilled professionals. Market gaps can also be identified in the field of promoting industrial symbioses (e.g. support network, software development, etc.). Also in the regulation of manufacturing sectors, increasingly ambitious energy efficiency, emission reduction and waste reduction targets are encouraging greater use of secondary raw materials in production processes. Product expectations (longevity, serviceability, modular design, energy saving, etc.) require continuous technological development. The demand for state-of-the-art technologies and continuous innovation are also reflected at all levels of the waste hierarchy as well as in related industries.

The two levels of the waste management hierarchy, both prevention and re-use, are greatly influenced by the type of consumer behaviour that develops in society. But significant changes in household demand also affect production processes (supply). Social opinion-forming on waste, which is still in its infancy in Hungary, should therefore be given higher priority. The tasks related to the change of attitude will also be manifested in financial sources, which at the same time may provide an opportunity for new companies to enter the market.

Examining the supply side of becoming an entrepreneur, we can say that in Hungary, in general, the intention of students to be entrepreneurs is low and is even lower among students in the technical field. Increasing this requires complex intervention. Career opportunities for students need to be addressed more intensively, and students need to be made aware of them so that they can think in time and prepare according to their plans. In order to be able to turn their business ideas into well-developed business plans, they also need economic/business/entrepreneurial knowledge or peers who can perform these tasks in the planned business. The institutional framework for this needs to be created within the university, which also requires stronger communication and collaboration between faculties.

We conducted interviews with a total of ten stakeholders who had relevant knowledge about the sector and with seven students. Because of the limited number of interviews and the characteristics of the methodology our results may not be generalizable. When interpreting the results, the constraints arising from both the methodology and the number of respondents should be taken into account. However, these also indicate potential for further research. Both increasing the number of respondents and broadening the sectors covered by the study can contribute to our current results.

ACKNOWLEDGEMENTS

The article came into being within the project no. 18197 entitled 'LIMBRA Decreasing the negative outcomes of brain drain in the raw material sector - EIT RawMaterials Project'.

The authors would like to thank the interviewees for their openness and helpfulness.

REFERENCES

Aid, G., Eklund, M., Anderberg, S. & Baas, L. (2017). Expanding roles for the Swedish waste management sector in inter-organizational resource management. Resources, Conservation and Recycling, 124, 85–97. doi: 10.1016/j.resconrec.2017.04.007

Autio, E. & Wennberg, K. (2010). You think, therefore, I become: Social attitudes and the transition to entrepreneurship. Paper presented at DRUID Summer Conference 2010, Imperial College London Business School, 16–18 June 2010, London

Baron, R.A. & Ensley, M.D. (2006). Opportunity Recognition as the Detection of Meaningful Patterns: Evidence from Comparisons of Novice and Experienced Entrepreneurs. Management ScienceVol. 52, No. 9, https://doi.org/10.1287/mnsc.1060.0538

Carree, M. A. & Thurik, A. R. (2010). The Impact of entrepreneurship on Economic Growth. In: Zoltan Acs & David Audretsch (eds.) International Handbook of Entrepreneurship Research, 2nd edition. Springer New York: Springer, 557–594

Davidsson, P. (2015). Entrepreneurial opportunities and the entrepreneurship nexus: A re-conceptualization. Journal of Business Venturing, Volume 30, Issue 5, Pages 674–695, https://doi.org/10.1016/j.jbusvent.2015.01.002.

Drucker, P.F. (1985). Innovation and entrepreneurship. Practice and Principles. Harper & Row, New York

Egerová, D., Eger, L. & Micik, M. (2017). Does entrepreneurship education matter? Business students' perspectives. Tertiary Education and Management 23(1), 1–15.

Gauthier, J.F., Stangler, D., Penzel, M., Morelix, A. & Ortmans, J. (2018). Global Startup Ecosystem Report 2018. Succeeding in the New Era of Technology. Startup Genome and Global Entrepreneurship Network (GEN). Retrieved February 12, 2019, from https://startupgenome.com/reports/2018/GSER-2018-v1.1.pdf

Grégoire, D.A. & Shepherd, D.A. (2012). Technology-Market Combinations and the Identification of Entrepreneurial Opportunities: An Investigation of the Opportunity-Individual Nexus. Academy of Management Journal Vol. 55, No. 4 https://doi.org/10.5465/amj.2011.0126 753–785

Gruber M, MacMillan IC, & Thompson JD. (2012). From Minds to Markets: How Human Capital Endowments Shape Market Opportunity Identification of Technology Start-Ups. Journal of Management. 2012;38(5):1421–1449. doi:10.1177/0149206310386228

Gubik, S. Andrea (2013). A magyar hallgatók vállalkozásindító szándékát befolyásoló tényezők modellje – Ajzen tervezett magatartás elméletének kiterjesztése (Model of the Hungarian students' business start-up intention influencing factors – Extending of Ajzen's Theory of Planned Behavior). Vezetéstudomány, 44(7-8.), 5–17.

Gubik, S.A. & Farkas, Sz. (2019). Entrepreneurial Intention in the Visegrad Countries. DANUBE: LAW AND ECONOMICS REVIEW 10: 4 pp. 347–368., 22 p.

Hope, K. (ed.) (2016). Annual Report on European SMEs 2015/2016. SME Recovery Continues. European Commission. DOI 10.2873/76227

Horváth, Á. & Bereczk, Á. (2019). Az ipari szimbiózis szerepe a fenntartható erőforrásgazdálkodásban (Role of the industrial symbiosis in the sustainable corporate resource management) Észak-Magyarországi Stratégiai Füzetek XVI(3), 99–109.

Kirzner, (1973). Competition and entrepreneurship. The University of Chicago Press, Chicago and London

Kolstad, I. & Wiig, A. (2015). Education and entrepreneurial success. Small Business Economics, 44(4) 783–796.

Krueger, N. & Dickson, P.R. (1994). How Believing in Ourselves Increases Risk Taking: Perceived Self-Efficacy and Opportunity Recognition. Decision Sciences Volume25, Issue3, Pages 385–400, https://doi.org/10.1111/j.1540-5915.1994.tb00810.x

Ling, H. & Venesaar, U. (2015). Enhancing Entrepreneurship Education in Engineering Students to Increase Their Metacognitive Abilities: Analysis of Student Self-Assessments. Inzinerine Ekonomika-Engineering Economics, 26(3), 333–342.

Maresch, D., Harms, R., Kailer, N. & Wimmer-Wurm, B. (2016). The impact of entrepreneurship education on the entrepreneurial intention of students in science and engineering versus business studies university programs. Technological Forecasting and Social Change, 104(3), 172–179.

Meager, N., Bates, P. & Cowling, M. (2003). An evaluation of business start-up support for young people. National Institute Economic Review, 186(1), 59–72.

Nowiński, W., Haddoud, M.Y., Lančarič, D., Egerová, D. & Czeglédi, Cs. (2017). The impact of entrepreneurship education, entrepreneurial self-efficacy and gender on entrepreneurial intentions of university students in the Visegrad countries. Studies in Higher Education, 44(2)1–19.

Shane, S. (2000). Prior Knowledge and the Discovery of Entrepreneurial Opportunities. Organization Science, Vol. 11, No. 4 Pages 367–472 https://doi.org/10.1287/orsc.11.4.448.14602

Shane, S., & Venkataraman, S. (2000). The Promise of Entrepreneurship as a Field of Research. The Academy of Management Review, 25 (1),217–226. Retrieved January 22, 2021, from http://www.jstor.org/stable/259271

Shane, S., Kolvereid, L. & Westhead, P. (1991). An Exploratory Examination of the Reasons Leading to New Firm Formation Across Country and Gender. Journal of Business Venturing, 6(6), 431–446.

Stevenson, H.H., J.C. Jarillo (1990): A paradigm of entrepreneurship: Entrepreneurial management, Strategic Management Journal, 11, 17–27.

Szerb, L. & Lukovszki, L. (2013). Magyar egyetemi hallgatók vállalkozási attitűdjei és az attitűdöket befolyásoló tényezők elemzése a GUESSS-felmérés adatai alapján – Kik is akarnak ténylegesen vállalkozni? (Entrepreneurial attitudes of the Hungarian students and the analysis of the factors influencing attitudes based on the data of GUESSS survey – Who want to undertake really?) Vezetéstudomány, 44(7-8.) 30–40.

Thomas, A. S. & Mueller, S. L. (2000). A Case for Comparative Entrepreneurship: Assessing the Relevance of Culture. Journal of International Business Studies, 31(2), 287–301.

Thurik, R. & Dejardin, M. (2012). Entrepreneurship and Culture. In Marco van Gelderen, & Enno Masurel (eds). Entrepreneurship in Context. Routledge, Routledge Studies in Entrepreneurship. 175–186.

von Graevenitz, G., Harhoff, D. & Weber, R. (2010). The effects of entrepreneurship education. Journal of Economic Behavior and Organization, 76(1), 90–112.

Zahra, S.A. (2008). The virtuous cycle of discovery and creation of entrepreneurial opportunities. Strategic Entrepreneurship Journal, Volume2, Issue3, Pages 243–257 https://doi.org/10.1002/sej.47

Zhao, X., Li, H. & Rauch, A. (2012). Cross-country Differences in Entrepreneurial Activity: The Role of Cultural Practice and National Wealth. Frontiers of Business Research in China, 6(4), 447–474.

ANNEXES

Questions for stakeholders

1. What business opportunities do you see for waste management in the areas of prevention, re-use, recycling, energy recovery, and disposal?
2. At what level of the waste management hierarchy (prevention, re-use, recycling, energy recovery, and disposal) do you see the best chance for newly graduated students to become entrepreneurs?
3. What market challenges does the sector face in these areas?
4. What barriers to entry can be identified in the sector? What are the main barriers for start-ups?
5. What characterizes the regulatory (and support) environment? Do they hinder or even support business opportunities?
6. What is the technology requirement of each activity? Is there a technology gap that makes it difficult for a start-up entrepreneur to enter the market?
7. Is the necessary infrastructure available for entrepreneurs to successfully manage business opportunities?
8. Are there incubators/business facilitators?
9. Are investor networks available to SMEs?
10. Are funding sources (public or private) available to entrepreneurs?
11. Do entrepreneurs receive support (public or private) for labor, wage subsidies or job creation?
12. In many cases, innovations related to waste management and their results do not appear in the waste management sector. What role can the waste sector play in achieving waste management goals?
13. Do you see an opportunity to create a network of intermediaries supporting the promotion of industrial symbiosis, e.g. between waste donors and acceptors?
14. How can the environmental and social benefits of effective waste management be measured?
15. Do you see a need to support a change in social attitudes? What role can actors in the sector play in this?
    Do you have any other comments related to the topic?

Questions for students

1. Did you have any courses related to entrepreneurial knowledge? If so, would you characterize them? (List some strengths and weaknesses). Have you heard of the Agora program of the University of Miskolc? (Entrepreneurship Agora for Young People)

2. Have you ever considered becoming an entrepreneur? Are the economic/entrepreneurial subjects studied and the knowledge gained influencing your opinion?
3. Do you have any entrepreneurial experience (own business or family owned business)? If so, in what area?
4. Do you have work experience? If so, in what area?
5. In which faculty and in which specialisation do you study? Do you see a business opportunity related to your field of study? Do you know the most important issues of waste management? If so, do you see a business opportunity in this area?
6. Can you imagine yourself as an entrepreneur in waste management? If so, which area of the hierarchy do you see as attractive from an entrepreneurial perspective? (prevention, reuse, recycling, energy recovery, and disposal)
7. If not, what is the reason for this?
8. Are you aware of the steps of starting a business and the tasks of the business process?
9. Do you know the current grant opportunities? (in connection with starting a business in general or in a specific field)
10. Have you already taken steps to start your business? (e.g. inventing an entrepreneurial idea, finding peers, business plan, market analysis, etc.) What kind of outside help do you think you would need?
11. Where do you want to be located after your studies (scope of activity and geographical area)?
12. What are the most important aspects of the decision to stay or leave the Northern Hungary region (or even Hungary) after completing your studies?

Ecology aspect of CSR—What is the social plastic?

G. Mélypataki

University of Miskolc, Miskolc, Hungary

ABSTRACT: Plastic used as packaging creates a lot of waste. Addressing this problem is not only the responsibility of the state, but also of businesses. The recycling of plastics is a central issue, as they pollute the sea and people's lives. One of the solutions to this problem is to develop solutions as a CSR task, since businesses are responsible for the packaging they use. One practice devised for this purpose is social plastics, which can promote a circular economy whereby the company gives compensation for the plastic it collects. It then reuses the recovered plastic as a raw material. In my presentation and in my paper I would like to explain the details of this.

1 INTRODUCTION

Corporate Social Responsibility (CSR) has a myriad of manifestations. CSR is a form of responsibility that is difficult to define in legal terms. It can be seen as a form of responsibility that can be seen as a matter of corporate conscience. It is not by chance that the roots of corporate social responsibility go back to the company directors. However, it was in the context of corporate social responsibility that the concept of corporate conscience emerged, suggesting that corporations are also organisations of individuals, functioning as part of society, interacting with their environment (Goodpaster & Matthews, 1982).

The levels of this complex system of economic responsibility are also determined by the strength of the linkages with each stakeholder group. At the heart of CSR is the recognition that the scope of a shoulder does not stop at the fence. The approach is based on the thesis that in the modern world, the boundaries of the company are not at the fence, and that corporate decision-makers have to manage a complex matrix of interests and values rather than the 'company', i.e. the set of employees and the narrow business environment of the company. This managed process involves everyone who has an impact on the realisation of the company's strategic goals or who is influenced by the company in the realisation of these goals (Braun, 2015). Accordingly, the company has an impact on its actual environment. The activities of companies have an impact on their ecological environment. It is therefore the responsibility of the company to reduce its ecological footprint. This applies specifically to companies that are involved in the production of products. (Szigeti et al. 2019).

Plastics and plastic packaging play a significant role in today's production. Plastic is treated as a material that dominates our daily lives and can be produced relatively cheaply, and is therefore used in significant scales by industry and households. Which means that plastic is becoming part of everyday life, part of the daily cycle. More and more plastic waste is being generated, which in many places has already led to an ecological disaster. Where it is not, it is also a big problem, as it is constantly polluting the environment and destroying people's environment. Plastic is accumulating as a waste product. This is because it takes a long time to

DOI: 10.1201/9781003259954-7

decompose. Plastic waste is generated at a much higher rate than it decomposes. Some types of plastic can take more than a hundred years to decompose.

However, the accumulation of plastic in the world's seas and other places creates not only ecological problems, but also related social problems. Public administrations and citizens in poor areas are unable to manage this huge amount. From this point of view, it is irrelevant whether they produce the waste themselves or whether it ends up in their land and water in other ways. Some states do not have large supplies of drinking water. Even the little that is available can easily become contaminated. In many cases, these countries are vulnerable because of the presence of large multinational companies, many of which do not comply with regulations. They are heavily polluting and human rights are often violated. The above complex phenomena show that the problems are also clustered and need to be tackled together. If we take the fast fashion phenomenon as an example, it often reflects poor employment conditions, disregard for human rights and pollution. Responsibility on the part of businesses is essential to tackle these problems. Due to space constraints, I would like to briefly outline the issue of waste.

In all these respects, I would like to present the aspects of CSR that are linked to the problem of the management of technical waste. I will not, however, present this in isolation, but in the light of its social impact. Areas flooded with plastic waste have a very strong impact on the inhabitants of certain geographical areas, often creating social problems. I am looking for answers to the question of how companies can tackle these problems. For this reason, I would like to present the social plastic programme as a possible way forward and, of course, as a good practice.

As I am still in the early stages of my research I have mainly done secondary research. However, I believe that the practices I have explored are worthy of presentation and discussion. My research and thus this academic thesis focuses on enterprise solutions.

2 THE DEFINITION OF WASTE

One side effect of production processes is the generation of waste. One of the main problems for businesses is how to deal with all that waste? How can you reduce the waste generated during production? How can the amount of packaging material be reduced and how much recycled material can be used? To see all these issues in a coherent way, it is necessary to define waste. As I have argued in several previous studies, a distinction needs to be made between legal and technical approaches (Mélypataki, 2012). Technical approaches always consider the actual usability. If an object or material is no longer usable or recoverable, it is considered as waste. From a legal point of view, it is not possible to examine this issue. The legal approach is never based on use. There are two basic reasons for this. The first is the definition in the EU Waste Directive. It is not possible to deviate from the content of the Directive's published definition. Each case should always be examined on its own merits. This would make it considerably more difficult to apply. Waste is any substance or object which the holder discards, intends to discard or is about to discard. Recycling of waste is a formal obligation which in fact requires innovative solutions in terms of content.

Businesses are obliged to organise production in such a way as to reduce emissions and the production of pollutants. However, I do not believe that the company's half responsibility stops there. In many cases, waste is not generated directly by the company but by the consumer. The company is then indirectly involved, if we look at the strict legal framework. The product has been taken out of the company's possession at various stages, so of course the waste from this product is not its property either. In principle, the consumer will be the owner and holder of the waste, who will transfer it to the utility provider under the public service contract (Mélypataki G., 2012).

3 WHO IS RESPONSIBLE FOR WASTE? - THE CIRCULAR ECONOMY

The situation outlined above is presented in the legal framework. However, social responsibility goes beyond the legal framework. From a CSR perspective, ownership and tenure are important, but it is important what is covered by CSR. In examining this, there is an apparent conflict between legal and economic principles (Jakab & Ráczi, 2019). Along economic lines, corporate social responsibility can disrupt the ownership chain of the waste chain, but this does not mean direct intervention, but the introduction of elements that divert the waste path. Diversion here could mean the separate collection of certain types of plastics by the producer (Olajos, 2016). Why is it necessary to look at this? Because one of the basic principles of CSR is that the company's activities and their impact do not stop at the fence, but go beyond it. Accordingly, it has an indirect half-ownership of the life cycle of the products it manufactures, at least to the extent that they are environmentally friendly or less polluting. This does not mean that the company has to follow up every single product. It means either developing preventive measures to reduce its existing ecological footprint, or developing a policy that includes a significant element of waste management, or at least reuse. Because of my profession, I look at this issue through the lens of law. In this aspect, the responsibility of the company, as defined by CSR, can be understood in an ecological perspective, somewhat beyond the framework of law, but linked to it as an extended producer responsibility. CSR is the social and economic responsibility that embodies all the legal responsibilities associated with the operation of a company, both at the same time and beyond. In my view, this aggregate resp. If companies are serious about achieving the ecological goals they have set themselves in the CSR framework, I think it is important for them to see the need for a circular economy. They need to recognise that plastic is not only a potential waste but also a potential raw material.

An important step is for businesses to try to mainstream the circular economy theory in their CSR policies. They can do this in the form of the IKEA 2018 Sustainability Report. IKEA's medium-term goal in the report is to be a 100% circular economy company by 2030. This means raising sustainable buildings, using renewable energy sources and, interestingly, using less plastic (IKEA, 2018). For the purposes of our study, the latter is the one to be highlighted. IKEA sees plastic as a material that can be used and thinks of it as a durable material. Things made of plastic can be used for many years and even in many different ways. What is a disadvantage of plastic can also be an advantage. Products made of plastic are generally durable and therefore do not encourage frequent consumption because they are not single-use products.

Therefore, it is not legitimate for a plastic product to become waste after a single use. However, it should be added that this will quickly depend on the function of the product. In this context, it can be pointed out that the development of the circular economy is linked to the global systems of our time. This was also recognised by the European Union when it presented an action plan for the circular economy in March 2020 as part of the European Green Deal and the new industrial strategy. As one of the tools, the Commission Communication also mentions the review of the rules on extended producer responsibility (European Commisson, 2018). In addition, the EU aims to have all packaging made from recyclable plastics by 2030. Single-use plastic products and packaging make up a significant proportion of plastic waste. In this context, the circular economy is based on the idea that what would be waste can also become raw material. At the level of today's industrial techno-logy, we have the operations and processes to recycle plastics treated as waste into raw materials. In addition, the life cycle of plastics allows the same product or waste to be involved in several cycles.

This is why businesses should adopt this approach as soon as possible. Increasing pressure will mean increasing amounts of waste. An important factor will be that the market itself will now demand that businesses increasingly build on the circular economy and become environmentally aware and responsible themselves. Szabolcs Nagy points out that the social image of companies entering the market for environmentally friendly products generally improves in the short term. This of course depends on the quality of corporate communication and the level of commitment. He also adds that consumers perceive corporate responsibility to be almost as high as individual responsibility, which has important consequences (Nagy, 2005). The company should communicate its successes and failures on the environmental front to society through an environmentally conscious promotion mix. Communicating failures is important because it is the only way for a company to act ethically towards consumers. This is why the so-called dieselgate affair was such a big issue. The Volkswagen Group was the main party involved in Dieselgate. The scandal erupted in 2015, when Volkswagen used an irregular bypass device in the engine management of its diesel cars to circumvent US emissions standards. Cars fitted with the bypass were not only running in the US, but also in Europe. The seriousness of the situation is illustrated by the fact that of the nearly 2.6 million bypass-equipped cars sold in Germany.

Businesses need to communicate openly and clearly about their environmental responsibility. If the company does not do so, failures and mistakes will still come to light, but the social perception will not be nearly as favourable as in the first case. A company that does not take the clean road could easily end up like the companies involved in the Dieselgate scandal.

The circular economy is therefore, from our point of view, a system in which recyclable waste is constantly recycled back into production as a secondary raw material. This secondary raw material needs to be prepared and used in a cost-effective way with the minimum possible loss of material. And the social responsibility of business in this case is that, although there is a legal and technological route for waste, this route can be diverted and plastic can be channelled into the circular economy. This way of treating plastic waste has primarily ecological impacts. In itself, the fight for green goals can be seen as CSR in action.

The example of Kersia is a case in point. Kersia also attaches great importance to reducing pollution. The collection and recycling of plastic packaging waste is a prerequisite for a circular economy strategy (Code of Ethic of Kersia, 2019). The aim is to turn this social expectation into a real business model, using an approach that includes:

- purchasing packaging materials containing recycled plastic
- collecting the packaging materials
- recycling of packaging materials

However, there are several categories of waste. We can talk about municipal, inert and hazardous waste. In some cases, the collection of these is an important responsibility in itself. From a legal point of view, however, the concept of waste is broader than this. The term waste also includes "rubbish", i.e. materials that are not suitable for further use or recovery and are disposed of. It also includes materials that can be used for further recovery or as secondary raw materials. In the understanding of the concept of waste, it is the treatment of recyclable materials as waste and their regulation as such that causes most problems. Some materials and valuable assets may also be classified as waste. There is a very fine line between materials classified as waste and "valuable products (Csák, 2011). Maybe what is waste at the consumer can still be used as a secondary raw material by business and industry.

However, it should also be seen that this activity often has not only an ecological but also a social impact. This is particularly true in areas where the standard of living of the population is not high, but where the environment is increasingly flooded with rubbish in various ways. The key question is how to achieve both ecological and social responsibility? One solution currently in operation is the Social Plastic scheme. What is it? I would like to present its concept below as a good practice. The use of plastic goes beyond environmental issues. That is why the definition of waste also has a social dimension.

4 SOCIAL PLASTIC

In order to understand how Social Plastic works, we need to step outside the business. Social Plastic stands for the circular system that the founders of the Plastic Bank have devised and means specifically the plastic itself that is collected. Social Plastic, as a circular economic model, works on the basis that the plastic collected by people is essentially a convertible currency.

A Plastic Bank encourages people to send their plastic waste to collection points around the world for recycling. In return, they receive digital tokens (Plastic Bank). These digital tokens can be managed and used in a bank account accessible via a smartphone. People can use the 'funds' in the account to exchange for food, water, tele-phone minutes and other goods. By using recyclable materials and a blockchain token, Plastic Bank offers a secure, cashless method of financial inclusion. The system offers incentives that motivate them to collect and return their trash. Garbage collection and drop-off is one of the livelihood options. It is a source of livelihood that can help mainly in the countries of the Third World. There, too, it is mainly in areas that have a coastline or ocean shore. The reason is that seas and oceans harbour a lot of waste. Social Plastic is not only an economic model, but also a concrete plastic. As I said, it is both a currency and a potential raw material. This is where the business level comes in again with CSR activities. The companies participating in this scheme undertake to produce a new product or packaging from the plastic thus collected.

The Plastic Banks, in partnership with IBM, have united and strengthened the recycling ecosystems. They want to reduce plastic pollution in the ocean.

What are Plastic Bank and Social Plastic all about? Fighting ocean plastic and global poverty with blockchain-based token rewards. Scientists predict that by 2050, at this rate of plastic pollution in the oceans - there will be more polluting plastic in the ocean than there are fish in the ocean. In a bid to protect the natural world, Plastic Bank, working with IBM and service provider Cognition Foundry, is mobilising recycling entrepreneurs in the world's poorest communities to clean up plastic waste in exchange for life-changing goods. Powered by IBM technology, the Plastic Bank demonstrates the value of plastic waste, interrupts its flow to the ocean, and provides companies with a way to use it for new products. (Takács, 2018).

In this case, waste can be described as "social plastic", which provides a guarantee for access to products and services. Mostly plastic waste used as currency goes from the Plastic Bank to the users. Usually in the form of recycled plastic. Henkel has also joined this initiative and will make the packaging for its products from raw material obtained through the Plastic Bank. Henkel's long-term goal is to make its packaging 100% recycled plastic. We aim to reduce the amount of virgin plastics from fossil sources in the packaging of our consumer products by 50%. This is to be achieved by increasing the proportion of recycled plastic to over 30%, reducing the amount of plastic and increasing the use of bio-based plastic.[1]

5   SUMMARY - SOCIAL LIMITS OF THE SOCIAL PLASTIC?

Social Plastic as a system can be described as an increasingly efficient system. But it is necessary to highlight several things. More and more large groups of companies have joined the system. It is worth examining the potential of this concept and system to achieve other objectives in addition to the ecological ones. Can we look at Social Plastic as a social service? A social benefit that is not the result of the will of the state, but of the responsibility of the Azdakian sector? Can we expect governments to take responsibility in this form? The EU report on corporate social responsibility: accountable, transparent and responsible business conduct and sustainable growth. The report underlines that companies should not take over from public authorities the responsibility for promoting, implementing and monitoring social and environmental standards cannot replace the role of the state.

The legal guarantee is, of course, that companies go beyond the legal guarantees to carry out activities or provide services that can benefit society. The state cannot escape its responsibility by passing it entirely on to companies (Kun, 2009). This is not inconsistent with the view that corporate governance is an essential element of corporate social responsibility, in particular with regard to relations with public authorities, employees and their representative bodies, and corporate remuneration policies; considers that excessive remuneration or remuneration of managers is not compatible with socially responsible behaviour, especially when the company is in difficulty. (European Parlament, 2013). The report underlines that it supports the Commission's new definition which removes the distinction between voluntary and mandatory approaches. The definition in the Green Paper is in line with this, according to

---

1. https://www.henkel.hu/fenntarthatosag/fenntarthato-csomagolas, 2021. 03. 30.

which companies voluntarily integrate social and environmental considerations into their partnerships and business relations.

In conclusion, Social Plastic can be understood as an ecological responsibility in terms of CSR activities, which means the production, processing and use of secondary raw materials. The tokens collected and the services that can be bought for them are a means of providing social benefits, which can be a means of combating social poverty. However, we must bear in mind that this after-market activity is limited, as it can play a secondary role to that of the state. Companies cannot be expected to do more than this, even if some multinationals have revenues that exceed the budget of some countries. The social contribution can at best be additive.

The Social Plastic project is a very good initiative, which tries to address the issues of environment and poverty in a complex way. However, the limitations of the programme must also be recognised. The layers of meaning outlined above build on each other but are not a complete solution. The Social Plastic programmes can first and foremost help those living in countries with a coastline. Here, a steady supply of waste is guaranteed.

Countries with only land borders are at a disadvantage because access to waste is more limited. It would be worthwhile to specialise the system for non-coastal countries, because there is a lot of waste in these countries, but access is also much more difficult. Thus, the social function of Social Plastic in these countries is limited.

ACKNOWLEDGEMENTS

This paper supported by National Scientific Research Foundation in the frame-work of research „K 120158, K.16: The situation of the vulnerable party in the working relations."

REFERENCES

Braun, R. (2015). *Vállalati társadalmi felelősségvállalás - A vállalatok politikája*. Budapest: Akadémiai Kiadó.

Code of Ethic of Kersia. (2019). Letöltés dátuma: 2021. 10 25, forrás: https://www.kersia-group.com/wp-content/uploads/2019/12/CODE-OF-ETHICS-KERSIA-2019-06-19-EN.pdf,

Csák, C. (2011). A hulladék fogalmának értelmezése az uniós ítélkezési gyakorlat alapján. *PUBLICATIONES UNIVERSITATIS MISKOLCINENSIS SECTIO JURIDICA ET POLITICA, 29*, 423–434.

European Commisson. (2018). COMMUNICATION FROM THE COMMISSION TO THE EUROPEAN PARLIAMENT, THE COUNCIL, THE EUROPEAN ECONOMIC AND SOCIAL COMMITTEE AND THE COMMITTEE OF THE REGIONS A European Strategy for Plastics in a Circular Economy {SWD(2018) 16 final}. Letöltés dátuma: 2021. 11 1

European Parlament. (2013). Report on corporate social responsibility: accountable, transparent and responsible business behaviour and sustainable growth. Forrás: https://www.europarl.europa.eu/doceo/document/A-7-2013-0017_EN.html

Goodpaster, K. E., & Matthews, J. B. (1982). Can a Corporation Have a Conscience? *Harvard Business Journal*.

IKEA. (2018). IKEA's sustainable growth - Local sustainability report. Letöltés dátuma: 2021. 11 01, forrás: Local sustainability report

Jakab, N., & Ráczi, Z. (2019). Issues of Public Social Responsibility in Great Britain and Hungary. *ZBORNIK RADOVA PRAVNI FAKULTET (NOVI SAD), 53*(2), 603–611. doi:10.5937/zrpfns53-22780

Kun, A. (2009). *A multinacionális vállalatok szociális felelőssége: CSR-alapú önszabályozás kontra (munka)jogi szabályozás*. Budapest: Ad Librum.

Mélypataki, G. (2012). Der Abfall als Eigentum in dem neuen Abfallgesetz. *Journal of Agriculture and Environmental Law*, 51–58.

Mélypataki, G. (2012). Hulladék vagy nyersanyag- A hulladék fogalma és kezelésének németországi és hazai gyakorlata. In C. Csilla (Szerk.), *Jogtudományi tanulmányok a fenntartható természeti erőforrások témakörében* (old.: 123-130). Miskolc: Miskolci Egyetem.

Nagy, S. (2005). Környezettudatos marketing. Miskolci Egyetem: Miskolci Egyetem.

Olajos, I. (2016). The legal problems related to re-use of metallic wastes. *Journal of Agriculture and Environmental Law, 20*, 91–102. doi:10.21029/JAEL.2016.20.91

Plastic Bank. (dátum nélk.). Forrás: https://plasticbank.com/about/

Szigeti, C., Szennay, Á., Lisányi Endréné Beke, J., Polák-Weldon, R. J., & Radácsi, L. (2019). Vállalati ökológiai lábnyom-számítás kihívásai a KKV. szektorban. *Vezetéstudomámy, L*(7-8), 63–69. doi:10.14267/veztud.2019.0706

Takács, J. (2018). Blockchain - CSR szempontjából. Letöltés dátuma: 2021. 10 25, forrás: https://csrhungary.eu/csrblog/blockchain-csr-szempontjabol/

Analyzing entrepreneurship-growth nexus across high and low income countries

Buah Aku-Sika

Institute of Economic Theory and Methodology, University of Miskolc, Miskolc, Hungary

ABSTRACT: The emergence of large industries (the industrialization era) were considered the key drivers of economic growth in the mid-18th century through to the early part of the 19th century (Bruns, 2011). During this period, most of these large scale industries enjoyed economies of scale and this made them more efficient. Due to this, most economies, particularly the developed ones paid so much attention to the growth and expansion of large firms whiles micro, small and medium scale enterprises as well as entrepreneurship were thought out to impede economic growth and development. However, in recent years, entrepreneurship has become a central issue and as such the focus and attention has been shifted from large scale manufacturing and industrialization towards entrepreneurship. This could be attributed to advancement in the service sector, technological change, the quest for people to have their own businesses, to mention a few. This paper therefore examines the role entrepreneurship plays in economic growth and development across some selected high and low income countries. A longitudinal estimation technique is adopted to make the comparison. This approach concurrently account for the dynamic effect of the entrepreneurship and economic growth nexus across the cluster of countries. Data on 39 high income countries as well as 24 low income countries from a period of 1999 to 2019 were considered. It was observed that entrepreneurship has a positive impact on growth across the selected high income group of countries but within the context of low income group of countries, entrepreneurship does not necessarily aid growth.

1 INTRODUCTION

More recently, the role of entrepreneurship on economic growth and development has received huge attention. Industrialization was considered as the key driver of growth some decades back, however, after series of events like the Great Depression, Credit crunch, World War I and II set in, most of the industries collapsed and gradually unemployment rate began to rise, revenue margins began to drop and there was massive loss of output (History crunch, 2018). Coupled with that, the industrialization period was well noted for poor working conditions, low wages and high level of environmental pollution. As such, economies started shifting the attention from industrialization towards small scale enterprises and entrepreneurship. In fact, the bigger economies like the United States (US) and United Kingdom (UK), saw the need to encourage growth of micro, small and medium scale enterprises. Their respective governments started to make policies that stimulated the pursuit of small business (Persson et al, 2006). Similar nations saw the impact of this move on the economy and have since then followed suit and cumulatively we see entrepreneurship playing a vital role in economic growth and development in these bigger economies. Turning the tables, it can also be observed that majority of the labor force in developing countries are unable to find employment in the

DOI: 10.1201/9781003259954-8

public or private sectors, and most of them in the quest to survive attempts to create their own businesses. As a result, shifting the focus away from the larger economies and looking at the position of entrepreneurship in smaller/peripheral countries is thought-provoking. According to Acs and Virgill (2009), developing countries have a tendency to use entrepreneurship to help them grow. Entrepreneurs, working across markets and supported by market-friendly institutions, are the best agents for achieving economic growth and development in the so-called periphery or developing countries. Thus, it is worthwhile to make a comparative analysis on the role of entrepreneurship in economic and development in developed and developing countries.

The statement of problem originates from a gap in the extant literature. There is an undoubtable fact that the number of studies and research works on entrepreneurship and growth is on the rise. However, evidence from the literature has shown that most of these works focus of the nexus between entrepreneurship and growth amongst developed countries. For instance, Acs and Varga, 2005; Armington, 2004; Carree and Thurik, 2008; Audretsch and Keilbach, 2004; etc elaborate on the high and significant impact of entrepreneurship on growth in developed countries. Interestingly, just a few authors focus on entrepreneurship growth nexus amongst developing countries, talk of the works of Folarin, 2018; Omoruyi et al, 2017; Adusei, 2016 and the like. Whereas some authors like Acs and Varga (2005), Carree and Thurik (2008) found an inverse relationship between entrepreneurship and growth in low-income countries, Adusei (2016), Omoruyi et al. (2017) have found a rather positive and significant effect. The brings about a mixed result in this line of research.

This paper will therefore investigate further into the role entrepreneurship plays in economic growth with much focus on some selected high and low countries. The countries are selected based on the World Bank's income group classification as well as availability of data in the database. The goal is however to draw own conclusions about the status quo and suggest some operational approaches to understanding or tackling it and also bring a novel perspective into the already existing literature. Most of the previous works on entrepreneurship and growth have identified synergies and generated new questions for further research. To achieve this aim, the study intends to extend the data used by previous authors, select different variables, adopt a different methodology and generally try to expand on the scope and delimitations of other studies. In the light of this major problem, this study seeks to investigate further into this topic.

2 LITERATURE REVIEW

2.1 *Empirical literature*

Studying the impact of entrepreneurship on growth, Salgado-Banda (2005) uses data on self-employment and productive entrepreneurship as the two main measures to examine how entrepreneurship affects economic growth. Using 22 OECD countries, the author finds out that, self-employment has a negative relationship with economic growth where as productive entrepreneurship has a positive relationship with economic growth. According to Salgado-Banda (2005), productive entrepreneurship is simply the degree of innovativeness of the entrepreneur as inspired by Baumol (1990), whiles self-employment is starting up or owning a new business. Due to the nature of his research questions he employs different methods to undertake each specific objective. For instance, he uses the Ordinary Least Square (OLS), Two-Stage Least Square (TSLS) and the Generalized Method of Moments (GMM) to make a cross- sectional analysis using the data from 22 OECD countries within the period 1980-1995. First, the OLS is used to test the impact of the two main variables (self-employment and productive entrepreneurship) on growth. The results indicated that self-employment was negative and statistically insignificant however that of productive entrepreneurship was positive and statistically significant. Although the TSLS can easily combine multiple instrumental variables, and it also makes including control variables easier, the Generalized Method of Moments (GMM) which provides a more robust estimator was also used to test the impact of two main measures mentioned above on growth. The GMM approach has also been used by authors like Porta et al. (1997, 1998) and Levine (2000) to discuss topics on financial development and growth and according to them this method also caters for the problem of heteroscedasticity. Lastly, Salgado-Banda (2005) also used the Dynamic Panel Data estimation to examine the impact of self-employment and productive entrepreneurship on growth. This method is best for taking full advantage of every single data point. By using panel data, it is easy to analyze how variations in the variables over time in the selected sample affect economic growth.

Using the Generalised Method of Moments (GMM) as an adopted methodology, Thanti and Kalu (2018) illustrate how institutions and human capital facilitate entrepreneurship, which in turn aids economic growth and development. It is interesting how Thanti and Kalu (2018) first create a robust support for the well-known notion by Adam Smith and Joseph Schumpeter, that for the economy to grow in the long run there is the need to improve human capital and institutions. With the Generalised Method of Moments as the base model, they develop the Entrepreneurship Orientation (EO), which consist of innovativeness, risk taking and proactiveness. With a sample of 93 countries and a period between 1980 and 2008 they use the Generalised Method of Moments (GMM) to examine institutions and human capital as potential determining factor of the so called Schumpeterian entrepreneurship. The GMM is basically a generic method of estimating parameters in statistical models and in this instance the authors use this methodology to illustrate how institutions and human capital serve as key drivers of entrepreneurship so as to aid economic growth. From the broader literature however, institutional variables and human capital act as major determinants of growth (Barro, 2000; King and Levine, 1993; Acemoglu et al., 2001) but from the work of Thanti and Kalu (2018), the major conclusion drawn is that institutions and human capital are seen as catalysts which boost entrepreneurship and in turn aids growth. From the work of these authors, we can critically observe that the causal trend for growth to occur is from institutional growth to human capital growth and then to productivity enhancing entrepreneurship. According to them once this pattern is followed then we are gradually approaching economic growth. With the help of the GMM the overall sample of 98 countries suggest that the quality of institutions, which is reflected in the reduction of corrupt activities and the development of the banking sector enhances Entrepreneurship Orientation (EO). Human capital, on the other hand, has a strong positive correlation with EO, and is robust to controlling for institutional quality, and all together generates growth in the economy.

In the work of Bruns et al. 2017, for instance, the Multilevel growth regression and Latent class analysis are used to show that if ecosystems vary in quality across regions, then we should be able to disclose the existence and relevance of entrepreneurial ecosystems and its impacts on economic growth. In this context, the multilevel modelling is preferred because, it is an approach that can be used to handle clustered or grouped data (Browne et al, 2004). The main aim is to know the impact of entrepreneurship on growth, but within the entrepreneurial ecosystem there are some factors which also affect entrepreneurship. Hence this methodology is appropriate to handle such clusters or grouped data and the explanatory variables can be defined at any level. According to Pinheiro and Bates (2000) the multilevel group regression or multilevel modelling is preferred to the simple multiple regression for the following reasons; it allows us to generalize a wider population, fewer parameters are needed when we have a complex model yet have limited amount of data and information can be shared among groups.

3 METHODOLOGY

3.1 *Empirical model and econometric issues*

Since the study focuses on a cluster of 39 high and 24 low income group of countries, panel estimation is adopted. The variations in the variables over time in a country which affect economic growth can be accessed using panel data where more degrees of freedom are deduced by adding the time series dimension. Within the context of this paper panel descriptive analysis is first employed to help us understand the selected variables. The descriptive statistics allows us to quantify and characterize the fundamental properties of a data set. Also a panel trend analysis on the entrepreneurship growth nexus across the cluster of high and low countries is conducted.

Arellano and Bond (1991) Dynamic Panel Data approach was popularized in the work of Holtz-Eakin, Newey and Rosen (Econometrica, 1988). It is based on the idea that the instrumental variables approach does not exploit all of the information available in the sample. In that effect, the Generalized Method of Moments (GMM) construct more efficient estimates of the dynamic panel data model. Arellano and Bond argue that consistency, fails to take all of the potential orthogonality conditions into account. Notably, there is the assumption that the necessary instruments are 'internal': that is, based on lagged values of the instrumented variable(s). The estimators allow the inclusion of external instruments as well. Arellano and Bond (1991) therefore presented a panel data analysis based on a GMM-type estimator called the "system estimator", to answer some of the potential econometric problems that emanates with working with DPD.

3.2 *Data sources and description*

In order to analyze the entrepreneurship-growth nexus among the cluster of high and low income group of countries a panel data which captures data across 39 high income countries and 24 low income countries from 1999 to 2019 were considered. The data set on the variables of interest used in the study is built from several databases. More specifically, data was obtained from the World Development Indicators (WDI) database, ILOSTAT database, and other OECD databases. The study employs two main variables; Self-employment which was used as a proxy or measurement for entrepreneurship and Gross Domestic Product (GDP) per capita which was used as a proxy for economic growth. GDP per capita is the dependent variable while Self-employment is the independent variable. Based on evidence from the literature (Arin et al., 2014; Omer and Sarra, 2014; Backman & Karlsson, 2013) other variables like Domestic Credit to Private Sector (DCPS), Employment Population Ratio (EPR), Unemployment (UNEMP), Business Disclosure Index (BDI), Time required to start a business, Inflation (INF), Savings (SAV), Labor Force Participation Rate (LFPR) and Economic Openness (EO) are used as controlled variables.

4 RESULTS

This section presents and discusses the results of the study. The aim is to understand the entrepreneurship-growth relation amongst the cluster of high and low income countries. The results show that the contribution of entrepreneurship to economic growth is diverse across countries. Every country is unique, with different degrees of development, different macroeconomic environments and even different cultures, hence the impact of entrepreneurship on growth will not be the same.

4.1 *Descriptive analysis*

The table above shows a juxtaposition of the descriptive analysis for the selected high income and low income countries. The white box to the left depicts results for high income group of countries whiles the grey box to the right depicts results for low income group of countries. In the white box it can be observed that the average Gross Domestic Product per capita of the high income countries is approximately 25.85 per cent. This means that collectively over the period 1999 to 2019, the respective economies have grown at an average rate of 25.85 per cent. On the other side, it can be observed that the average growth rate for the low income countries is approximately 6.17 per cent over the same period. Comparatively, it can be concluded that the average annual growth rate of the selected low income group of countries is lower than

Table 4.1. Panel descriptive analysis for high and low income countries.

High-Income Countries	Mean	Std. Dev.	Min	Max	Low-Income Countries	Mean	Std. Dev.	Min	Max
lnGDPPCG	25.849	1.9800	21.805	30.695	lnGDPPCG	6.1697	.55783	4.6308	7.5547
lnSELF	2.5589	.61262	.05826	3.8310	lnSELF	4.3665	.21460	3.3648	4.5556
lnDCPS	4.3804	.5651	1.9636	5.7332	lnDCPS	2.1791	.73144	-.9098	3.7173
lnEPR	4.0430	.13139	3.7360	4.4042	lnEPR	4.1401	.2441	3.4616	4.4752
lnUNEMP	1.7379	.58492	-.3566	2.9907	lnUNEMP	1.4041	.81729	-1.139	2.8604
BDI	6.1213	2.4483	1	10	BDI	4.9027	2.1500	0	8
Time	16.838	14.805	1.5	113	Time	38.133	46.215	2.5	260.5
lnINF	.72069	.93074	-4.790	3.8665	lnINF	1.8446	1.0987	-3.206	6.2420
lnSAV	3.2615	.37889	1.8198	4.1155	lnSAV	2.1295	1.0215	-5.843	4.0395
lnLFPR	4.1124	.11244	3.8653	4.4281	lnLFPR	4.1984	.20654	3.6063	4.4891
lnEO	4.6063	.59085	2.9095	6.0927	lnEO	3.9945	.43846	2.8135	5.7409

Source: Author's own calculations

that of the high income group of countries. Interestingly, values on self-employment took a different turn when comparing the results. As it can be observed, entrepreneurship or self-employment as used in the context of this study is a percentage or fraction of total employment who are working on their own account. The results show that the average self-employment for high income countries is 2.56 whiles that of low income countries is 4.37. This means that comparatively the share of total employment within an economy who work on their own account is somewhat higher in low income countries than high income countries. It is therefore not difficult to arrive at the conclusion that a large quantum of the economically active people in low-income countries do not easily find jobs in the public or corporate entities and as such decide to venture into their own business. Surprisingly, the results from the study reveals that it is not about the quantity of entrepreneurs that matters but the quality. In the low income countries, the figures show that more people venture into self-employment but the impact on growth was very minimal. The opposite is the case for the high income countries. This could be attributed to the type of entrepreneurship being practiced, ie, necessity based entrepreneurship or opportunity based entrepreneurship, productive or unproductive entrepreneurship, etc.

The disparity between other variables of interest like employment to population ratio and labor force participation rate which are considered as factors which influence entrepreneurship were not so wide. Respectively, the averages of employment to population ratio and labor force participation rate for high income and low income countries were 4.04 and 4.14. As it can be observed, the minimum number of days required to start a business across the cluster of high income countries is 1.5 (one and half days) and the maximum number of days are 113. Alternatively, a minimum of 2.5 (two and half days) and a maximum of 260.5 days is required to start a business in low income countries. Provision and availability of domestic credit to the private sector is typically higher in high income countries than in low income countries. On average domestic credit to private sector in high income countries hovers around 4.38 whiles that of low income countries is around 2.18. Again, savings amongst the high income countries is higher than the low income countries with a typical value of 3.26 and 2.12 respectively. All in all, the cluster of high income countries has a much open economy with an average value of 4.61 compared with the low income countries with an average economic openness of 3.99, where economic openness in this context refers to the sum of imports and exports as a share of GDP.

4.2 *Trend analysis of entrepreneurship and growth across high and low income group of countries–scatter plot with overlaid linear prediction*

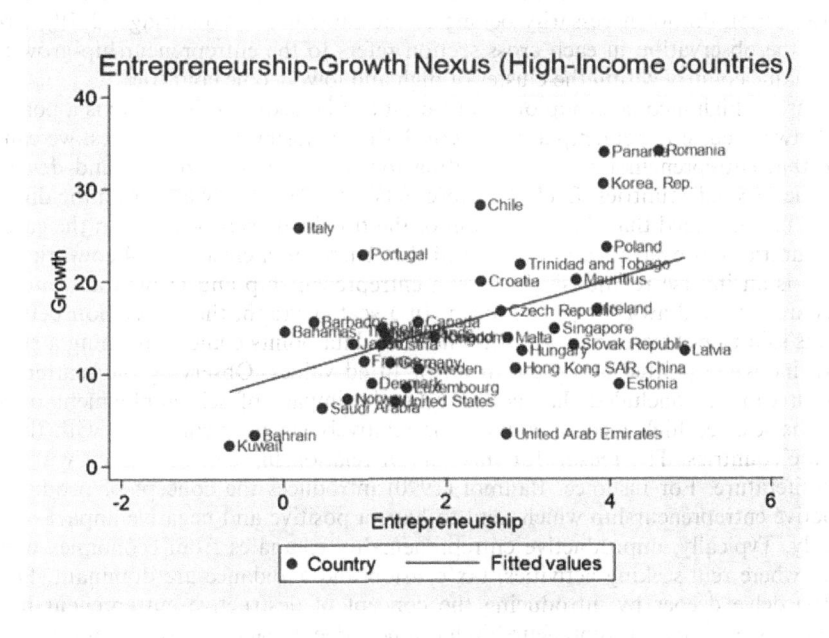

Figure 1. Trend analysis of entrepreneurship and growth across high income group of countries.

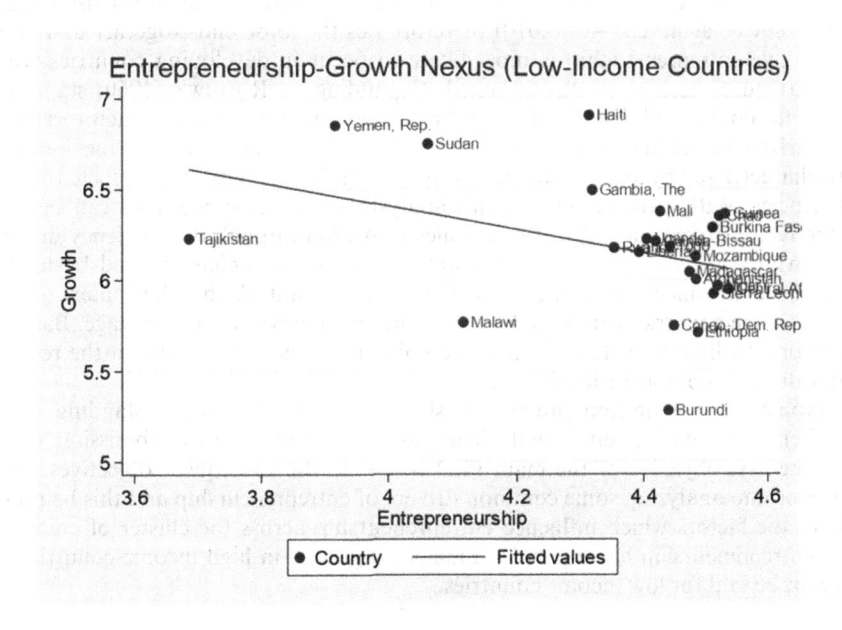

Figure 2. Trend analysis of entrepreneurship and growth across low income group of countries.

To understand the entrepreneurship-growth nexus among the selected high and low income group of countries there is the need to have a general visualization among the two variables. The scatter diagram reveals an interesting relationship between entrepreneurship and growth

81

among the selected high income countries and low income countries. Before illustrating the scatter diagram, some caveats were taken into consideration. First, we consider a pooled OLS for panel estimation where we have a "time series of cross sections," but the observations in each cross section do not necessarily belong to the same unit (Wooldridge, 2010). From the foregoing, the observation in each cross section refers to the entrepreneurship-growth nexus for each unique country within the cluster of high and low income countries.

In the case of high income group of countries, it can be deduced that there is a positive correlation between entrepreneurship and growth. Using a cluster of 39 countries, we can boldly conclude that entrepreneurship is contributing towards economic growth and development amongst the selected countries. Each dot represents a single country and from the direction of flow it can be concluded that the correlation of the fitted values is positive. In the case of low income countries however, it can be observed that based on a cluster of 24 countries, collectively there is an inverse relationship between entrepreneurship and growth and most of the countries are scattered away from the mean. In a scatter graph, the correlation between two variables is said to be stronger or weaker when the data points come to forming a straight or dispersed line when plotted along the mean or fitted values. Observing the scatter diagram carefully, it can be concluded that collectively, the impact of self-employment on growth amongst the selected high income countries is relatively stronger compared with that of the low income countries. The reason for this sort of relationship can be backed with evidence from the literature. For instance, Baumol (1990) introduces the concept of productive and unproductive entrepreneurship which tend to have a positive and negative impact on growth respectively. Typically, unproductive entrepreneurship emanates from economies with weak structures where rent-seeking activities, tax evasion and avoidance are dominant. Desai and Acs (2007) delve deeper by introducing the concept of destructive entrepreneurship. They delineate that destructive entrepreneurship has a negative impact on Gross Domestic Product. More often than not destructive entrepreneurship stifles innovation. According to Schumpeter's theory however innovation or creativity drives entrepreneurship which in the long term results in growth. Hence if innovation is suppressed, then entrepreneurship is discouraged and growth will not be achieved. Acs (2010) therefore ties the loose ends together and concludes that destructive entrepreneurship is most likely to occur in developing countries where the incentive structures need to be strengthened. Expanding on Rostow's (1960) stages on economic growth, Porter et al. (2002), identify three stages on growth namely factor-driven stage; efficiency-driven stage; and innovation-driven stage. Countries found in the factor-driven stage are characterized by agricultural self-employment, low income and compete through low cost efficiencies. Within the context of this analysis, low-income countries can be classified among the factor-driven stage. Most economies transition through the efficiency driven stage to the innovation driven stage. The innovation driven stage is characterized by high value-added industries in which entrepreneurial activity is important. Within the context of this analysis, high-income countries can be classified among the innovative-driven stage. Based on the evidence from the literature stated in the fore going it can be concluded that the results from the scatter diagram conform with theory.

The graphical representation provides a simple framework to understanding the actual impact of entrepreneurship on growth. The paper presented in this submission is only an aspect of the first objective of the main PhD thesis. In the subsequent objectives, the study delves deeper into analyzing some common drivers of entrepreneurship and this help us better understand the factors which influence entrepreneurship across the cluster of countries and also why entrepreneurship has a positive impact on growth in high income countries but the same cannot be said for low income countries.

5 CONCLUSION

In analyzing the role of entrepreneurship on growth amongst the selected high and low income countries, the main conclusion that could be drawn is that entrepreneurship has a positive impact on growth in the high income group of countries but in the low income groups of countries entrepreneurship does not aid growth. Hence, it is worthwhile for governments of the respective developing countries to make policies which will change the entrepreneurship ecosystem. For instance, policies to reduce long bureaucratic procedures before starting up a business could be implemented. From the results, when longer time periods are required to start up a business it impedes growth. Again, when majority of the populace are self-employed or have their own businesses, it influences growth positively. Hence, the governments of the respective countries should create a conducive environment which will encourage more people to startup their own businesses. For instance, giving out financial aids, tax exemptions for businesses which are less than two years and inculcating entrepreneurship into the education curriculum could boost self-employment amongst the selected cluster of countries. Economic openness, which is the sum of exports and imports, employment to population ratio and savings were also key variables which influences growth positively. Hence policies which can boost these factors can also help to attain growth.

REFERENCES

Ács, Z.J. & Varga, A. 2005. Entrepreneurship, Agglomeration and Technological Change. Small Business Economics. April 2005, Volume 24, Issue 3

Ács, Z.J. & Virgill, N. 2009. Entrepreneurship in developing countries. Jena Economic Research Papers, No. 2009,023, Friedrich Schiller University Jena and Max Planck Institute of Economics, Jena

Acemoglu, D., Johnson, S. & Robinson, J.A. 2001. Reversal of fortune: geography and institutions in the making of the modern world income distribution. No. 8460, National Bureau of Economic Research, Cambridge, MA.

Adusei, M. 2016. Does Entrepreneurship Promote Economic Growth in Africa? African Development Review, Vol. 28, No. 2, 2016, 201–214

Armington, C. 2004. Employment Growth and Entrepreneurial Activity in Cities', Regional Studies Acs, Z. J. (2006). How is entrepreneurship good for economic growth? Innovations, 1 (1), 97–107

Audretsch, D. B. and Keilbach M. 2004. Entrepreneurship Capital and Economic Performance', Regional Studies, Vol. 38

Arellano, M. and Bond, S. 1991. Some tests of specification for panel data: Monte carlo evidence and an application to employment equations. The Review of Economic Studies, 58: 277–297.

Arin K. P., Huang V. Z., Minniti M., Nandialath A. M., Reich Otto F. M. 2014. Revisiting the Determinants of Entrepreneurship: A Bayesian Approach, Journal of Management Vol. 41 No. 2

Backman M. & Karlsson C. 2013. Determinants of entrepreneurship. Is it all about the individual or the region? CESIS Electronic Working Paper Series Paper No. 338

Barro, R.J. 2000. Inequality and growth in a panel of countries, Journal of Economic Growth, Vol. 5 No. 1, pp. 5–32

Baumol, W. J. 1990. Entrepreneurship: Productive, Unproductive and Destructive. Journal of Political Economy, 80 5:893–921.

Browne, W. & Rasbash, J. 2004. 'Multilevel Modelling', in Hardy, M. and Bryman, A. (eds.), Handbook of data analysis, Sage Publications.

Bruns, P. 2011. Entrepreneurship and small business, New York, Palgrave Macmillan

Bruns K., Bosma N., Sanders M. & Schramm M. 2017. Searching for the existence of entrepreneurial ecosystems: a regional cross-section growth regression approach. Small Business Economics, DOI 10.1007/s11187-017-9866-6

Carree, M. and Thurik R. 2008. The Lag Structure of the Impact of Business Ownership on Economic Performance in OECD Countries', Small Business Economics, Vol. 30

Drucker P. F 2007. Innovation and Entrepreneurship; Practice and Principles. Classic Drucker Collection Edition 2007.

Dilanchiev, A. 2014. Relationship between Entrepreneurship and Unemployment: The Case of Georgia Journal of Social Sciences; ISSN: 2233-3878; Volume 3, Issue 2, 2014

Folarin, O. 2018. The role of Entrepreneurship as a driver of economic growth; A Nigerian Case Global Entrepreneurship Monitor (GEM Reports)

Hornaday R.W 1992. Thinking about entrepreneurship: A fuzzy set approach, Journal of Small Business Management.

Holmes, R., McCord A., & Hagen-Zanker J. 2013. What is the evidence on the impact of employment creation on stability and poverty reduction in fragile states? Overseas Development Institute. http://www.odi.org.uk/

History crunch 2018. https://www.historycrunch.com/negatives-of-the-industrial-revolution.html#/

King, R.G. & Levine, R. 1993. Finance, entrepreneurship and growth. Journal of Monetary Economics, Vol. 32 No. 3

Kirzner, I. M. 1997. Entrepreneurial discovery and the competitive market process: An Austrian approach. Journal of Economic Literature.

Miller D. 1983. The Emergence of the Entrepreneurial Orientation (EO) construct. Foundation Research in Entrepreneurship; Journal of Management Sciences.

Omer, S. & Sarra, S. 2014. An Appraisal of the Determinants of Entrepreneurship in Developing Countries: The Case of the Middle East, North Africa and Selected Gulf Cooperation Council Nations African Journal of Social Sciences. Volume 4 Number 4 (2014) 63–74 ISSN 2045-8452 (Print) ISSN 2045-8460 (Online)

Omoruyi E, Olamide K. S, Gomolemo G and Donath O.A 2017. Entrepreneurship and Economic Growth: Does Entrepreneurship Bolster Economic Expansion in Africa? J Socialomics 2017, 6:4 DOI: 10.4172/2167-0358.1000219

Persson, O., Cornelius, B., Landström, H. 2006. Entrepreneurial Studies: The Dynamic Research Front of a Developing Social Science, Entrepreneurship Theory and Practice, Volume30 (3):375–398.

Pinheiro, J.C. and Bates, D.M. 2000. Mixed-Effects Models in S and S-PLUS, Springer.

Porter, M., Sachs, J., & McArthur, J. 2002. Executive summary: Competitiveness and stages of economic development. In M. Porter, J. Sachs, P. K. Cornelius, J. McArthur, & K. Schwab (Eds.), The global competitiveness report 2001_2002 (pp. 16_25). New York: Oxford University Press.

Salgado-Banda, H. 2005. Measures and Determinants of Entrepreneurship: An Empirical Analysis." Chapter 3, PhD Thesis, University of London

Schumpeter, J.A 1934. The Theory of Economic Development. Cambridge, MA: Harvard University Press

Stevenson, Howard and Jarillo, J. Carlos 1990. A Paradigm of Entrepreneurship: Entrepreneurial Management. Strategic Management Journal, Vol. 11.

Shane, S. And Venkataraman S. 2000. The Promise of Entrepreneurship as a Field of Research. Academic Management Review. Vol 25 (1)

Thanti, M. & Kalu, O. 2018. Institutions, human capital and entrepreneurial orientation: implications for growth policy. Journal of Entrepreneurship and Public Policy, https://doi.org/10.1108/JEPP-D-18-00002

Wooldrige J.M, 2010. Econometric Analysis of Cross Section and Panel Data, 2nd ed. P. cm. ISBN 978-0-262-2325806

High Income countries: Austria, Bahamas, Bahrain, Barbados, Belgium, Canada, Chile, Croatia, Czech Republic, Denmark, Estonia, France, Germany, Hong Kong SAR China, Hungary, Iceland, Ireland, Italy, Japan, Korea Republic, Kuwait, Latvia, Luxemburg, Malta, Mauritius, Netherlands, Norway, Panama, Poland, Portugal, Romania, Saudi Arabia, Singapore, Slovak Republic, Sweden, Trinidad and Tobago, United Arab Emirates, United Kingdom, United States.

Low Income countries: Afghanistan, Burkina Faso, Burundi, Central African Republic, Chad, Congo Dem Rep, Ethiopia, Gambia, Guinea, Guinea Bissau, Haiti, Liberia, Madagascar, Malawi, Mali, Mozambique, Niger, Rwanda, Sierra Leone, Sudan, Tajikistan, Togo, Uganda, Yemen Republic.

Entrepreneurship in the Raw Materials Sector – Bartha et al. (Eds)

Business model analysis for the scope of entrepreneurship in a solar drying field in the European region

Baibhaw Kumar
Institute of Energy Engineering and Chemical Machinery, University of Miskolc, Miskolc, Hungary

László Berényi
Institute of Management Science, University of Miskolc, Miskolc, Hungary

Zoltán Szamosi & Gábor L. Szepesi
Institute of Energy Engineering and Chemical Machinery, University of Miskolc, Miskolc, Hungary

ABSTRACT: The transition towards using renewable sources of energy from traditional sources is inevitable in the 21st century. Many agro-based industries are now developing innovative solutions to transform their energy utility. These modern approaches are not only energy saving but economical also. In this study, the authors investigated the potential role of solar drying in the entrepreneurship of low and mid-scale agriculture-based businesses. The business canvas model and value proposition canvas are analyzed to understand better the business development related to solar dryers. The article proposes using a P-graph for cost-effectiveness and process optimization in business models related to solar drying.

Keywords: Solar Drying, Entrepreneurship, Business canvas Model, Value Proposition

1 INTRODUCTION

In academic etymology, the word "Entrepreneur" and "Entrepreneurship" is a bit complex by definition itself. There are various schools of thought, which describe entrepreneurship in various ways possible. Barton and Joe suggested six schools of thought to summarize the definition of "Entrepreneurship." These schools are comprised of various dimensions of thoughts involved in this process. Based on the focus of the investigation, researchers may choose the type, which consists of personal traits, recognizing potentials, adaptability, and action in managing things.(Cunningham and Lischeron, 1991) Entrepreneurship in the agricultural sector is evolving rapidly, mostly in developing nations, but the strategic focus remains high in developed nations for food production.(Dias, Rodrigues and Ferreira, 2019) On the one hand, entrepreneurship is growing, but at the same time, the new businesses face energy shortages or deal with very high energy costs. These trends hamper the growth of new inventors in the business supply chain. Renewable energy sources are an emerging solution for energy scarcity in the modern world. Solar energy is abundant in nature is being used extensively in various agricultural applications. Due to unsuitable storage and climatic conditions, many small and mid-level farmers face huge post-harvest losses in fruits, vegetables, and crops. In such cases, solar dyers have emerged as a boon for low-income farmers. Regular innovations are being made to enhance the efficiency of these solar dryers to promote better storage for post-harvest security.(El-Sebaii and Shalaby, 2012) Solar thermal technologies use, and growth has seen evident

DOI: 10.1201/9781003259954-9

growth in the context of the European region in the last few decades. The major concern faced by entrepreneurs and people in business in solar thermal technologies is the lack of good marketing strategies and awareness among people regarding environmental concerns (Tsoutsos, 2002).

Spatial and geographical parameters have affected rural entrepreneurship in the European Union (EU) for a long time. A study suggests competent and practical policies are required for entrepreneurial growth in the rural areas of the EU (Stathopoulou, Psaltopoulos and Skuras, 2004). The future policies related to rural entrepreneurship should not be unidimensional. A broad sustainable strategic framework is recommended for the long-term growth model in this sector. Sustainability is extensive in nature to consider various facets of development and ecological prosperity in the entrepreneurial environment progress.(Gholamrezai, Aliabadi and Ataei, 2021) An empirical study in Nigeria suggests that training programs for young agricultural entrepreneurs could significantly impact their entrepreneurial performance. In the long run, such community-based programs help in making a direct connection with the community. Such models make the community more aware with direct interaction and make the new technologies more adoptable by the rural masses.(Adeyanju, Mburu and Mignouna, 2021) Sustainable development is an important aspect in today's product development and innovation management process in any field. Sociocultural and economic growth are two main pillars that support the societal acceptance of entrepreneurship. General and social entrepreneurship trends contribute to economic growth, but social entrepreneurship has a larger impact on sustainability.(Méndez-Picazo, Galindo-Martín and Castaño-Martínez, 2021).

On the macro level, various factors or latent parameters could directly or indirectly influence the promotion of using renewable sources for entrepreneurial ventures. Hence an analysis of these governing factors can bring clarity to the future scope of entrepreneurial growth in this sector. Several other versions of PEST analysis, e.g., PESTLE, SLEPT, could be extended by adding parameters such as legal and environmental aspects to the study. PEST is an acronym used for political, economic, social, and technological aspects of a study (Brockwell and Davis, 1994). The article attempts to provides insight into not only the political and economic frameworks. Also, it proposes the business canvas and value proposition canvas for the business models in the solar drying field.

2 SOLAR DRYING IN THE EUROPEAN REGION

The European region has experienced significant growth in solar-based innovative technologies in the last few decades. Various technologies based on solar thermal utilities also witnessed technological advancements. The environmental and climatic conditions no doubt affect the operating conditions and efficiency of the product, yet economical and market analysis of the area can not be neglected (Tsoutsos, 2002). A good market analysis can help the product mature financially. It can also help discover new opportunities in the drying sector of various agricultural products such as wood chips, fruits, crops, etc. Solar drying has utility in drying not only agricultural products but is helpful in solid wastewater management as well. Poland and Germany together dispose of around 20,000 tonnes of wet sludge per year. Austria, Germany, and Poland thus have developed many solar drying facilities to address this issue (Boguniewicz-Zablocka, Klosok-Bazan and Capodaglio, 2021). Fruits drying has been a long-practiced common Hungarian tradition. Hungary has a rich cultivation of various varieties of fruits. To prevent these fruits from post-harvest waste, sometimes due to prevention of mold growth. The fruits were dried using dryers for long-run usage (Surányi, 2017).

Experiments suggest good drying results not only in fruits but other agricultural products such as wood chips (Baibhaw, Szepesi and Szamosi, 2021). An excellent solar dryer can provide better calorific value and make the boiler plants more efficient in terms of energy. In addition, the southern part of central Europe and Hungary receives a good amount of solar insolation in the summer season, which could be a good reason for small-scale farmers to promote this technology (Kumar et al., 2021).

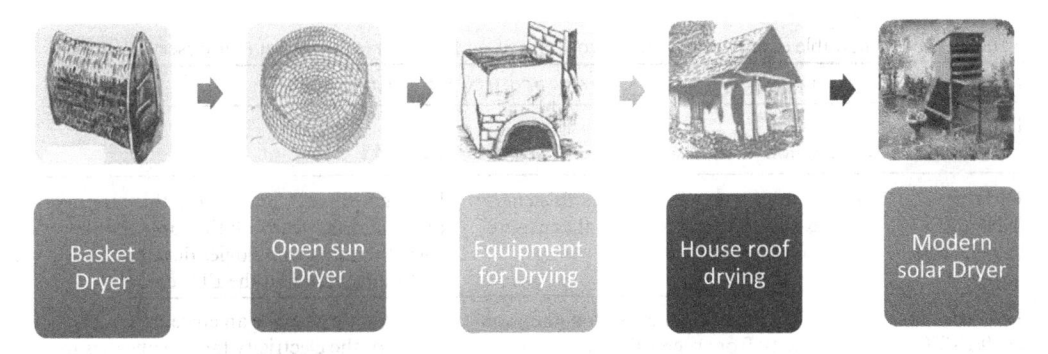

Figure 1. Evolution of solar drying equipment in the last century (Surányi, 2017).

As shown in Figure 1. Solar drying technology has evolved in the last few decades. The technology has matured enough for a market presence of all sizes and shapes. The modern age dryers are majorly classified into two categories active and passive. It has been found in studies that active hybrid dryers are more efficient in comparison to passive ones (Prakash and Kumar, 2013). Hence, hybrid dryers supported by photovoltaic and thermal backup are recommended for new-age entrepreneurs in the field of agricultural drying.

3 METHODOLOGY FOR STUDY

3.1 *Status of political framework*

Political factors can directly or indirectly have a considerate effect on the business modules of any sector. It is recommended to be updated with the government's policies in the region to business and entrepreneurial persons. The influence could vary from macro to micro level. The analysis could be done on a regional level. Policies regarding growth for renewable energy-specific for solar energy sector could be different at the European Union (EU) level and that of any specific country. The national action plans of the country must be studied for fiscal and trading analysis in the solar sector. The entrepreneurs could also get information on some funding and grants the government may be sponsored to promote the industry. The bilateral relations between nations on trading legislation could also provide future trading options for the business. Some of the recent policies regarding solar energy industry support in the European region are mentioned below.

3.2 *Useful economic assessment*

Any entrepreneurial venture is mainly dependent on the economic sustainability of the product and the manufacturing costs related to it. The commercialization of the drying systems needs thorough investigations on the raw material and deliverable outputs, which govern the capacity remunerations for the business model. The initial investments and the relative returns could vary for the various products depending on their market value and transportation costs related to it. The design and development costs also are comparable to the modernization and comfort for the end-use customer. The entrepreneurs should also consider minimizing the maintenance costs as the prime users of these systems would be medium and low-income farmers. Govind and Tiwari gave some economic cost analysis assessments designed for solar drying systems, and these could be helpful in cost analysis for new entrepreneurs are compiled below in Table 2 (G.N. Tiwari, 1984).

Table 1. EU renewable energy policy framework based on Eurobserver factsheet (Eurobserver, 2020).

EUROPEAN UNION RENEWABLE ENERGY POLICY FRAMEWORK

Directive of EU policy	Description	Remarks
Directive 2009/28/EC, Article 5(6)	Defines the "energy from renewable energy sources (RES)" and "gross final consumption of energy"	It is important to understand this terminology in order to check the category of solar thermal technologies development and transmission in the EU region
Directive 2009/28/EC, Article 5(3)	In this article, the final gross consumption of electricity from renewable sources is defined for the member states.	The policy can make an entrepreneur aware of the electricity tariffs subsidies in their state and subsidies related to it.
Directive 2009/28/EC, Article 5(4),	Provides information about the final gross consumption of energy from RES for heating and cooling purposes	This article focuses on the cooling and heating deployment and its consumption of member states
Directive (EU) 2018/ 2001	Annex IX indicates compliance for meeting sustainability criteria for biofuels.	Solar drying of biofuels such as wood chips and its sustainability criteria could be understood through this directive.
Directive 2009/28/EC Article 3(4)	Annex III defines energy consumption by transport fuels their calorific values by weight and volume.	In biofuels, the higher calorific value could be achieved by removal of moisture from the fuel through solar drying. Hence, insights of these could help in setting up new ventures in drying biofuels.

Table 2. Economic analysis calculation tool for solar drying entrepreneurs.

Economic Parameter	Formula	Abbreviations
Capital recovery factor (CRF)	$CRF = \frac{r(1+r)^n}{(1+r)^n-1}$	r-annual interest rate n- Number of useful years
First annual cost of the system	$CRF * P$	P- Initial investment cost
Sinking fund factor	$SFF = \frac{r}{(1+r)^n-1}$	r-annual interest rate n- Number of useful years
Annual cost	Annual cost = first annual cost + annual maintenance cost-annual salvage value.	
Annual Product yield	$Y = \frac{M \, X \, T}{\tau}$	Y-Annual product yield M-Mass of the product τ-Drying time T- Harvesting time
Cost of Drying per unit mass of product	C/Y	C- Annual cost Y-Annual product yield

3.3 Business model canvas

Osterwalder and Pigneur described the business canvas as "a shared language for describing, visualizing, assessing, and changing business models" (Osterwalder *et al.*, 2010). They also proposed the nine building blocks as essential parameters for the canvas model. Before this, the business models were using the outside-in or inside-out approaches for innovation and entrepreneurship models (Baden-Fuller, 1995). In the context of the analysis of new technologies such as solar dryers, it becomes inevitable to envisage the future sustainability of the business model. Solar dryers are not so common in usage, and their promotion for Agri-based products is an arduous task. At the same time, it holds the possibility to replace and grow

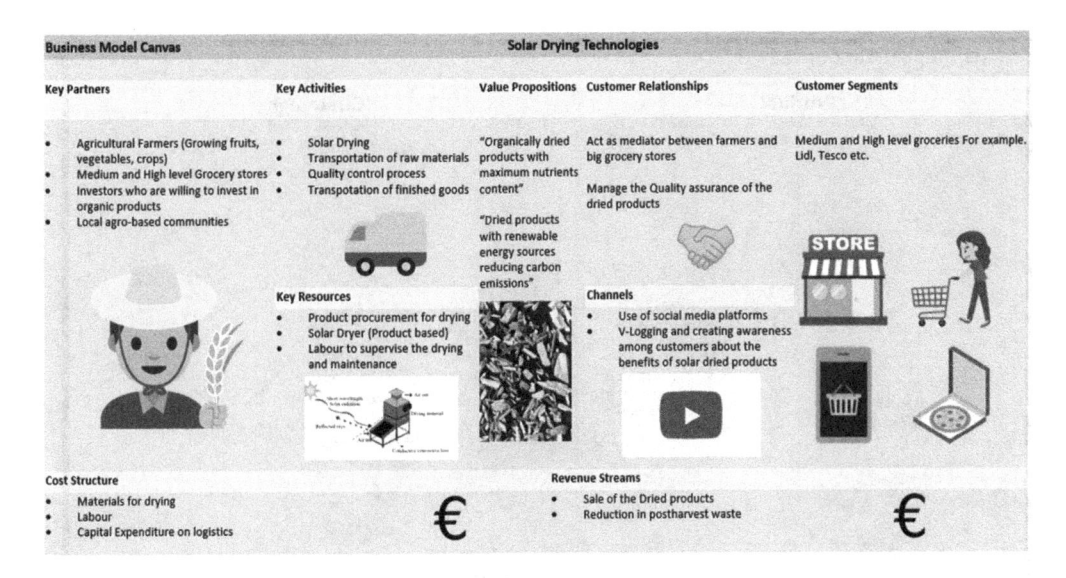

Figure 2. Business model canvas for solar drying technologies (*strategyzer*, 2021).

with respect to the traditional drying techniques. We further discuss the key concepts and the building blocks involved in our proposed canvas for the solar dryers in Figure 2.

The business canvas model describes the essential resources, channels, activities, and channels involved in the solar drying business. The canvas also provides insights into the use of social media platforms for the promotion of the technology. The revenue-generating parameters are projected in brief. It also gives a glimpse of an idea about customer relationship management and targeted customer block. This visualization and approach could help the entrepreneurs to develop a broad spectrum of their business in the solar drying field.

3.4 *Value proposition of solar drying technologies*

The customer perceptions about the dried products have a substantive effect on the value proposition of the products in the market. The benefits of the solar-dried product should reach the customer segment in the farmer's market and in the big supermarket houses. The relationship between the product, customer, and the substitutes is briefly shown in Figure 3. It depicts the mindset of the customer as well as the business producer side. The benefits and fear are associated on both sides, and the value proposition brings clarity on such parameters. Pokorna et al. (Pokorná *et al.*, 2015) studied the value propositions for the farmers market and suggested further development of value proposition for supermarkets. Figure 3 proposes the gap-filling in this regard and provides insights into the relationship of customer demand and the business approach of entrepreneurs associated with solar drying technologies.

3.5 *P-graph for business models related to solar drying*

The P-graph framework is part of the PNS (Process Network Synthesis) which is a flowsheet design used generally in process optimization in various complex problems associated with industries. In the 1990s, Cabezas et al. (Cabezas *et al.*, 2015) developed the P-graph tool for the PNS-related optimization problem. The P-graph in Figure 4. depicts the process flow for various sections of solar-dried products. The PNS Draw was used to generate the graph from www. p-graph.com and the raw material and process are shown in Figure 4. This process model is proposed for entrepreneurs or business startups in solar drying. In the proposed graph, the cost analysis in the process flow of solar-dried products can be performed by using the algorithm tree in the software. The

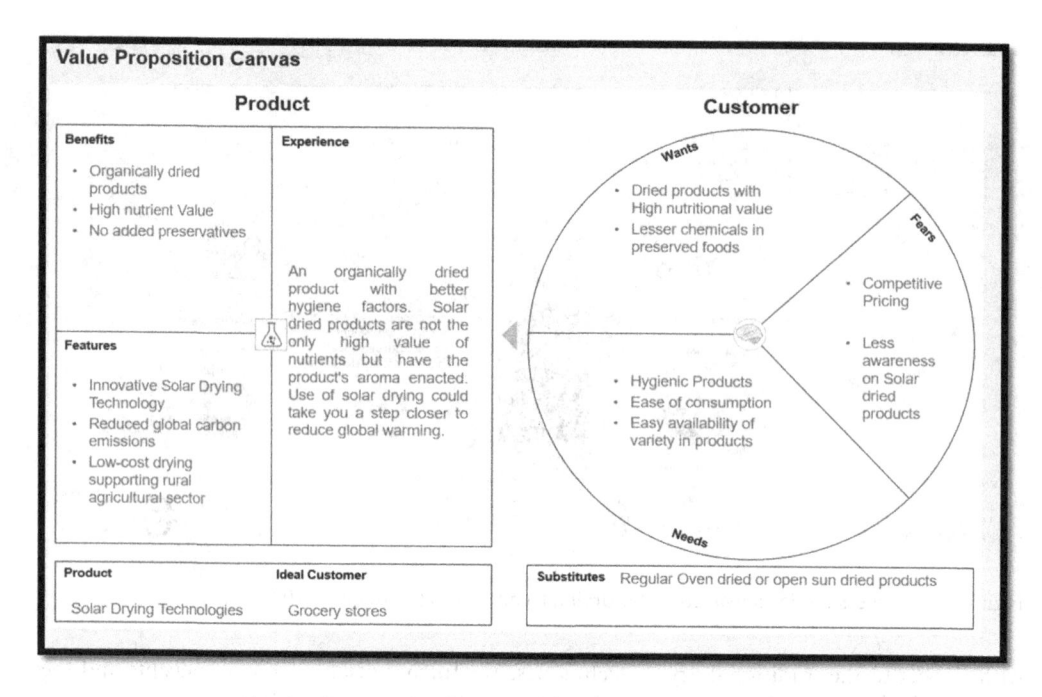

Figure 3. Value proposition canvas for solar drying technologies (*strategyzer*, 2021).

raw materials, intermediate materials, finished goods, and the processes involved in solar drying can be fed to the system as raw material, processes, and finished products. Parallel, the economic values associated with every step could be added. This generates the solution for the process. The software allows pricing analysis in between the processes involved. The optimization could help in the visualization of process flow and gives the heuristic viewpoint to the entrepreneur.

4 CONCLUSIONS

Today, global warming and carbon emissions are a major threat to the climatic conditions of the world. In such a scenario, all renewable energy-based technologies must be supported by all the pillars of society. Apart from this, on the one hand, the food crisis is a significant problem in some parts of the world, and on the other hand, many farmers are struggling to minimize post-harvest waste. In these backgrounds, the modern solar dryers could have a substantial impact in fighting these concerns. The solar drying field has a broad range of applications ranging from drying food, crops, biofuels, food waste, pharmaceuticals, and others. In addition, solar-dried products are more hygienic and have better quality in comparison to industrial drying. Some of the recommendations based on our analysis for upcoming entrepreneurs are mentioned below.

- For the European region, entrepreneurs in solar drying must understand the European directives related to the renewable energy policy framework for a broad understanding. On the state level, national action plans and energy policies for information related to subsidies, tariffs, and licensing-related information.
- The authors recommend analyzing business models related to solar drying to understand the risks and commercialization opportunities. A focused strategy can minimize the financial risk involved in entrepreneurship.
- Social adaptability is a relevant challenge for the solar drying business model. However, the benefits related to solar drying should be used to create awareness among the masses. Social media influencers could play an important role through their Vlogs and posts.

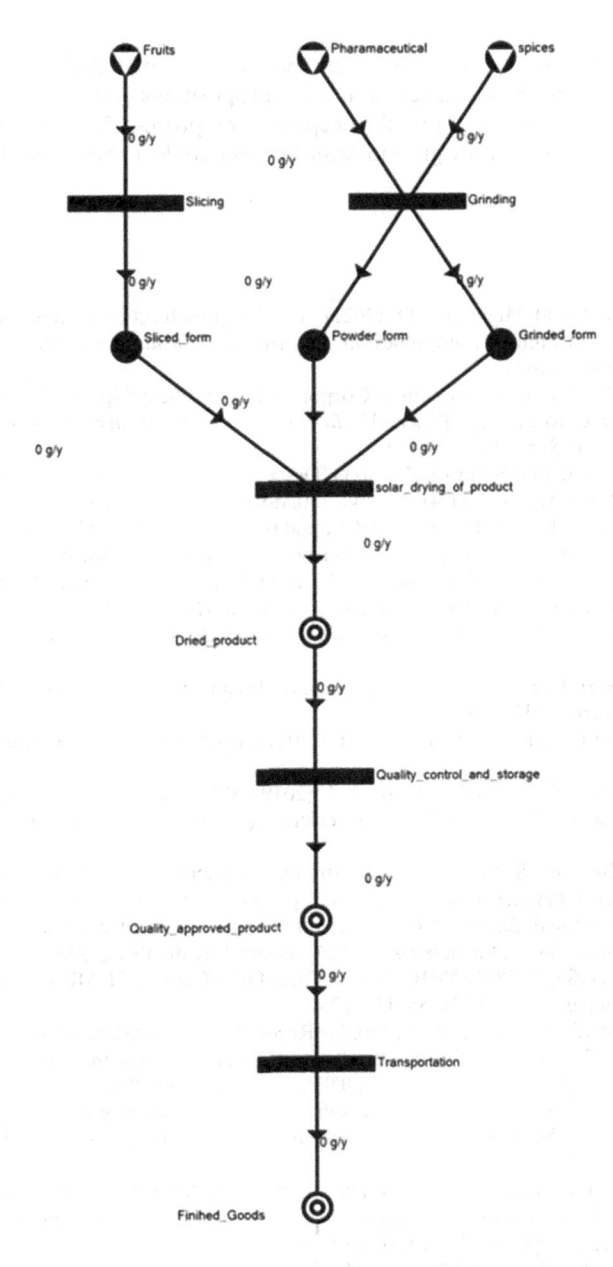

Figure 4. P-graph for the process flow of solar drying of various products.

- The business canvas model presented in the paper emphasizes essential issues in the field The value proposition is an extensive analysis of the business canvas providing the inter-related correlation between the product and the customer's mindset towards the company or the startup and their associated products.
- The Proposed P-graph could be used for the business model optimization by accounting for the various parameters and process flow involved in solar drying technologies. It can help in the cost-effectiveness of the model in the long term.
- On the technical grounds, more funding is required to take the technology beyond the efficiency of the dryers beyond the upper limit of 25%. University collaborations with the industry partners could yield fruitful results in this direction.

The article offers a heuristic overview of the potential of solar drying technologies in the entrepreneurial sector. Business canvas and value propositions provide insights to a certain level. The p-graph could serve as a tool for deep cost and process flow analysis. Further work and surveys with interaction with ground-level farmers could provide substantive results in this field of study.

REFERENCES

Adeyanju, D., Mburu, J. and Mignouna, D. (2021) 'Youth agricultural entrepreneurship: Assessing the impact of agricultural training programmes on performance', *Sustainability (Switzerland)*, 13(4), pp. 1–12. doi: 10.3390/su13041697.

Baden-Fuller, C. (1995) 'Strategic Innovation, Corporate Entrepreneurship and Matching Outside-in to Inside-out Approaches to Strategy Research', *British Journal of Management*, 6(December), pp. S3–S16. doi: 10.1111/j.1467-8551.1995.tb00134.x.

Baibhaw, K., Szepesi, G. L. and Szamosi, Z. (2021) 'Design and Development of natural convective solar dryer', *Multidisciplinary Sciences*, 11(4), pp. 144–150. doi: https://doi.org/10.35925/j.multi.2021.4.18.

Boguniewicz-Zablocka, J., Klosok-Bazan, I. and Capodaglio, A. G. (2021) 'Sustainable management of biological solids in small treatment plants: overview of strategies and reuse options for a solar drying facility in Poland', *Environmental Science and Pollution Research*. Environmental Science and Pollution Research, 28(19), pp. 24680–24693. doi: 10.1007/s11356-020-10200-9.

Brockwell, P. J. and Davis, R. A. (1994) 'Pest', *ITSM for Windows*, pp. 9–59. doi: 10.1007/978-1-4612-2676-5_2.

Cabezas, H. *et al.* (2015) 'Use the P-graph framework to design supply chains for sustainability', *Chemical Engineering Progress*, 111(1), pp. 41–47.

Cunningham, J. and Lischeron, J. (1991) 'Defining Entrepreneurship', *Journal of small business management*, 29(1), p. 45.

Dias, C. S. L., Rodrigues, R. G. and Ferreira, J. J. (2019) 'What's new in the research on agricultural entrepreneurship?', *Journal of Rural Studies*. Elsevier, 65(November 2018), pp. 99–115. doi: 10.1016/j.jrurstud.2018.11.003.

El-Sebaii, A. A. and Shalaby, S. M. (2012) 'Solar drying of agricultural products: A review', *Renewable and Sustainable Energy Reviews*. Elsevier Ltd, 16(1), pp. 37–43. doi: 10.1016/j.rser.2011.07.134.

Eurobserver (2020) *Renewable Energy Policy Factsheet*. Available at: https://www.eurobserv-er.org/eurobserver-policy-files-for-all-eu-28-member-states/ (Accessed: 1 September 2021).

G.N.Tiwari, G. and (1984) 'ECONOMIC ANALYSIS OF SOME SOLAR ENERGY SYSTEMS', *Energy conversion management*, 24(2), pp. 131–135.

Gholamrezai, S., Aliabadi, V. and Ataei, P. (2021) 'Recognizing dimensions of sustainability entrepreneurship among local producers of agricultural inputs', *Journal of Environmental Planning and Management*. Routledge, 0(0), pp. 1–59. doi: 10.1080/09640568.2021.1875998.

Kumar, B. *et al.* (2021) 'Trendline assessment of solar energy potential in hungary and current scenario of renewable energy in the visegrád countries for future sustainability', *Sustainability (Switzerland)*, 13(10). doi: 10.3390/su13105462.

Méndez-Picazo, M. T., Galindo-Martín, M. A. and Castaño-Martínez, M. S. (2021) 'Effects of sociocultural and economic factors on social entrepreneurship and sustainable development', *Journal of Innovation and Knowledge*, 6(2), pp. 69–77. doi: 10.1016/j.jik.2020.06.001.

Osterwalder, A. *et al.* (2010) *You're holding a handbook for visionaries, game changers, and challengers striving to defy outmoded business models and design tomorrow's enterprises. It's a book for the... written by.*

Pokorná, J. *et al.* (2015) 'Agris on-line Papers in Economics and Informatics Value Proposition Canvas : Identification of Pains, Gains and Customer Jobs at Farmers ' Markets', VII(4), pp. 123–130.

Prakash, O. and Kumar, A. (2013) 'Historical review and recent trends in solar drying systems', *International Journal of Green Energy*, 10(7), pp. 690–738. doi: 10.1080/15435075.2012.727113.

Stathopoulou, S., Psaltopoulos, D. and Skuras, D. (2004) 'Rural entrepreneurship in Europe: A research framework and agenda', *International Journal of Entrepreneurial Behaviour & Research*, 10(6), pp. 404–425. doi: 10.1108/13552550410564725.

strategyzer (2021). Available at: https://www.strategyzer.com/ (Accessed: 1 October 2021).

Surányi, D. (2017) 'Fruit drying traditions in Hungary', *International Journal of Horticultural Science*, 23 (1–4), pp. 7–10. doi: 10.31421/ijhs/23/1-4./1193.

Tsoutsos, T. D. (2002) 'Marketing solar thermal technologies: Strategies in Europe, experience in Greece', *Renewable Energy*, 26(1), pp. 33–46. doi: 10.1016/S0960-1481(01)00096-9.

Bio-solution for global sand crisis and sustainable organic agriculture in desert states

D. Štyriaková
ekolive s.r.o., Košice, Slovakia
Slovenian National Building and Civil Engineering Institute, Ljubljana, Slovenia

I. Štyriaková & J. Šuba
ekolive s.r.o., Košice, Slovakia

Felix Föhre
FB Flüssigboden GmbH, Leipzig, Germany

ABSTRACT: Sand is an important component of many everyday items, and currently sand is the second most extracted resource on earth after water, but it is not sustainable: we are running out of sand! The black market is booming, and the sand mafia is mining sand at any price. Desert sand is unusable, even Dubai must import it. The smooth surface and iron impurities prevent its industrial use. In this study, bacteria in the bioleaching test attacked the surface of the mineral grains and dissolved impurities including iron through organic acids. Furthermore, the liquid residue containing dissolved iron, organic acids and bacteria stimulated the growth plant what can be a valuable biofertilizer and biostimulant for organic agriculture. Desert states have fertility problems. Despite this, Qatar, for example, is aiming for self-sufficiency in vegetables "in five years". Results showed that bioleaching combined with magnetic separation resulted in iron removal of 73.23%. The sand after treatment can be suitable to produce clear flat glass, coloured container glass, insulating glass fibres or ceramics. The integrated technology based ecological study revealed overall as utilization potential of the desert sand and the liquid residue could support glass and food production in desert states.

1   INTRODUCTION

Sand is one of the main components of the modern glass, foundry, refractory, ceramic and construction industries. In recent years, there has been a sharp increase in demand for high-purity quartz for semiconductor chips, solar batteries, photovoltaic and flat panel displays, which are classified as advanced technology products. Quartz is one of the most important raw materials used in many industries. There are four types of sand: river sand, sea sand, desert sand and machine-made sand. Desert sand, as the name suggests, is sand from the desert.

1.1   *Industrial sand*

Sand is the main ingredient in the entire glass industry. The purity of the sand determines the colour, clarity, strength and other physical advantages of the glass products. The main glass

DOI: 10.1201/9781003259954-10

products that use sand include colourless and coloured containers such as bottles and glasses, flat glass for windows and automobiles, glass fibre, glass fibre reinforcement, light bulbs, fluorescent tubes, televisions and computer screens. Its special applications include products such as piezoelectric crystals, optical products and glassy silica.

The Asia Pacific region accounts for 47% of global sand needs. Mitsubishi's Cape Flattery in Queensland is currently the largest high-grade silica operation in Australia, delivering ~2.5 million tons per year to Asian countries. In recent years, several regions in which sand is produced have been restricted for environmental reasons. In the past, sand was extracted from environmentally sensitive coastal, river or delta regions such as the Mekong Delta in Vietnam or the Yangtze River in China. Based on estimated world production the United States was the world's leading producer and consumer in 2018 and 2019 of industrial sand and gravel (Table 1). It is difficult to collect definitive data on silica sand and gravel production in most nations because of the wide range of terminology and specifications found among different countries. The United States remained a major exporter of silica sand and gravel, shipping it to almost every region of the world. The high level of exports was attributed to the high quality and advanced processing techniques used in the United States for many grades of silica sand and gravel, meeting virtually every specification. Estimated global demand for in 2020 sand by region is showed in Table 2.

Table 1. World mine production of industrial sand and gravel (USGS).

State		% of Global demand
United States	2018 (kt) 121,000	2019 (kt) 110,000
Australia	3,000	3,000
Bulgaria	7,250	7,300
Canada	2,500	2,500
France	9,310	9,300
Germany	7,500	7,500
India	11,900	12,000
Indonesia	5,540	5,500
Japan	2,520	2,500
Korea	4,300	4,500
Malaysia	10,000	10,000
Mexico	2,360	2,400
Netherlands	54,000	54,000
New Zealand	2,320	2,300
Poland	5,120	5,000
South Africa	2,400	2,400
Spain	35,500	36,000
Turkey	13,500	14,000
United Kingdom	4,000	4,000
Other countries	17,200	21,300

Table 2. Estimated demand for sand by region (source: Freedonia group).

Region	% of Global demand
Asia pacific	47%
North America	20%
Western Europe	16%
Eastern Europe	8%
Africa/Middle East	5%
Central and South America	4%

The Arabian Desert is the second largest desert in the world. The only two different types of construction sand available in Arabian Desert are fluvial sand (for concrete work) and aeolian dune (for mortar work). The scarcity of sand necessitates quality management of these deposits to ensure its availability for as long a period as possible. In addition, the desert states restrict the use of imported sand in all construction works. The desert sand is mainly composed of more than 95% quartz and long-lived minerals such as zircon, tourmaline, rutile and small amounts of feldspar and muscovite. With rapid industrial development, the demand for sand resources is increasing rapidly, but at the same time, sand resources on Earth are limited.

The petrography and heavy mineral content of various dune sands have been described in detail in an article by authors Pastore et al. (2021) with the following composition: Quartz, feldspar, plagioclase, lithic grains (volcanic, carbonate, other sedimentary and metasedimentary) and transparent heavy minerals, including: Zircon + Tourmaline + Rutile, Apatite, Titanite, Epidote, Prehnite + Pumpellyite, Garnet, Staurolite, Kyanite, Amphibole, Pyroxene, Olivine and others (Anatase, Sillimanite, Andalusite, Monazite, Topaz, Brookite). The chemical composition of the raw quartz sands (especially the content of SiO_2, Fe_2O_3 and Al_2O_3) is most important for their use and physical properties. The sand in the desert is formed by weathering and accumulation, and the pollutants cannot be removed as in river or sea sand, resulting in a high pollutant content in the sand, which is very slippery and does not meet the standards and limits for industrial use. To increase the purity of quartz and reduce the content of impurities to the desired levels, various physical and chemical processes are used industrially (Tuncuk & Akcil 2014).

As there will be around 9.3 billion people on earth in 2050 (Sahara Forest Project, 2012), the problem of providing sufficient food for these people will be enormous. Therefore, we need to think critically about new strategies to expand our ability to produce food in the future. Food production remains a challenge, especially for desert countries. Many Gulf countries have learned from the 2008/2009 food crisis that they cannot import food simply because they have the financial capacity to do so. Therefore, it is crucial to find new ways to produce as much food as possible locally to minimise the burden of food imports (Mbaga 2013).

1.2 *Quality improvement of silica sand and increasing of soil fertility*

The purification of silica sand is extremely important for many industries. Several techniques are available for the treatment of silica sand through the partial removal of iron, e.g., flotation, heavy separation, or magnetic separation. Other available techniques are based on the use of sulphuric acid, hydrochloric acid and phosphoric acid as demonstrated by (Tuncuk & Akcil 2014, Suratman & Handayani 2014, Zhang et al. 2012). These methods are very efficient in removing metal contaminants, but they are generally expensive and have significant environmental impacts.

Biological methods are also effective for the surface chemistry of clay minerals and the release of iron minerals from quartz particles (Štyriaková et al. 2012), and these methods have gained interest in recent years. Organic acids dissolve iron oxides by direct attack of H+ ions on the mineral matrix and keep them in solution by forming soluble complexes and chelates. Organic acids can be produced by fermentation using heterotrophic bacteria and serve as leaching agents for dissolving the iron oxides. This biotechnological route, using microorganisms to remove metal contaminants, could prove to be more cost-effective and environmentally friendly, resulting in effluents that are not harmful to nature and can be easily purified.

This process refers to the removal of unwanted mineral components from a silica sand through interaction with a microorganism that causes their selective dissolution (removal), thereby improving their quality and the possibilities of their industrial utilisation. Previous laboratory studies have shown that bacteria and fungi can be effectively used to remove iron from silica sand, kaolin, bauxite, and silica sand (Štyriaková et al. 2015, Šuba & Štyriaková 2015).

Consumers are increasingly concerned about food safety, rising residues in food and environmental issues as they become more concerned about their health. This is driving the need for organic inputs such as biofertilizers and biostimulants to improve soil fertility and crop yields. The use of chemical fertilisers and pesticides causes numerous environmental and health problems. Loss of soil structure and fertility is one of the main causes of soil degradation. Safe and environmentally friendly technologies could help in the sustainable restoration of degraded soils and fertilisation of crops and plants. Innovative, safe, and environmentally friendly technologies could help in the sustainable restoration of degraded soils. Bacteria with dissolved nutrients from natural minerals such as silica sand can restore the fertility of degraded soils. These microorganisms increase the bioavailability of nutrients by fixing nitrogen and mobilising key nutrients (phosphorus, potassium, and iron) in crops, and optimise soil structure by improving its aggregation and stability. Organic acids, produced naturally by bacteria, support growth, and yield and protect plants from diseases.

The aim of the present study was to investigate the removal of impurities, especially iron oxides, from silica sand using biological and physical methods to obtain a product of higher quality and purity. This product can be used in the glass industry and at the same time a biofertiliser is produced that can be used to improve soil fertility and help solve the problem of high food imports in desert countries.

2 MATERIALS AND METHODS

2.1 Desert sand

The desert sand used for the bioleaching experiment was obtained from the sand dunes of the Arabian Desert. Table 3 shows the chemical properties of this desert sand. The chemical analyses were carried out using a portable Vanta X-ray fluorescence spectrometer (XRF), which allows rapid and accurate elemental analyses of solid and liquid phases in laboratory quality.

Table 3. The chemical composition of desert sand.

SAND	Al	Si	S	Ti	Fe	Mn	Ca	Cu	Zn
(mg/kg)	7791	204,318	4403	469	2640	61	98,493	13	6

2.2 Bioleaching

Biological removal of iron from desert sand was done by culturing heterotrophic bacteria *microlive*® in parallel flasks containing 1.200 g of desert sand samples and 1.200 ml of the liquid medium *ekocomplex*®. Bioleaching consisted of exchanging fresh medium (1.000 ml) five times during incubation of the flasks under static conditions for 45 days at 21°C. The leachate was stirred to homogenise the solution before sampling. After centrifugation at 7.000 rpm for 15 minutes, the leachate was separated from the sample. The liquid supernatant was collected ten times (10 ml) for rapid elemental analyses of the bi-leaching experiment. The chemical abiotic controls were not given an inoculum but were otherwise incubated under similar conditions. The bioleaching experiments were performed in two replicates and the average values were recorded. The solution concentration data in the figures for each leachate sample is the average of three measurements. Redox potential and pH were measured with platinum and silver chloride electrodes (In-Lab Expert Pro, Mettler Toledo).

2.3 Magnetic separation

Dry electromagnetic separation was carried out using a laboratory high gradient magnetic separator with the induction of magnetic field at 1.3 T.

3 RESULTS AND DISCUSION

3.1 *Bio-solution of sand quality improvement*

Desert sand consists mainly of rounded quartz grains covered with brown hematite films. The roundness of the desert sand particles is non-circular and subangular, and sub angularity is not uncommon. Smaller grains are more angular than larger ones, and there appears to be considerable variability between the roundness of the sand and the intensity of iron coverage (Figure 1A).

A   B   C

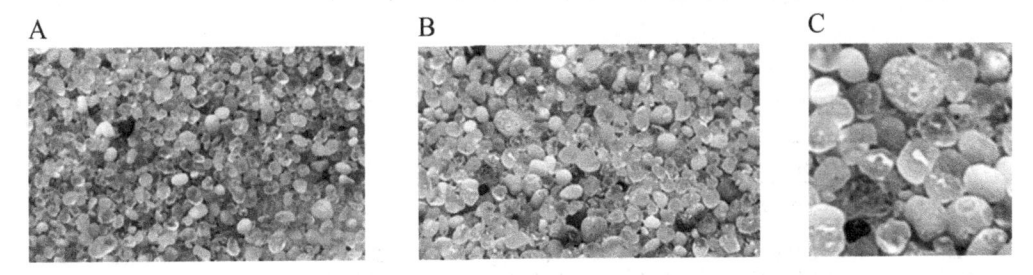

Figure 1. Grains of desert sand before (A) and after bioleaching (B), details of corrosive holes after bioleaching (C).

Desert sand from the Ardhuma deposit in Iraq was treated using growth culture solutions of the mould *Aspergillus niger* in combination with 10% HCl and a pH adjustment to 0.5 as an acidic biochemical leach to remove iron oxide contaminants. The Fe removal efficiency by biochemical leaching was 79.1% and the Fe_2O_3 content was 0.0125%. The combination of magnetic separation and biochemical leaching increased Fe removal to 85.8%, and Fe_2O_3 content was 0.0085%. Desert sand improved by biochemical leaching and magnetic deposition had a low iron oxide content and can therefore be used for optical applications, crystal glass, solar cells, and semiconductors (Mustafa et al. 2011).

Hydrochloric acid is an extremely aggressive chemical and must be handled and recycled safely. This process is not an ecological way of processing sand, so only the process of heterotrophic bioleaching with magnetic separation was tested to increase the quality of the raw material. The yield for the removal of each element is given in Table 4. The chemical analysis of the solid phase confirmed the significant removal of Fe, S, Mn of over 50% after bioleaching and the increase of Fe, S, Mn removal to over 65% after subsequent magnetic separation. The biogenic elements Cu, Zn, Ca were also removed during bioleaching with increasing Si content. These elements were found in the leachate and are important sources of nutrients (Fe, S, Mn, Zn, Ca, Cu) for plant stimulation. Quartz grains coated with hematite are biologically leached (Figure 1B), and corrosive holes are observed in some surfaces after clay detachment (Figure 1C).

Due to high melting temperatures and/or large waste streams from processing, about half of the desert sand samples studied contain more than 90 wt% silica, making it difficult to use as a raw material for glass, while sands with larger proportions of carbonates and/or feldspars form a melt at less than 1650°C when the SiO_2 content is less than 55 wt%. For desert sand glass with a thickness of 3 mm, a light transmittance of 85% at a wavelength of 550 nm has been demonstrated when the Fe_2O_3 content is less than 0.1 wt%, while for the same transmittance across the effective spectrum of silicon-based solar cells, the iron content needs to be further reduced (Minkels 2020).

Bioleaching with heterotrophic bacteria in static medium (Figure 2) in combination with magnetic separation resulted in an iron removal of 73.23%. The sand after treatment is suitable for the production of clear flat glass, coloured container glass, insulating glass fibres or ceramics and the liquid residue could support food production in desert states.

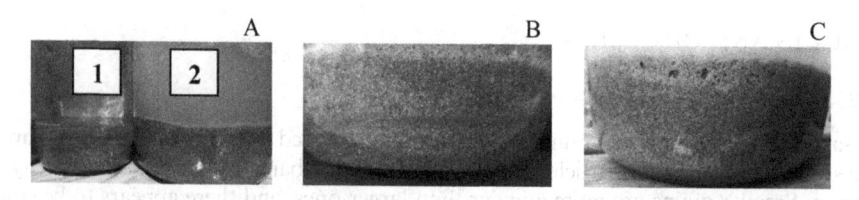

Figure 2. Desert sand leaching (A, 1 - abiotic control, 2 - bioleaching) and details desert sand color after 1 day of bioleaching (B) and after 1 months of bioleaching (C).

Table 4. The percentage of elements removal after bioleaching (BL) and magnetic separation (MS).

SAND	BL		MS	
	Content (mg/kg)	Yield (%)	Content (mg/kg)	Yield (%)
Al	6018	-23	2879	-63
Si	236,817	+14	213,804	+4
S	1675	-62	1500	-66
Ti	293	-38	247	-47
Fe	995	-62	707	-73
Mn	30	-51	20	-67
Ca	79,387	-19	88,268	-10
Cu	9	-31	11	-16
Zn	4	-41	0	-100

3.2 *Bio-solution of leachate utilization*

After each media change, the collected leachates contained different extracted biogenic elements K > Ca > S > Fe (Figure 3), except N (160 mg/l), P (11 mg/l), Na (517 mg/l) and Mg (46 mg/l), which are particularly important for plant health and development, by the media additions. In addition, organic acids (Table 5) and increased heterotrophic bacterial cells, mainly probiotic lactic acid bacteria (Table 6), were obtained from the leachates, which can be used for biostimulation of plants in conventional, organic or vertical agriculture.

Leachate has been registered by the FIBL Institute as *ekofertile™ plant* in the category of microbial biostimulants and biofertilizers for organic farming and has been confirmed to increase plant growth and yield by up to 100% and plant dry matter by 400% (Figure 4,5). The global market for biostimulants and biofertilizers has reached a value of €4 billion and is showing a strong growth trend. There is also a high demand due to the increasing production of organic food (increase of 89%).

Biofertilizers and biostimulants *ekofertile™*, produced by a new ecological process for leaching minerals by ekolive's bacteria *microlive®*, help by:

- Renewing soil microflora through plant growth promoting bacteria to increase nutrient bioavailability and uptake through nitrogen fixation and mobilisation of key nutrients, optimising soil structure and promoting root, flower and fruit growth and development, increasing crop yields, and eliminating toxic contaminants (oil, cyanides, phenols, pesticides, heavy metals, and other toxic substances) through the bioremediation effect.
- Naturally produced organic acids that strongly support plant development and growth and replace pesticides.

- Important micro and macro nutrients from dissolved natural minerals.

Desert soils and desert sands usually have high pH values. Such reactivity can have a negative impact on the availability of nitrogen, phosphorus, and micronutrients to plants, as

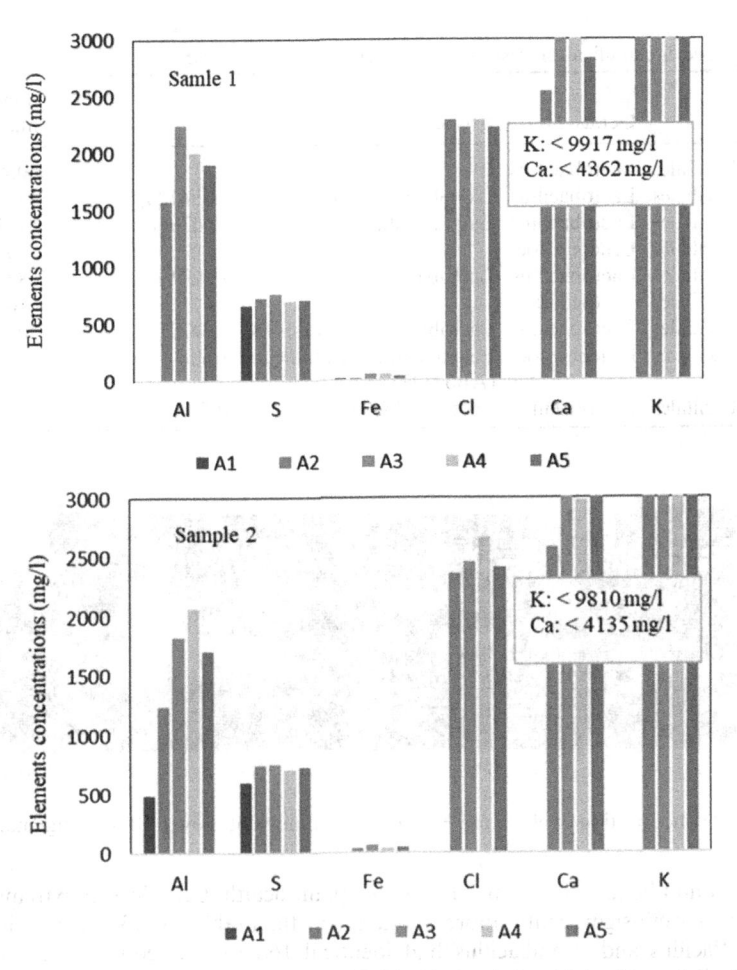

Figure 3.   Chemical analyses (A1, A2, A3, A4, A5) of leachates during bioleaching of the desert sands in the parallel conditions (Sample 1, Sample 2).

Table 5.   Concentration of organic acids in concentrated leachate by HPLC method.

| Sample | mg/L | | | | | |
	lactic acid	acetic acid	butyric acid	methanol	ethanol	propanone
Average concentration in concentrated leachate	20547.33	1327.23	221.97	688.62	0.00	822.41
Standard deviation	57.01	126.16	313.91	355.55	0.00	68.03

these are not in solution at pH > 7. The second problem with desert sand and soil is the lack of organic carbon. In the leachates, the pH dropped to 5.5 ± 0.5 after 4 days of bioleaching, and the admixture of organic matter in the medium contributed to the formation of organic acids, which can improve the availability of nutrients to plants.

The conversion of desert states into arable land is a global vision, and desert agriculture is a rapidly growing area of agriculture worldwide. In one of the best-known examples of organic desert farming in Sekem (Egypt), a drastic change in bacterial communities in the desert soil was observed after long-term farming (30 years). Bacterial communities in farmed soil showed

Table 6. Top species classification results of 16S Metagenomics analyse.

Class	Order	Genus	Species	num hits	%hits
Bacilli	Lactobacillales	Lactobacillus		60,478	45.442
Bacilli	Lactobacillales	Lactobacillus	Lactobacillus harbinensis (AB196123)	15,710	11.804
Bacilli	Lactobacillales	Lactobacillus	Lactobacillus diolivrans (AF264701)	8121	6.102
Bacilli	Lactobacillales	Leuconostoc		7006	5.264
Bacilli	Lactobacillales	Lactobacillus	Lactobacillus satsumsis (AB154519)	6877	5.167
Bacilli	Lactobacillales	Lactococcus		6569	4.936
Bacilli	Lactobacillales	Lactobacillus	Lactobacillus iwatensis (AB773428)	4079	3.065
Bacilli	Lactobacillales	Leuconostoc	Leuconostoc pseudomesenteroides (AB023237)	3473	2.610
Bacilli	Lactobacillales	Lactobacillus	Lactobacillus perolens (Y19167)	1733	1.302

0%   10%   50%   100%

Figure 4. Used concentration of ekofertile™ and its effect on plant growth (BDC, England, 8 weeks).

higher diversity and better ecosystem function for plant health, but a loss of extremophilic bacteria. Firmicutes were significantly more abundant in the arable soil (37%) than in the desert sand (11%). Bacillus and Paenibacillus had identical 16S rRNA sequences in the amplicon library and isolate and accounted for 96% of the antagonists against phytopathogens. Compared to the desert sand, the proportion of antagonistic strains in the field was twice as high (21.6%/12.4%); the disease-suppressing bacteria were particularly enriched in the plant roots. On the other hand, several extremophilic bacterial groups such as *Acidimicrobium*, *Rubellimicrobium* and *Deinococcus-Thermus* disappeared from the soil after agricultural use. The N-fixing *Herbaspirillum* group was found only in desert soils. The abiotic factors of water supply and pH had a strong influence on the soil bacterial communities (Koberl et al. 2011).

The application of leachate with a pH of 5.5 ± 0.5 containing organic acids, macronutrients, micronutrients and lactic acid bacteria and their metabolites can help to increase crop yield and health. The accumulation of salt ions in the soil is due to high evaporation rates and low rainfall, and saline soils have serious consequences in terms of osmotic stress, ion toxicity and imbalance for desert-dwelling plants. Excessive amounts of sodium (Na^+) and chloride (Cl^-) ions have negative effects on plant membranes and enzymes, disrupting energy balance and protein metabolism (Shrivastava & Kumar 2015).

Bioleaching reduced the concentration of chloride (Cl^-) ions in the desert sand because the leachate contained these elements, which can be removed from solution by precipitation before the leachate is used for plant biostimulation.

4 CONCLUSION

The laboratory bioleaching experiment for iron removal with heterotrophic bacteria on desert sand were conducted to explore a simple cyclic operation for potential use at the industrial scale. The bioleaching test involved organic acid attack, resulting in the solubilization of Fe from the quartz surface and releasing biogenic elements to liquid residues. By this way it was possible to recover desert sand quality improvement and biofertilizer tested on basal. The bioleaching of desert sand by heterotrophic bacteria may be of commercial interest to glass, mining and agriculture industries.

Several studies have demonstrated the potential of biofertilizers to increase the yield and quality of various crops. However, market prices for low-value crops usually make the use of biofertilizers unprofitable.

Our solution offers the opportunity to solve two global problems at once. Improving the quality of silica sand by removing the main unwanted Fe impurities can be important for the future more versatile use of desert sand as a raw material for different industries. At the same time, biofertilizers with enormous value for future sustainable and safe food production are created.

Technology is currently under ecological technology verification ETV process, developed on TRL6 with the latest application on 150 and 300 tons of silica sand in the pilot operation in Slovenia. Biofertilizer from silica sand was tested on TRL5 on different crops (tomatoes, potatoes, herbs, strawberries, blueberries, bananas) and is listed in Dutch Organic Agriculture input list by FIBL institute as ekofertile™plant. Commercialization strategy is represented by licencing in desert states.

The biological solution to the two problems is another step towards a possible solution to the global sand crisis and sustainable agriculture in desert states.

REFERENCES

Koberl, M. et al. 2011. Desert Farming Benefits from Microbial Potential. Arid Soils and Promotes Diversity and Plant Health. In PLoS ONE 6(9): e24452. doi: 10.1371/journal.pone.0024452

Mbaga, M. D. (2013) Alternative mechanisms for achieving food security in Oman. Agriculture and Food Security, 2, 1–11.

Mbaga, M. D. (2013) Alternative mechanisms for achieving food security in Oman. Agriculture and Food Security, 2, 1–11.

Minkels, J.A. 2020. Glass production from desert sand: Proof of concept and characterization. Master theses. Delft University of Technology. TU Delft Mechanical, Maritime and Materials En-gineering. http://resolver.tudelft.nl/uuid:62b1ae5a-c071-4501-b670-835965866450

Mustafa, M. K. et al. 2011. Biobenefication of silica sand for crystal glass industry from ardhuma location, iraqi western desert. Iraqi Bulletin of Geology and Mining Vol.7, No.1, 77–86.

Pastore, G. et al. 2021. Provenance and recycling of Sahara Desert sand. Earth-Science Reviews. Vol. 216, 103606, ISSN 0012-8252, https://doi.org/10.1016/j.earscirev.2021.103606.

Sahara Forest Project 2012. The Impact Potential of The Sahara Forest Project – a scenario towards 2050. Accessed on the 11th of September 2012 at 17: 00. Available at: http://www.circleofblue.org/waternews/wp-content/uploads/2012/02/Sahara-Forest-Project.pdf

Shrivastava, P. & Kumar, R. 2015. Soil salinity: a serious environmental issue and plant growth promoting bacteria as one of the tools for its alleviation. Saudi J. Biol. Sci. 22, 123–131. doi: 10.1016/j.sjbs.2014.12.001

Suratman & Handayani, 2014. Beneficiation of Sambiroto silica sand by chemical and biological leachings. Indonesian Mining Journal, 17(3), pp. 134–143. http://jurnal.tekmira.esdm.go.id/index.php/imj/article/view/318.

Štyriakova, I. et al. 2012. Bioleaching of clays and iron oxide coatings from quartz sands. Applied Clay Science, 61 pp. 1–7.

Štyriaková, I. et al. 2015. Second pilot-plant bioleaching verification of the iron removal from quartz sands. Procedia Earth and Planetary Science, 15, pp. 861–865. doi: 10.1016/j.proeps.2015.08.138.

Šuba, J. & Štyriaková, D. 2015. Iron minerals removal from different quartz sands. Procedia Earth and Planetary Science, 15, pp. 849–854. doi: 10.1016/j.proeps.2015.08.136

Tuncuk & Akcil, 2014a. Removal of iron from quartz ore using different acids: a laboratory-scale reactor study. Mineral Processing & Extractive Metall. Rev, Vol. 35, No. 4, 217–228.

Zhang et al. 2012. High efficiency iron removal from quartz sand using phosphoric acid. International Journal of Mineral Processing, Vol. 114, No. 117, 30–34.

Recovering oxides from construction waste as an alternative raw material for the production of cement clinker

Katarzyna Styk & Olga Świniarska

Faculty of Civil Engineering and Resource Management, AGH University of Science and Technology, Kraków, Poland

ABSTRACT: In line with the concept of a Circular Economy, one of the leaders of the cement industry in Poland has decided to search for alternative sources of raw materials for cement clinker production under the Limbra project. The students forming the project team from AGH UST, as one of the solutions, proposed the recovery of oxides from construction waste as an alternative raw material to produce cement clinker. To determine the viability and feasibility of this proposal, it was necessary to conduct a market analysis of potential raw material suppliers. This paper presents the results of the analysis.

1 INTRODUCTION

Circular Economy represents a significant challenge for all industries, especially for heavy industries. Recommendations and indications contained in the European Green Deal are implemented in the legislation of the individual Member States of the European Union, having an increasing and significant impact on manufacturing companies. Therefore, to meet the challenges posed by legislators, but also to act responsibly and sustainably, manufacturing companies are looking for alternative sources of raw materials for their production processes.

This paper addresses the use of alternative raw materials in the cement industry, specifically the cement clinker production process. The research presented in this article was conducted by students of the AGH University of Science and Technology in Krakow as part of a case study commissioned by Limbra, a leading cement manufacturing company in Poland. The article presents the essence of the problem, i.e. the case commissioned by the company and the algorithm of its solution including market analysis, analysis of data obtained from potential suppliers, SWOT analysis and conclusions from the conducted research.

2 CIRCULAR ECONOMY ON CEMENT BUSINESS SEGMENT

There are many definitions of a Circular Economy, but in principle, it can be presented as an industrial system focused on closing the loop of material and energy flows and contributing to long-term sustainability. The Circular Economy incorporates principles and strategies for more efficient use of energy, materials and water while emitting minimal waste into the environment [1, 3].

As the definition indicates, the Circular Economy is overwhelmingly based on closing the cycle of the flow of materials, raw materials and products. Figure 1 shows the product life cycle maintained by the circular concept. It indicates 7 stages:

DOI: 10.1201/9781003259954-11

1. Acquisition of raw materials,
2. Design/improvement of a product or production technology,
3. Production,
4. Distribution,
5. Consumption/use,
6. Collection,
7. Disposal/Recycling.

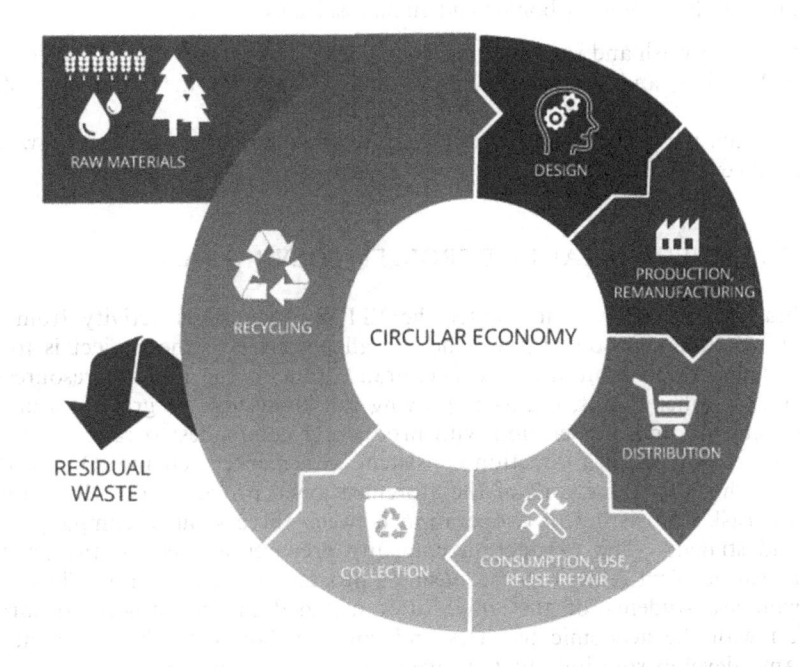

Figure 1.   Product life cycle in line with the Circular Economy concept.
Source: [3]

For this article, we will focus on the first of the steps, the sourcing of raw materials. To make the sourcing of raw materials as sustainable as possible, it is necessary to adhere to a few key principles: choosing renewable, recyclable or biodegradable materials; reclamation of degraded areas; sustainable and responsible sourcing of raw materials [8, 11]. One of the 3 principles of the Circular Economy proposed in November 2015 by the Ellen MacArthur Foundation is: Preserve and enrich natural capital by controlling finite stocks and balancing renewable resource streams. The basis of this principle is to control the management of renewable, non-renewable resource streams and their stocks. The most important assumption of this principle is to minimize the demand for non-renewable resources and substitute them with renewable resources. Moreover, if it is necessary to use a non-renewable raw material, the system should make a careful selection and choose the technology in such a way as to maximize the efficiency of the selected raw material. Such action is expected to help reduce environmental degradation and allow, for example, soil regeneration [5, 9]. Therefore, sourcing raw materials for production is one of the most important elements of the product life cycle.

This paper aims to present alternative sources for the production of cement clinker. To make a proper introduction to the following research section, it is necessary to present the definition of cement as well as the clinker itself. According to the technical definition, cement is a hydraulic binding material obtained from mineral resources (marl, limestone, clay) by firing and subsequent grinding of the resulting sinter [3]. Cement clinker, on the other hand, is the basic ingredient in the production of cement and is responsible for its setting. It is produced by firing ingredients (most commonly calcium carbonate, aluminosilicates and other admixtures) at high temperatures in a rotary kiln [9, 10]. There are three basic types of clinker in the cement production process:

- barium - they are obtained from raw materials containing calcium and barium carbonates and aluminum silicates,
- aluminum - they are obtained from bauxite and calcium or from bauxite and limestone,
- portland - for the production of Portland cement; they are obtained from raw materials containing mainly calcium carbonate and aluminosilicates.

Currently, slag, fly ash and raw materials containing a high proportion of such compounds as CaO, SiO_2, Al_2O_3 and Fe_2O_3 are most commonly used for the production of cement clinker.

For the project, the research team focused on finding alternative sources of raw materials for cement clinker production.

3 LIMBRA PROJECT – REAL LIFE PROBLEM SOLVING TASK

The Limbra project is a venture under the EIT RawMaterials activity from 2019 to 2022 by an international consortium. The overall objective of the project is to develop multi-level solutions to limit the so-called brain drain in the mineral resources sector through, among other things, events improving the knowledge of graduates in the field of entrepreneurship and cooperation with production companies to raise the competencies of future employees in a direction consistent with market demand. One of the tasks carried out within the framework of the aforementioned project is the "Real Life Problem Solving Task" consisting of cooperation between three groups: company, academic teachers and students. The production company prepares a task for the participants, which is a real problem related to the business process of the company. Then the participants, who are students of the universities included in the project consortium, in cooperation with the academic teachers and collaboration with the representatives of the company, develop solutions to the given problem. The whole project lasts about 4 months and is completed with the evaluation of the work by a committee that includes representatives of the company commissioning the task with a significant voice.

In 2020, the organizer of RLPS was a Polish university - AGH UST in Krakow. A company that is one of the leading manufacturers of cement, aggregates and concrete in Poland and a leader in the Polish construction market was invited to cooperate. At the same time, Company X is a global leader in building materials and solutions, operating in four business segments: Cement, Aggregates, Ready-Mix Concrete and Solutions & Products. As part of the RLPS, Company X provided a task for project participants that involved one of the cement plants in the group. Because of the changing market and the expected significantly lower production of steel (slag reduction) and thermal coal (fly ash reduction) in Poland in the coming years, Company X is seeking to acquire and use for the production of cement clinker alternative raw materials containing clay oxide (Al_2O_3), iron oxide (Fe_2O_3) and decarbonised calcium oxide (CaO), which in the future will replace the materials currently used as the basic raw material for cement clinker production (slag, fly ash). Another factor in the creation of this task, apart from the changing market, was the desire to implement solutions compatible with the Circular Economy in the operations of cement plants.

The final task for the participants was to propose an alternative mineral raw material for the production of cement clinker, together with an indication of the effectiveness and profitability of the solution. The challenge for the project team was to find an alternative source of raw material and conduct a market study that would ultimately show the profitability of using the chosen source.

This paper presents a study of the problem prepared by a group of participants from the Faculty of Civil Engineering and Resource Management at AGH UST (Olga

Świniarska, Julia Krućko, Krzysztof Bocheński, Konrad Słowiński) in collaboration with the group supervisor (Katarzyna Styk). The authors of the project were strongly involved in the implementation of the project, Olga Świniarska was the leader of the project team, Katarzyna Styk as an academic teacher took care of a group of students and was a kind of advisory body.

4 CASE STUDY - OPPORTUNITIES TO SOURCE AND USE ALTERNATIVE RAW MATERIALS FOR THE PRODUCTION OF CEMENT CLINKER

During the preliminary design work, all project participants generated 11 problem solution proposals, which were consulted with Company X. As interesting and worthy of further work, the ordering company selected 4 topics, including one concerning the recovery of oxides from construction waste, which was developed by a group from AGH. After receiving all 4 proposals for substitute raw materials, Company X undertook a comparison of these solutions and a calculation of their cost-effectiveness for implementation, this activity took place without student teams.

Even before starting to work on developing a solution to the problem, the group had to become familiar with the technology of cement clinker production, existing knowledge of the composition of the raw material mix, learn about the chemical composition of cement clinker and the ingredients of the raw material mix. Only after acquiring the above-mentioned information and knowledge - publicly available or made available by Company X - it was possible to start research work. An algorithm was developed to conduct the work, which included a market analysis for companies producing construction waste in Poland or its close vicinity. The next step was to select the companies that would go on to further analysis and to choose the key according to which the elimination would be carried out. The next step is to contact the companies already selected and try to obtain data on the amount of raw material they have, its origin, composition and price. Based on the obtained data, it was necessary to conduct a numerical analysis, then a SWOT analysis, and finally to select the best company for cooperation. The algorithm for conducting the work is shown in Figure 2.

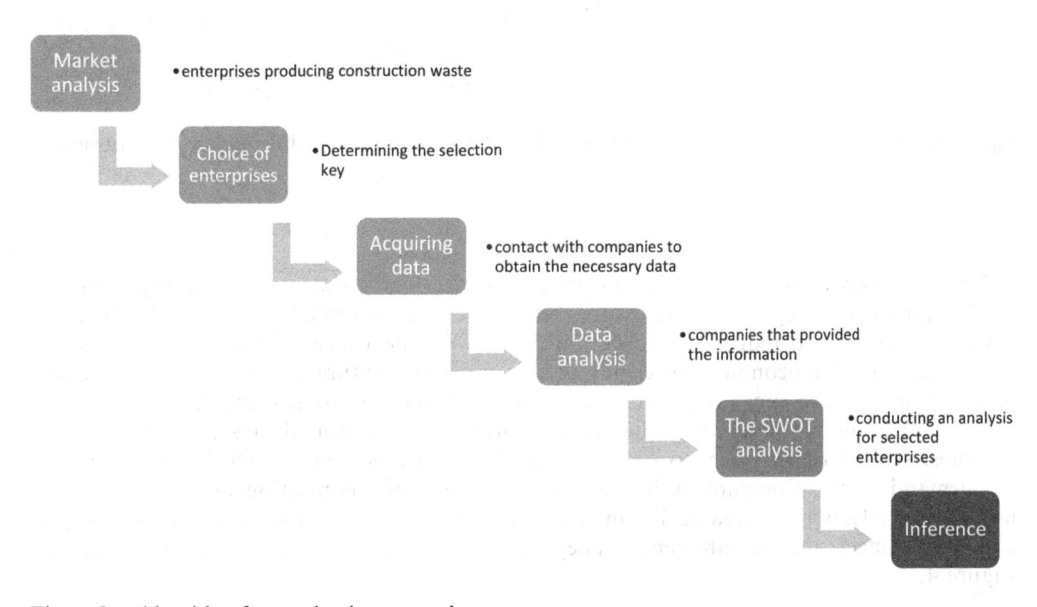

Figure 2.   Algorithm for conducting research.

4.1 Market research

In this study, the market analysis was divided into three steps, as shown in green in Figure 3. The first activity was to analyze the market for construction waste distribution companies. The team was looking for companies in the vicinity of large urban areas such as Warsaw, Krakow and Katowice, as companies in this area were likely to have a steady and stable supply of construction waste. A combination of 26 companies involved in distribution of construction waste from Poland and neighbouring countries was prepared: 15 companies from Poland, 6 companies from Ukraine, 3 companies from Germany, 1 company from the Czech Republic. The location of some of the mapped companies is indicated on the map presented in Figure 3. The summary was written in tabular form, in which data were collected on the country in which the company is located, the exact address, website, contact information (e-mail address or link to the contact form) and an attempt to determine the approximate size of the company on the basis of publicly available data (internal scale was adopted: small, medium, large).

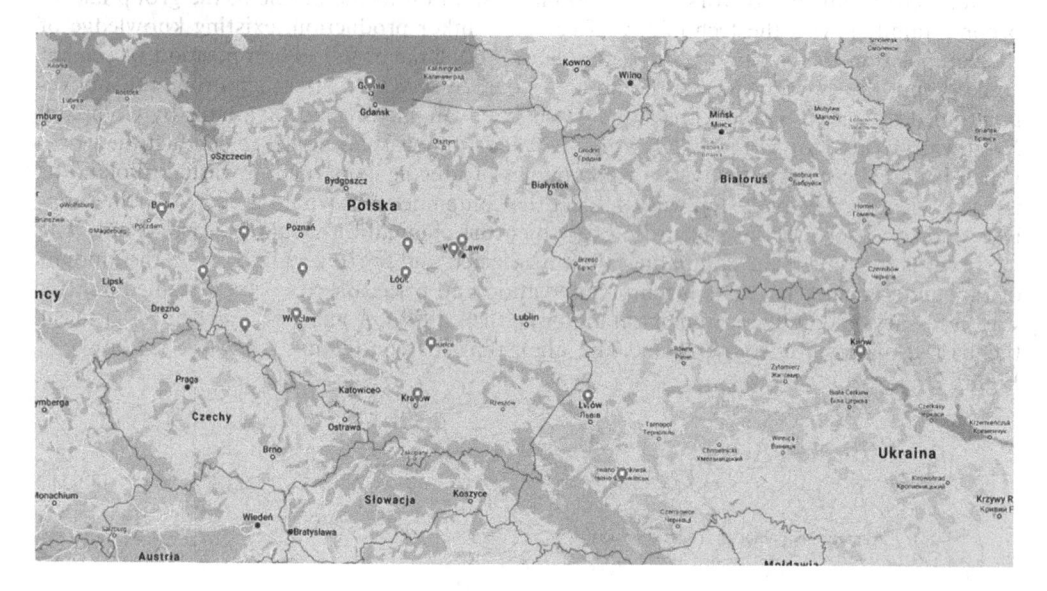

Figure 3. Map with marked companies involved in the acquisition and distribution of construction waste.

The next step involved the selection of companies for further analysis along with the establishment of a key for this selection. As a key, it was decided to choose the distance from Company X to reduce the costs associated with the transportation of raw material and to increase the economic efficiency of the potential venture and the size of the company. However, the most important selection criterion was to get acquainted with the product offering of these companies (the information was not always available on the websites, so it was necessary to contact them by phone or e-mail), which had to match the demand of the Company X in terms of the chemical composition of the raw material. After analyzing the created list in terms of these 3 factors, it turned out that only 5 companies meet the requirements. They are summarized on the map presented in Figure 4.

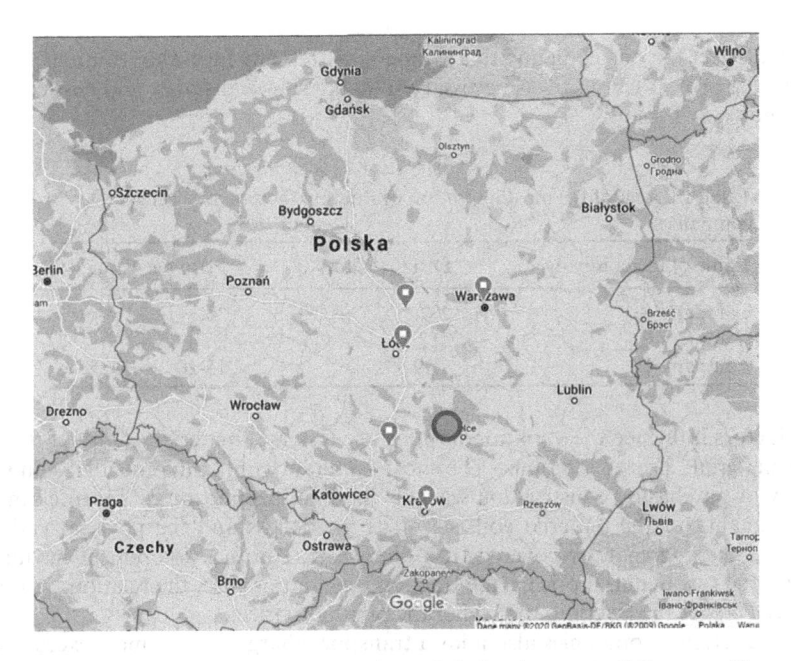

Figure 4.   Map of Poland with 5 selected companies and the headquarters of Company X.

The final action in this step was to contact the selected companies to obtain the necessary data. It was decided to undertake contact by email and in case of no response by phone. Statistical data from the last year on the amount of demolition raw material processed and how it was disposed of, as well as information on the price per unit of raw material offered, were requested.

4.2   *Analysis of chosen company data*

Aftermarket analysis and contacting selected companies, only 3 of them met the expectations set by the project team. For this article they will be named as follows: Company A, Company B, Company C. Figure 5 shows the location of the selected companies on the map of Poland within the distance from the production plant of Company X.

Figure 5.   Map of Poland with 3 selected companies and the headquarters of Company X.

In order to select the one company that would most reliably meet the requirements of Company X and the project team, it was necessary to make simple distance and cost comparisons, which are shown in Table 1.

Table 1. List of the most important evaluation factors of selected companies.

Name of the company	Distance [km]	Price per 1 tone [zł]
Company A	207	30
Company B	217	9-64
Company C	92,9	15-20

Several factors influence the variation in price per tonne of material: purity of the material, quality of material, size of fractions. The most common contamination that eliminates the profitability of purchasing construction waste is the high proportion of red brick in the total waste. The quality of the material consists of its brittleness and the physical and chemical parameters of the aggregates recovered from the waste. Another component having a direct influence on the raw material price is the fraction size, in this case, the relation is directly proportional, the bigger the fraction, the higher the purchase price.

Each of the selected companies also adds a transport charge for distances exceeding 15 km, due to which the price of the raw material itself is raised in addition to the transport cost borne by Company X at the time of purchase. This cost was not approximated by the project team due to the lack of estimates for the size of the contract and the mode of transportation.

Another criterion for supplier selection was the raw material itself, for which the project team created several categories:

• The level of contamination of the raw material with other chemical compounds,
• The size of the fraction to be delivered,
• Continuity in the supply of raw material.

The information indicated was provided by the companies interviewed, the team could not physically and chemically test the samples.

4.3 *SWOT analysis*

SWOT analysis is the second key criterion to select the company that most accurately met the requirements set by Company X and the project team.

The name of the analysis itself is an acronym from the English words Strengths, Weaknesses, Opportunities and Threats. Based on the four areas, a proposal is developed to adopt one of the strategic plans, which were developed by H. Weihrich [8]:

• Strengths-Opportunities - aggressive strategy (maxi-maxi),
• Weaknesses-Opportunities - competitive strategy (mini-maxi),
• Strengths-Threats - conservative strategy (maxi-mini),
• Weaknesses-Threats - defensive strategy (mini-mini)

First SWOT analysis is for Company A, shown in Table 2.

In the above analysis, the prevailing elements are Weaknesses and Opportunities. The key weaknesses of Company A are its inability to supply continuously, due to the seasonal nature of its business. Moreover, the company is not able to maintain a constant quality of the waste it offers since it takes on demolition jobs of varying types. These are some of the key parameters when selecting a supplier for Company X.

The second factor with a relatively high proportion in the analysis is opportunity. The most important of these is the company's proximity to major metropolitan areas, which may

Table 2. SWOT analysis for Company A.

Strengths	Weaknesses
• The company has been on the market since 2005, • Extensive demolition experience • Wide range of products extraction, production sale and transport of aggregates.	• Lack of delivery stability, • The company is unable to provide a constant level of quality of the raw material, • Company prefers orders for short distances.
Opportunities	**Threats**
• The proximity to large urban agglomerations can ensure constant supplies of raw material from construction waste, • Loyalty program for lower prices for wholesale orders, • Attractive discounts for the clients who order more than one service.	• Company is further away from cement plant, • Long waiting for good quality raw material, • The distance exceeding 15 km forces you to hire an intermediary in the form of a transport company.

increase the chance of a steady supply of raw materials due to the relatively higher volume of demolitions.

The development strategy of Company A, based on this analysis, is defined as a Competitive Strategy.

Second SWOT analysis is for Company B, shown in Table 3.

Table 3. SWOT analysis for Company B.

Strengths	Weaknesses
• The company has been on the market since 2001, • Extensive demolition experience, • Conducting selection of construction waste, • Efficient node-crushing sorting.	• Lack of delivery stability, • Limited rock yard with a large number of different factions, • The dominant product is construction waste with a large admixture of bricks.
Opportunities	**Threats**
• A wide range of products increases the company's competitiveness on the market, • Company recognition on the market, • Better material handling after demolition.	• Company is further away from cement plant, • A limited amount of raw material of the right quality, • Long waiting for good quality raw material.

The dominant factor in the SWOT analysis for Company B is its strengths and opportunities. The company has many years of experience in demolition and sorting of construction waste. Possession of know-how directly influences greater competitiveness of the company on the market.

The project team identified improved handling of waste material after demolition as some of the most important opportunities in the table above. This is the proper sorting, cleaning, crushing and securing of raw materials. Based on its own technology, the company selects and cleans material according to the requirements of its customers. With the present technology, the weakness due to the high proportion of bricks in the waste is no longer a key factor for the company and the purity of the material.

Unfortunately, due to the time-consuming nature of the cleaning process, Company B is threatened by the long waiting time for the material ordered by the customer. This process needs to be optimized and the timing of raw material deliveries needs to be properly arranged.

The development strategy of Company A, based on this analysis, is referred to as the Aggressive Strategy.

Third SWOT analysis is for Company C, shown in Table 4.

Table 4. SWOT analysis for Company C.

Strengths	Weaknesses
• The company has been on the market since 2003, • Extensive demolition experience, • One of the leaders on the demolition market in Poland, • The company's extensive marketing network, • A wide range of activities including demolition, earthworks, scrap trading and aggregate sales.	• Lack of delivery stability, • The company is unable to provide a constant level of quality of the raw material, • Distance in excess of 15 km from the cement plant, • They only offer one size of aggregate fraction.
Opportunities	**Threats**
• Company is the nearest away to the cement plant, • The lowest price of raw material, • High recognition of the company on the market, • A large group of trusted customers.	• If the recovered material contains a high percentage of bricks, recycling is not profitable, • Construction waste containing the highest percentage of concrete is still contaminated with other aggregates, • The distance exceeding 15 km forces you to hire an intermediary in the form of a transport company.

The strengths of Company C are its vast experience in the demolition business and its wide range of activities including demolition, earthmoving, scrap metal trading and aggregate sales. The company carries out the demolition work itself, then carries out the process of selection of materials and finally sells them as raw materials.

The most important opportunities for Company C are its closest proximity to the cement plant and the lowest raw material price. What is more, the company has a strong position on the market and high recognition, which positively influences building trust as a supplier.

A recurring weakness with each of the selected companies is the inability to maintain a steady supply. This is due to the nature of the demolition industry, which is seasonal.

Nevertheless, threats are also a strong factor for Company C. The technology they have is not capable of recovering material with a high percentage of brick, it is an unprofitable process for the company, the same with other contaminants.

In addition to this threat, the strategy for Company C based on this analysis is defined as an Aggressive Strategy.

4.4 Conclusions from the research

After a thorough analysis of the market for aggregates from construction waste, it can be concluded that construction waste cannot be identified as a reliable substitute for the production of cement clinker due to the seasonal availability of the material, the heavy contamination of the material and the often uneconomical treatment and costly transportation due to the long distance between the companies and the cement plants.

Nevertheless, construction waste can be one of several sources for obtaining raw material for clinker production. Because of the glaring risks resulting precisely from the lack of consistency of supply and the variability of the quality of the material, this source cannot constitute the basis for obtaining raw materials but may be a good supplement to supply because of the much lower price of the raw material.

5 SUMMARY

Circular economy at present is one of the most important development goals for manufacturing enterprises, including heavy industry. The search for new sources of raw materials for key intermediates was a casa goal to be solved by the students. A thorough understanding of the requirements and the production process allowed us to propose several potential solutions, which required a thorough testing and examination of its potential performance. After receiving all four proposals, the company was able to determine on its own the profitability and feasibility of these solutions in the cement plant.

Students of the AGH University of Science and Technology chose a solution which was to obtain raw material from construction waste. After conducting a thorough market research and various analyses, the students concluded that basing raw material intake solely on the indicated source would not meet the quantitative, qualitative and performance expectations of the company. Due to the recurring problem of maintaining stability of supply and quality of raw material, construction waste cannot be a substitute for natural raw materials. The only way to use this source efficiently is to order raw material at the time of increased production volumes and treat it as a back-up source.

REFERENCES

Camacho-Otero J., Boks C., Nilstad Pettersen I., Consumption in the Circular Economy: A Literature Review, NTNU Norwegian University of Science and Technology (2018).
Chmiel B., Grzegorczyk W., Cement production - Materials for conversational classes preceding the technical trip to the "Chełm" Cement Plant, learning materials (2008).
Ed. Scientific Kulczycka J.: Circular Economy in Politics and Research, Publishing house IGSMiE PAN, Kraków (2019).
European Parliament, Circular economy: the importance of re-using products and materials, https://www.europarl.europa.eu/news/hr/headlines/economy/20150701STO72956/kruzno-gospodarstvo-ucin kovitim-koristenjem-resursa-do-odrzivog-rasta, 28.10.2021.
Farong Qiao, Nan Qiao, Circular Economy: An Ethicaland Sustainable Economic Development Model, Akademia Leona Koźmińskiego (2013).
Gierszewska G., Romanowska M., Strategic analysis of the enterprise, Polish Economic Publishing House, Warszawa (2003).
Pewny cement, What is cement clinker and what is it necessary for?, https://pewnycement.pl/2015/04/czym-jest-klinkier-cementowy-czego-jest-niezbedny/, 28.10.2021.
Pikoń K., Circular Economy in a holistic approach, Publishing House of the Silesian University of Technology (2018).
The Ellen MacArthur Foundation, Towards a Circular Economy: The Business Rationale for Accelerated Change, The Ellen MacArthur Foundation (2015).
Yiqing Zhao, Li Zang, Zhongxue Li, Jiexuan Qin, Discussion on the Model of Mining Circular Economy, University of Science and Technology Beijing (2012).
Zarębska J., A circular economy as a path to sustainable development, Support Systems in Production Engineering (2017).

The Circular Economy in Polish industry—analysis of the issue and opportunities for implementation

K. Zybała

AGH University of Science and Technology, Kraków, Poland

ABSTRACT: The article first discusses the importance of Circular Economy. The importance of waste management in the context of environmental protection has been emphasized. The importance of the choice of manufacturing technologies and materials used for the implementation of the Circular Economy is presented. The issues of necessary investments, legislative and organisational works have been discussed. The next chapter discusses the Circular Economy system in Poland. The fundamental aspects, which would accelerate Poland's path towards the Circular Economy, are described. The importance of actions taken by the government, local authorities, shareholders and mutual cooperation between companies is highlighted. The next chapter presents a concrete example of implementing Circular Economy in the Polish mining sector based on the example of KGHM Polska Miedź. The research objective of this chapter is to analyze assumptions and solutions related to Circular Economy in the largest Polish copper mine. The next chapter discusses implementation tools that support the transformation process, such as: proper credit risk assessment, using indicators that measure the degree of project compliance with the model of economic, social and environmental benefits, project finance instruments. The last chapter is a summary of considerations.

1 INTRODUCTION

Nowadays, caring for the environment is situated at a high level. The raw materials used today have an adverse effect on the environment, which is why it is so important to keep them in the Economy for as long as possible. The appropriate use of resources and the maximum reduction of their adverse impact on the environment are the main objectives of the Circular Economy (Bachorz 2017). We identify the Circular Economy (Figure 1) as the consumption of resources through the minimisation of waste, the preservation of their value for as long as possible and, above all, closed cycles in the use of necessary raw materials (Bachorz 2017).

When defining the Circular Economy, the description provided by Ellen MacArthur Foundation s quoted most often: "Circular Economy is an industrial system that is restorative or regenerative by intention and design. It replaces the "end-of-life" concept with restoration, shifts towards the use of renewable energy, eliminates the use of toxic chemicals, which impair re-use, and aims for the elimination of waste through the superior design of materials, products, systems, and, within this, business models." (Kulczycka 2017) The definition indicates that initiating action and implementing the principles of the Circular Economy should be considered a priority worldwide. In Poland, it is necessary to define these

DOI: 10.1201/9781003259954-12

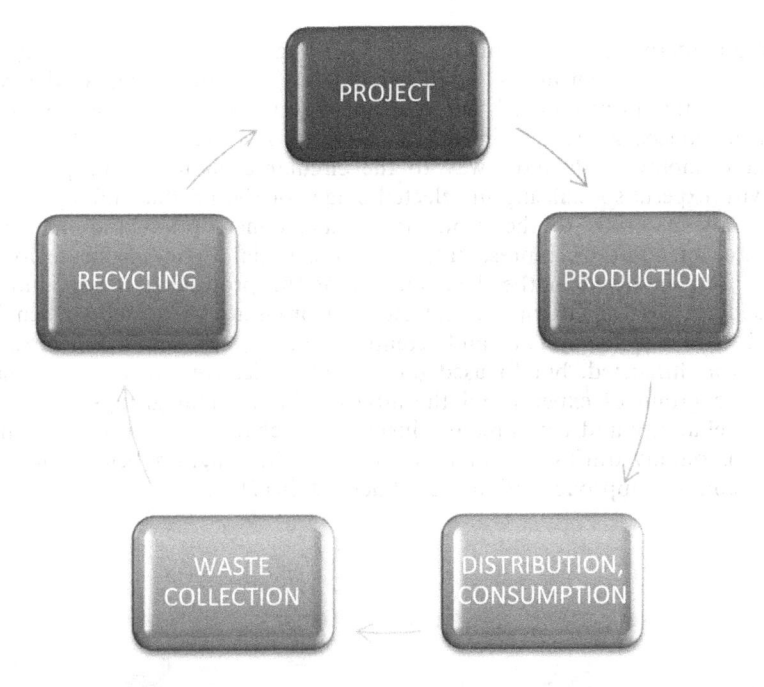

Figure 1. Diagram of the circular economy.
Reference: own study.

activities as economic development with appropriate economic and legal instruments. Using indicators to monitor the progress of its implementation and relying on the latest IT solutions. The global development model is based on its, two main assumption (Burkowicz et al. 2013):

1. The added value of raw materials, materials and finished products is maximised along the value chain (from designer to consumer).
2. The waste generated is minimised, while the waste produced is managed in accordance with the requirements (prevention of large quantities of waste, preparation for re-use, recycling and disposal).

In the Circular Economy model, the use of raw materials from secondary sources was pointed out. The proposed solutions address many areas of economics, energy efficiency, increased repair and reuse services, the imposition of producer responsibility rules and the assessment of the durability and lifespan of a product. All proposals are directed towards expanding recycling. Introducing the principles of Circular Economy into a company contributes to the development of new jobs, expands access to raw materials and favours the environment (European Commission 2011).

The idea of the Circular Economy requires a great deal of investment, but also legislative and organisational measures. All recycling activities must go through the required waste procedures. This is providing quite a lot of control over raw materials, but it definitely hinders the work of developing economic symbiosis (European Commission 2011).

2 CIRCULAR ECONOMY IN POLAND

Poland is implementing circular economy system very slowly. This is due to the diversity of organisation of each group seeking to implement the changes. The solution may be to build an international system for implementing the Circular Economy in Polish enterprises, so that the scheme is based on one main strategy and at the same time incorporates all the principles of the economic cycle. The European Environmental Bureau has introduced a project aimed at creating this strategy, entitled "Poland's way to a circular economy". "Poland's way to the circular economy". The project was co-developed with experts specialising in selected stages of the product life cycle. From the sourcing of raw materials to the production, sale, consumption and management of residual waste. In addition, representatives of the social Economy, a sociologist and a clergyman were involved in the development of the project. It is very important to keep excluded groups, social capital and cultural orientations in mind when intending to overhaul the current system and create a new plan. Each conversation that takes place is multifaceted, but focused on a single objective. An international project developed by a group of experts and the advice of individual groups is an additional guarantee of reliability and can already illustrate the challenges you face when entering the Circular Economy during the planning phase. The diagram below shows the original linear economy approach (Figure 2) (Bachorz 2017).

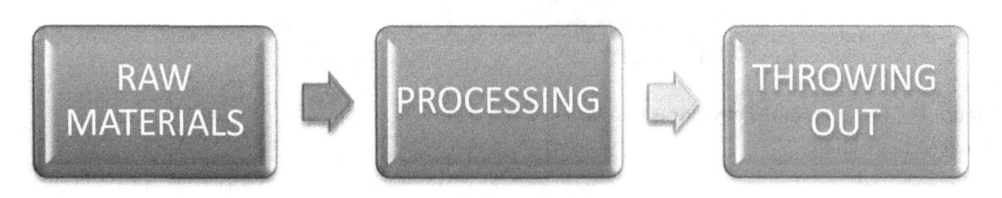

Figure 2.   Diagram of the linear economy.
Reference: own study.

The development of the Circular Economy in Poland will largely depend on the decisions of stakeholders. The attitude of local government officials to the new rules may influence positively or negatively the further development of the Circular Economy in all organisations and enterprises. In addition, the opinions of stakeholders often influence the decisions of the government, which may be guided by their views in taking further action. There has been a lot of support for circular economy idea from both sides so far. The idea of Circular Economy is supported, above all, by critics of the current system existing in Poland, the so-called linear Economy, which, in short, means extraction, then use and finally discard of a given product (Bachorz 2017), (Zarębska, Zarębski 2018).

Currently, the idea of the Circular Economy is gradually being implemented in Polish industrial enterprises. Introducing changes in factories is always initially difficult and requires a lot of work. The changes involve a new organisation of the site, the assignment of responsibilities to an employee and a reliable control of the project. A closed circuit should be in operation, at every stage of production work. A key aspect in this topic is that companies support each other and work towards one goal - caring for the environment (Zarębska, Zarębski 2018).

The Circular Economy concept is not limited to the reuse of waste within a single company. The full effectiveness of the solution is made possible by inter-company agreements on waste management. The photograph below shows the re-use of rain gutters to organise space in an electronics plant.

Figure 3.   Reuse of rain gutters.
Reference: Electronic equipment factory Omega Sp. z o.o.

Summarising all the planning and research on circular economy model, we can conclude that it is no longer a mere concept but a fundamental economic model. the Circular Economy system has been developed in the ISO standard and other documents of international organisations. All assumptions point to one goal - to minimise resource consumption along the value chain. It is important to remember that achieving the goal also focuses on parts of the entire value chain, starting with the introduction of waste management or source technology solutions. The introduction of Circular Economy into the European Union has greatly increased the number of its definitions. Currently, the concept is comparable to clean production, sustainable development, industrial parks and a zero waste strategy. Noting the considerable number of understandings of the Circular Economy, the following one should be the most important (Zarębska, Zarębski 2018):

1. Maximum extraction with minimum wastage. Industrial reuse and recycling, i.e. moving towards the complete closure of material cycles,
2. The introduction of the assessments of the Circular Economy in the value chain, which includes both suppliers and customers of a specific product and is the basis for creating cyclicality and new business models, which should be based on cooperation and responsibility between actors. The design phase plays the most significant role in this case, while the objectives of the Circular Economy should be included as criteria for project evaluation.
3. Seeking a solution that contributes to economic development while minimising environmental impact. The action requires policy support and continuous promotion of new economic and environmental methods.
4. The Circular Economy linked to innovation and new environmentally friendly technologies.

New technologies in various fields of science are making a move towards the Circular Economy increasingly innovative. Often there are barriers that need to be addressed in terms of purchasing practices, scaling rules and financial models, and then guided by cities and industry towards the Circular Economy (European Commission 2011), (Zarębska, Zarębski 2018).

Reports and studies that have been prepared for corporate financial models may initially show that Economy generates higher costs, given its pioneering nature, but the return on investment and productivity may ultimately prove to be much higher. Public procurement is an instrument that can decisively support the move towards the Circular Economy. With their help, cities or communes will be able to influence the market and at the same time stimulate production and service provision in line with the idea of the Circular Economy. Projects targeting public procurement typically include maintenance and repair, while also creating long-term relationships with the use of new business models. Such actions lead to competition with companies offering services in the idea of the linear Economy. Companies indicate a strong interest in reuse, repair and recycling. The willingness to move in this direction is constantly growing, however, there is still a lack of research on the evaluation and indicators of the Circular Economy at the micro level (European Commission 2011), (Zarębska, Zarębski 2018).

3 THE CIRCULAR ECONOMY IN THE POLISH MINING SECTOR

Mineral raw materials are the basis for the development of the world economy and the demand for them is therefore constantly increasing. It is important to note that as the extraction of mineral resources increases, the range of mineral processing increases and the amount of mining and processing waste increases. Poland is one of the largest producers of post-mining waste, 11.2% of this waste is generated here in relation to the whole world. In addition, the management of mineral resources depletes resources in existing sources. This is related to the linear production model, so attention has been directed to appropriate waste management, resulting in a closed cycle of raw material extraction and processing (Brzozowski 2016), (Sukiennik et al. 2021).

The mining system contributes to the rapid economic and social development of the region. But then again, it causes negative impacts on the environment (e.g. water and landscape). The exploitation of mineral deposits is usually accompanied by the extraction of waste rock. This activity is noticed in the form of landfills on the surface of the land, which occupies agricultural and forest areas, while posing a threat to water and soil quality.

The formal and legal regulations applicable in Poland governing the handling of mining waste oblige the mining company to subject it to recovery processes. If this is not possible or cannot be economically justified, the waste may be disposed of in dedicated facilities. The polluter is obliged to obtain a permit to operate a separate extractive waste facility and to keep ongoing quantitative and qualitative records in accordance with the waste catalogue. In view of the waste produced by the mines and the amount of landfill, it is reasonable to look for possibilities to manage it. In relation to mining, the main objective of the Circular Economy is to explore the possibility of effectively returning the raw materials accumulated in the waste to the mining industry (Sukiennik et al. 2021).

In mining, KGHM Polska Miedź S.A. is the largest domestic producer of waste. The waste generated can be divided into two categories: waste resulting from mining activities and ore processing, which accounts for approximately 92% of all other waste. There are numerous difficulties in introducing different ways of using waste. The copper industry can leave behind large stockpiles of materials that may become useless ballast for the environment, or become the region's raw material base for future use (Zarębska, Zarębski 2018), (Kowalczyk 2018) .

All phases of mining activities impose burden on the investor or plant owner to obtain the required permits for waste collection. Given how much is produced in mining, it is imperative that they are minimised or eliminated through the Circular Economy. Work related to the Circular Economy should be undertaken during joint change and co-created with other industries. The orientation of new solutions and technologies should result in the efficient use of waste (Kowalczyk 2018).

KGHM Polska Miedź is an example of implementing the Circular Economy. Efforts are constantly being made to develop effective waste recovery technology. The main direction for the recovery of flotation waste is its use on site. The waste reservoir is the Żelazny Most Reservoir with an area of 1,349 ha, which initially collected more than 700 million Mg of flotation waste (Figure 4) (Kowalczyk 2018).

Figure 4. Żelazny Most.
Reference: (Kowalczyk 2018).

The fine-grained tailings are used as sealing material for the bottom of the reservoir, while the coarse-grained tailings are used to build the facility dam. In this way, Europe's largest waste reservoir was created using the Circular Economy (Kowalczyk 2018).

Tightening the links between science and the industrial system brings, beneficial and effective solutions that facilitate the introduction of the Circular Economy. Opening up companies to innovation and cooperation plays a key role here. Encouraging these changes is the already present market for secondary raw materials, which facilitates the flow of waste (Kowalczyk 2018).

4 THE CIRCULAR ECONOMY TOOLS

The Circular Economy system, considers the impact on people, including: health, quality of life, frame of mind, and job distribution. In addition, the indicators take into account economic growth. There are a lot of factors influencing the newly introduced idea, but the basic condition for its development is a change in social behaviour. The European Economic and Social Committee reports that the indicators of the Circular Economy are heavily focused on waste, all based on reports and the lack of other options (Bachorz 2017).

The transformation of the introduction of the Circular Economy model requires many support measures. One of the main tools to support the Circular Economy financing is the right way to assess credit risk. The current calculation methods are not adapted to the model of the Circular Economy, and therefore modification of the current rules, or the development of new ones, are necessary when assessing credit risk. Financial tools should take into account potential negative externalities in the case of a linear economy, while, in case of the Circular Economy, the specifications and benefits in the long term (Bachorz 2017), (Sukiennik et al. 2021).

Another tool is an indicator measuring the degree of conformity of the project with the economic, social and environmental benefit model. A comparison of linear and circular economy projects can be used for this purpose. Due to the diversity of the Circular Economy model, there is no single indicator developed, so for the purpose of the adopted monitoring framework, the division of the Circular Economy into four groups was introduced (Bachorz 2017):

1. Production and consumption,
2. Waste management,
3. Secondary raw materials,
4. Competitiveness and innovation.

The first method is to observe how materials enter the Circular Economy, how they are used and how they are taken out of it.

In the supporting diagrams for the use of research, all raw materials used in the whole Economy are depicted (Bachorz 2017) (Dubiński 2013).

Tools to support the Circular Economy transformation process include project finance instruments that are based on risk sharing. Currently, the range of financing products is limited. Grants and loans are provided from national funds under the 2015 - 2020 programmes (e.g. the Circular Economy), EU 2014 - 2020 (Infrastructure and Environment) and State Budget Units accepting annual applications for the Circular Economy projects. There are institutions that have products specifically dedicated to green projects. One such institution is the Environmental Protection Bank, which has introduced subsidies for individuals, housing communities, businesses and local government units. In contrast, long-term financial support is provided by the European Investment Bank, and these are mainly loans to the public sector, corporate clients and energy companies. There are many banking institutions that have introduced support for green projects in their offer. Their support is very important in implementing the Circular Economy in Polish enterprises, but it is not sufficient. A key initiative could be an exemption from VAT for products and services that comply with the Circular Economy model. Such a tool could facilitate projects to a greater extent and broaden the area of interest (Dubiński 2013), (Zarębska, Zarębski 2018).

5 SUMMARY

Collecting the information presented above, the following conclusions emerge. Both Poland and other European countries should focus on:

- sustainable industrial production,
- sustainable consumption,
- bio-economy,
- new business models.

Introducing the Circular Economy principles will stabilise the waste collection situation and uphold the idea of sustainability for the common expectations of businesses. By using raw materials for as long as possible and distributing them appropriately, it is possible to reduce the amount of waste and thus minimise the negative impact of the Economy on the environment. An important aspect is the elimination of the use of toxic chemicals that may hinder reuse. Emphasis should be placed on appropriate design and selection of technologies that enable implementation of the Circular Economy. The efficiency of re-use also depends on the responsibility of producers and on the lifespan of products placed on the market.

The Circular Economy concept is not limited to the reuse of waste within a single company. The full effectiveness of the solution is made possible by inter-company agreements on waste management.

The introduction of the Circular Economy system in Poland is an evolutionary change - the slow one. The slow pace of change is affected not only by the large number of investment and legislative measures, but also by the lack of organisation of joint action by groups seeking to bring about change. The corrective measure is to build an international system for the implementation of the Circular Economy, which will allow the introduction of one main strategy for implementing the Circular Economy.

Implementing change is difficult, time-consuming and requires a series of consistent actions in many areas. Pursuing the common, overarching goal of caring for the environment is an idea that everyone must be aware of.

REFERENCES

Bachorz, M. 2017. *Poland's Way to the Circular Economy.*< http://igoz.org/wp/wp-content/uploads/2017/04/Polska_droga_do_GOZ_IGOZ.pdf > [accessed on 15 May 2021].

Burkowicz, A. & Galos, K. & Guzik, K. 2013. *Bilans Gospodarki Surowcami Mineralnymi Polski i Świata.* < https://www.minpan.krakow.pl/pliki/pracownie/pps/Bilans > Gospodarki Surowcami 2013. pdf [acsessed on 15 May 2021].

Brzozowski, T.T. 2016 *Idea of Sustainable Development in the Sphere of Global and Cultural Education* Foundations of Education Sustainable Development., 9, 11–23.

European Commission, 2011 Communication from the Commission to the European Parliament, the Council, the European Economic and Social Committee and the Committee of the Regions *Roadmap to a Resource-Efficient Europe* < https://eur-lex.europa.eu/legal-content/PL/TXT/?qid=1477938926695&uri=CELEX:52011DC0571 > [acsessed on 15 May 2021].

Dubiński, J. 2013. *Sustainable development of mining of mineral resources* 1–6,12.

Kowalczyk W. 2018 *Gospodarka obiegu zamkniętego w KGHM Polska Miedź S.A.*

Kulczycka, J. 2017 *Górnictwo i Energetyka jako elementy gospodarki o obiegu zamkniętym*

Sukiennik, M. & Zybała, K. & Fuksa, D. & Kęsek, M. 2021 *The Role of Universities in Sustainable Development and the Circular Economy Strategies. Energies* 2021, *14*, 5365. < https://doi.org/10.3390/en14175365 >

Zarębska, J. & Zarębski, A. 2018 *Ecological Education towards Challenges of the Circular Economy* 2, 25–31. <https://doi:10.26325/genpr.2018.2.5.>

Entrepreneurship in the Raw Materials Sector – Bartha et al. (Eds)
© 2022 Copyright the Author(s), ISBN: 978-1-032-19596-4
Open Access: www.taylorfrancis.com, CC BY-NC-ND 4.0 license

Trends in material recovery of waste

L. Domaracká, M. Taušová & M. Janičkan
Department of Earth Resources Management, Faculty of Mining, Ecology, Process Control and Geotechnologies, Technical university of Košice, Slovakia

ABSTRACT: The need for the protection of the environment gets increasingly urgent. The paper focuses on municipal waste, which can be considered as one of the most problematic elements of the environment in many regions of our planet, as mentioned in the EAP, stating that waste should be treated as a source and demanding the reduction of waste creation per inhabitant. Energetic evaluation of waste will be limited to non-recyclable materials. Storage of waste that can be recycled or composted should be eliminated. To achieve this, it is necessary to promote and comply with environmental protection and the hierarchy of waste economy, which is considered the basis of European policy in the field of waste management. This basis is orientated towards minimizing the negative effects of waste on the living environment and increasing and optimizing sources in the waste economy. Waste economy hierarchy allows storage—only in case that there is no chance to avoid waste rising. This should be the priority of the waste economy. Moreover, repeated use and recycling of materials should be preferred within energetic waste evaluation from (possible and proper) environmental, technical, and economic perspectives. In the field of waste economy, Slovakia is significantly behind many EU countries due to the low level of recycling and a high level of municipal waste storage. According to the European Commission, the problem is in the system of collection and separation of waste.

Keywords: waste, management, assessment, material recovery

1 INTRODUCTION

Nowadays, issues surrounding the living environment, and its protection, present often discussed topics. Experts on this global theme most often refer to sustainability, considering all elements of the environment. Environmental aspects present a base for sustainable development on the Earth for current and future generations. This theme is incorporated into strategic documents and action plans at national and international levels. In the European Union (EU), the basic strategy in this field results from the need to provide intelligent, sustainable, and inclusive growth. One of these strategic priority demands is sustainable development—connected to the Seventh Environment Action Programme (EAP)—as a part of the long-term vision, strategy, and orientation of the EU in the areas of living environments and climate protection, until 2050. The EU's goal is to achieve a balance between the living and ecological conditions of the planet in 2050.

The increasing population of the Earth and the growing needs of modern society, as well as other diverse factors, are causing a marked increase in waste. Our ambition was to point out

DOI: 10.1201/9781003259954-13

that the volume of waste will increase in the future and therefore it is necessary to think about the possibilities of using waste as a secondary raw material.

In this paper we discuss the theoretical breakdown of waste from several perspectives. We define recycling and its process. We conclude the theoretical part with a subsection on the current state of recycling in Slovakia and the EU.

The case study was carried out in the city of Košice, which is the second largest city in Slovakia.Thanks to the data provided by KOSIT a.s. on the issue of waste collection and recovery, we analysed the data that helped us to define the trends in the development of collection and recovery of this commodity. On the basis of the analysis of the knowledge obtained from the internal data of KOSIT a.s., we have come to several findings: the amount of waste is increasing, but at the same time the amount of sorted waste collected is increasing. The ratio of total waste collected to material recovered is still low. It is clear that materially recovered waste accounts for less than 0.023% of the total waste collected.

2 WASTE

2.1 *Categorization waste*

Waste is divided according to the Waste Catalogue, which is established by Decree No. 284/2001 Coll., Decree No. 129/2004 Coll. and Decree No 409/2002 Coll., amending and supplementing Decree No 284/2001 Coll. of the Ministry of the Environment and Food of the Republic of Slovakia establishing the Waste Catalogue. According to Decree No 284/2001, §2(4), waste is divided into the categories of hazardous waste, denoted by the letter 'N', and other waste, denoted by the letter 'O'. Municipal waste is classified as other waste. Hazardous waste is waste which, by its properties (in particular toxicity, infectivity, irritability, explosiveness, flammability, chemical properties, carcinogenic (cancer-causing), teratogenic (damaging to the human foetus) and mutagenic (causing mutations in genetic information or cancer) properties) is or may be hazardous to the health of the public or the environment. This category includes waste produced by certain industries, radioactive waste, waste from slaughterhouses, rendering plants, hospitals and others. Each type of hazardous waste is also assigned a hazardous properties code according to the waste catalogue. Other waste is waste that does not exhibit any of the characteristics of hazardous waste. It is a group which does not pose a significant risk to the environment. Construction spoil, organic agricultural waste (straw) and others can be included in this category. This group of wastes is problematic mainly because of its large volume but not because of its chemical composition. Construction tailings are disposed of in landfills or on the sites of old abandoned mine workings. However, it is well used in road construction, where harmless treated material becomes part of embankments Wurpel et al, (2011).

Composition of municipal waste

The composition of municipal waste varies from country to country. These differences result from (among other things) the following:

- type of households (proportion of households with flats or gardens, etc.),
- the socio-economic level of the household (as this determines the tendency to purchase different products),
- the method of waste collection (as this influences the likelihood of finding different materials in the waste - here the provision of a zero marginal cost service for households to remove garden waste is particularly important, as this is the essence of reducing residual waste),
- the extent to which home composting is encouraged (influenced by the amount of waste from private gardens), the nature of the fuel used in households (e.g. if a household heats with coal, a large amount of ash can be expected in the winter months).

The composition of waste also varies according to the season, as the consumption of some items is different in winter and others in summer. This is particularly true for areas where the necessary measures have not been taken to minimize garden waste, but where there is a high proportion of households with gardens. There is relatively little statistical data on the composition of mixed waste in Slovakia. This is not surprising, as such figures are always difficult to obtain and attempts to create a re-presentative picture are always meaningful in the light of the realities affecting the composition of waste at local level. Some data appear in the Waste Management Programme of the Slovak Republic.

In most cases it can be stated that biodegradable waste, together with paper and cardboard, accounts for between 50 % and 65 % of residual waste. When comparing other countries, the relative share of biodegradable waste together with paper and cardboard varies slightly. In most countries, biodegradable municipal waste (but including textiles and nappies, papier-mache and cardboard) accounts for around 65% to 70%. In Slovakia, we assume figures in this range as well.

2.2 Waste collection management

Waste collection is part of the waste management of an urbanized area, and local conditions play an important role. The different areas that waste collection management manages are mainly related to:

- the amount of waste produced,
- the composition of waste (including in terms of commodities),
- the method of waste collection (random, containerized),
- the transport of waste (collection vehicles),
- waste recovery, and waste disposal.

To meet these requirements, integrated waste management systems called ISWM (Integrated Sustainable Waste Management) are being developed abroad. Thus, waste management is the sequence of operations that originate with the generation of waste at the producer and end at the point of treatment or disposal of the waste. Within the single-individual operations, waste removal can be considered as the most costly activity, with removal costs representing up to 70 % of the total costs required for waste disposal. The choice of waste collection and disposal system depends on the structure of settlements, topography of the area, transport, quantity, and type of waste.

The Waste Framework Directive has brought a new philosophy to the European Community's waste management. The focus is on waste prevention and an approach is introduced that considers the whole life cycle of products and materials, not just their waste phase.

The provisions of the Waste Framework Directive were transposed into Slovak law by an amendment to the Waste Act with effect from 1 January 2013. The new legislation establishes a new hierarchy of waste management (Figure 4.2). The basis of waste management is waste prevention and preparation for re-use. This is followed by recycling and recovery (e.g., energy recovery). Disposal is the last possible alternative. Hierarchy of waste management:

- Waste prevention,
- preparation for re-use,
- recycling,
- other recovery, e.g., energy recovery, disposal.

2.3 Waste management

Waste management includes waste collection, waste removal, waste recovery and waste disposal, including care of the disposal site.

The following waste management methods are distinguished:

- Waste disposal:
  - Landfilling,
  - Incineration.

Many types of solid waste and sludges, including some types of industrial and construction waste, are still disposed of only by landfill. For most smaller towns and cities, landfilling is the only form of waste disposal. Also in cities equipped with incinerators or composting plants, it is necessary to landfill unburnable or non-compostable residues that cannot be disposed of in any other way.

Waste recovery:

- material (recycling, composting),
- energy (incineration and pyrolysis).

Waste disposal is the management of waste in a way that does not cause damage to the environment or endanger human health. Waste contains substances that often threaten virtually all components of the environment, i.e., water, air, and soil quality. Waste management is governed by Slovak Government Regulation No 606/1992 Coll., which sets out all the conditions for waste management, special conditions for the management of hazardous waste, waste disposal and the requirements for the issue of a waste management permit.

Recycling is the process of reusing materials or products already in use, such as recycling paper, non-ferrous and other metals, glass, plastics. Recycling eliminates the waste of resources, reduces the consumption of raw natural materials, reduces the amount of stored waste and reduces energy consumption, thus contributing to the reduction of greenhouse gas emissions compared to the use of raw materials. Thus, recycling refers to the recovery of material that has already been used for a purpose and has become waste.

The Waste Framework Directive DIRECTIVE 2008/98/EC OF THE EUROPEAN PARLIAMENT AND OF THE COUNCIL of 19 November 2008 on waste and repealing certain Directives defines recycling as: "The term "recycling" means any recovery activity by which waste materials are reprocessed into products, materials or substances intended for their original purpose or for other purposes". It includes the reprocessing of organic material but excludes energy recovery and reprocessing into materials to be used as fuel or for backfilling activities. The materials thus recovered are used either on their own or mostly as an additive in the production of products from virgin raw materials, to reduce production costs and in some cases to improve the properties of the product itself.

The beginning of the recycling process is the most important because it lies in obtaining a specific raw material suitable for recycling. Waste management therefore plays a very important role in the process of obtaining this raw material, since raw materials such as glass, paper, etc. are either obtained from separate collection or collected from municipal waste, which is a mixture of all materials. The collection of individual types of materials from municipal waste is too costly and is mostly not practiced in Slovakia. Cities and municipalities have separate collection systems in place, using colour-coded containers into which waste is separated according to the type of material. Glass, plastic and paper are separated as standard. At the collection yards, individual commodities are further sorted into more narrowly specified commodities. For example, plastics are sorted into PET bottles separated by colour, film, packaging for cosmetics and kitchen products and possibly others. In industrial production, waste is much easier to sort, as there is no need to sort it or to get rid of contamination. Often this waste is recycled directly by the waste producer. The sorted waste is then sent to processors who reprocess it and recover it. This recovery is either to the level of the base material, which is sold back to the processors of the primary material, or the final product is produced directly.

The Ministry of the Environment of the Slovak Republic reports that the current municipal waste recycling rate in Slovakia has increased by 7 percentage points year-on-year. A press release dated 1 July 2019 quotes Deputy Prime Minister and Minister of the Environment of the Slovak Republic László Sólymos "Over the last three years, we have been intensively adjusting waste policy to make it worthwhile to sort and recycle in Slovakia. And a big thank you also goes to the growing number of citizens who sort honestly. Because without them, any waste policy could not be successful."

The setting of a new waste policy in Slovakia is increasingly visible in the statistics. While in 2015 more than two thirds of municipal waste ended up in landfills, in 2018 it was only

55 percent. In order to reach the European benchmarks, the enviroresort is going to favour recyclable products and define food waste. The year-on-year comparison of municipal waste recycling underlines the changes for the better. While about 29% of municipal waste was recycled in 2017, last year it was already 36%. By 2035, countries need to recycle up to 65 percent of municipal waste, says Pavol Szalai of euroactiv.sk. However, according to the minister, it should be remembered that Slovakia wants to reach a recycling rate of 50% of municipal waste by 2020. Several measures have contributed to the positive changes. Among the European acts that will be incorporated into Slovak law are the directives on waste and landfills, which set future European targets. Since January 2017, an obligation has been introduced for municipalities to ensure that biodegradable municipal waste is also managed. A year later, an obligation was added to provide brown bins or composters also for residents of complex housing developments with green space at the request of the landowner (that is, if the landowner requests it). Millions of euros in fines have been introduced for landfill operators who do not comply with the rules, lightweight plastic bags have been charged, reporting of collected metals has been streamlined and other measures have been introduced. However, the environment ministry expects 2019 to be even more successful. It was in January 2019 that the anti-landfill package came into force. Among other things, it set landfill fees to financially favour municipalities that sort honestly. In February 2019, the Slovak Waste Prevention Programme for 2019 to 2025 came into force. The latter, among other things, pays attention to the quantitative collection of waste. That is, a system where households are directly financially favoured for sorting. There is also legislation in Parliament introducing the deposit of beverage packaging or a ban on the marketing of single-use plastic products. In general, European regulations have led to an increase in the rate of separation and recycling of municipal waste. However, Slovakia has failed to introduce eco-design of products to prevent waste, writes Tomáš Kolenčík.

3   CASE STUDY OF THE CITY OF KOŠICE

The amount of waste collected within the city of Košice is increasing every year, as can be seen in Figure 1. The highest value of 68 514 921 tons was reached in 2020. One of the reasons for the possible sharp increase in the collected waste in 2020 compared to the previous year 2019 can be considered the epidemiological situation, and therefore the increased consumption of packaged food due to regulations and measures of the Government of the Slovak Republic.

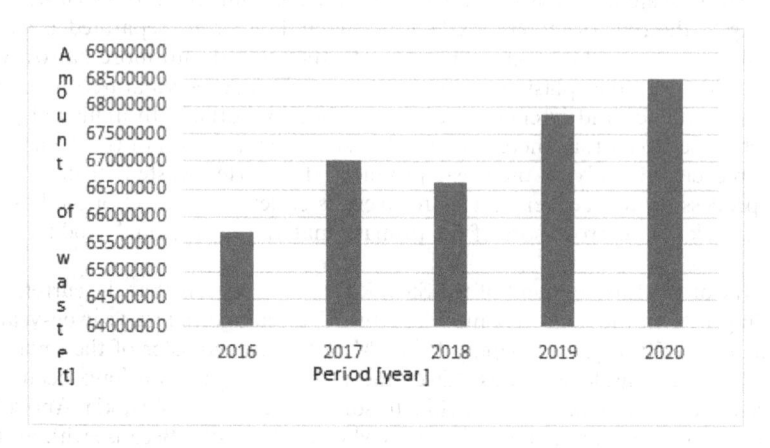

Figure 1.   Development of the amount of waste collected by KOSIT a. s. in the city of Košice for the period 2016-2020.

Source: Own elaboration according to internal materials of KOSIT a. s., 2021

The largest component of the total collected waste for the city of Košice in the period 2016-2020 is mixed municipal waste (see Figure 2.) with 73.25%. The plastic component, however, accounts for only 2.26% of the total and is therefore the fourth most collected item.

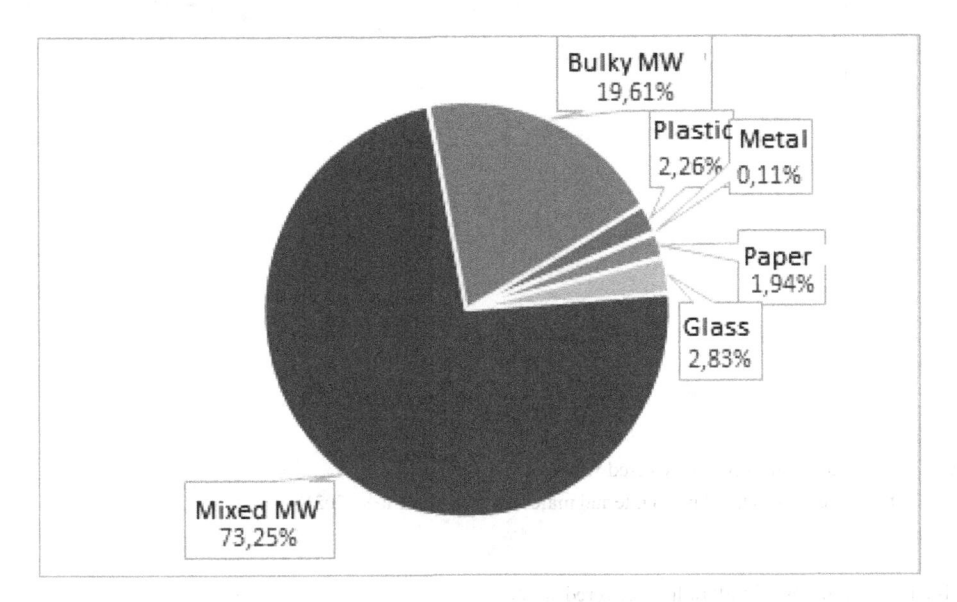

Figure 2. Percentage of components, total waste collected for the period 2016-2020 for the city of Košice.

Source: Own processing according to internal materials of KOSIT a. s., 2021

3.1 *Materially recovered waste - recycling*

KOSIT a. s. recovers waste such as paper, glass, metals, plastic, electrical waste and batteries. In Figure 3 we can see a graphical representation of the overall development of the above mentioned waste recovered for the provided years from the company's internal data and statistics. We would like to highlight the evolution of the amount of waste recovered, and specifically the increasing trend up to 2016, where the highest value of recovery so far was reached, namely 17,110 tons of waste. The reasons for this marked growth can be attributed to various influences such as:

- the evolution of prices of individual commodities,
- the efficiency of companies,
- greater demand for recovered waste.

In Table 1 we can see the material recovered components of waste for the years 2012 to 2020. The most significant item in the table is paper (51.76%), followed by glass (20.07%), metals (16.72%), plastic (9.15%), e-waste (2.13%) and oil (0.29%)j. From Table 1, we can see that the amount of waste recovered, specifically paper, has been increasing year on year from 2012 to 2016. In 2017, paper recovery reached a slight decrease. Based on the company's internal records, the reason for the slight decrease was the decreasing price of paper in the market, so there was less interest in sorting this waste commodity. Another possible factor for the decrease in the amount of paper recovered in 2020 is the decrease in the average price of paper by up to 30% compared to the previous year, i.e. 2019.

When defining the trend of individual commodities, it can be stated that over the 8 years analysed, an increase has been recorded for almost all commodities (see Figure 5). The exception is glass, which has seen a decrease of about 60 tonnes per year. The highest increase was recorded for the commodity paper by 422 tonnes/year, which has already been mentioned above in the description of Table 1.

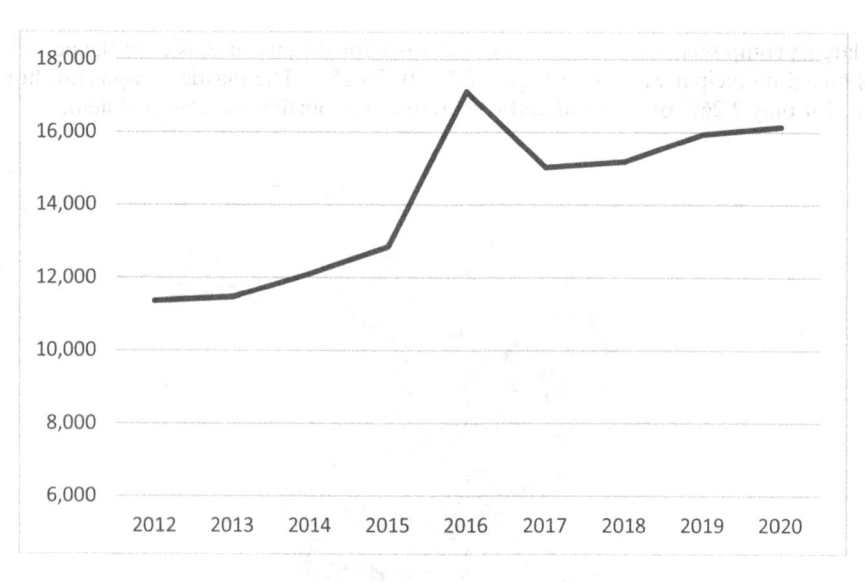

Figure 3. Total evolution of recovered waste.

Source: Own processing according to internal materials of KOSIT a. s., 2021

Table 1. Quantities of materially recovered waste.

Type of the waste [t]	2012	2013	2014	2015	2016	2017	2018	2019	2020
Paper	5 528	5 768	5 930	6 270	9 251	8 275	7 851	8 574	8 377
Glass	2 926	2 928	3 016	3 339	3 329	2 243	2 332	2 285	3 123
Plastic	1030	1 028	991	1489	1 539	1 630	1 557	1 383	985
Metal	1 605	1 501	1 891	1 418	2 603	2 500	3 024	3 314	3 158
Oil	37	31,6	43,5	21,5	35	50	67,2	39	38
E-waste	224	195,2	223,4	303	341	316	340,1	326	442
Batteries	10	10,1	7,1	5,4	12	11	11,3	21	19
Together	11 360	11 462	12 102	12 846	17 110	15 025	15 183	15 942	16 142

Source: Own processing according to internal materials of KOSIT a. s., 2021

The third largest recovery item is plastic (see Figure 5). Plastic is showing an increasing trend in the amount of waste recovered, up to 119 tonnes/year.

3.2 *Summary and discussion*

Based on the analysis of the obtained knowledge on the given issue from the internal data of KOSIT a. s. we have come to several findings.

1. The amount of waste is increasing

The graphical representation of the development of the amount of waste collected by KOSIT a.s. in the city of Košice for the period 2016 to 2020 shows that there is an annual increase in the amount of waste collected. Overall, the most collected waste is:

- mixed municipal waste,
- bulky municipal waste,
- glass,
- plastic,
- paper,
- metal.

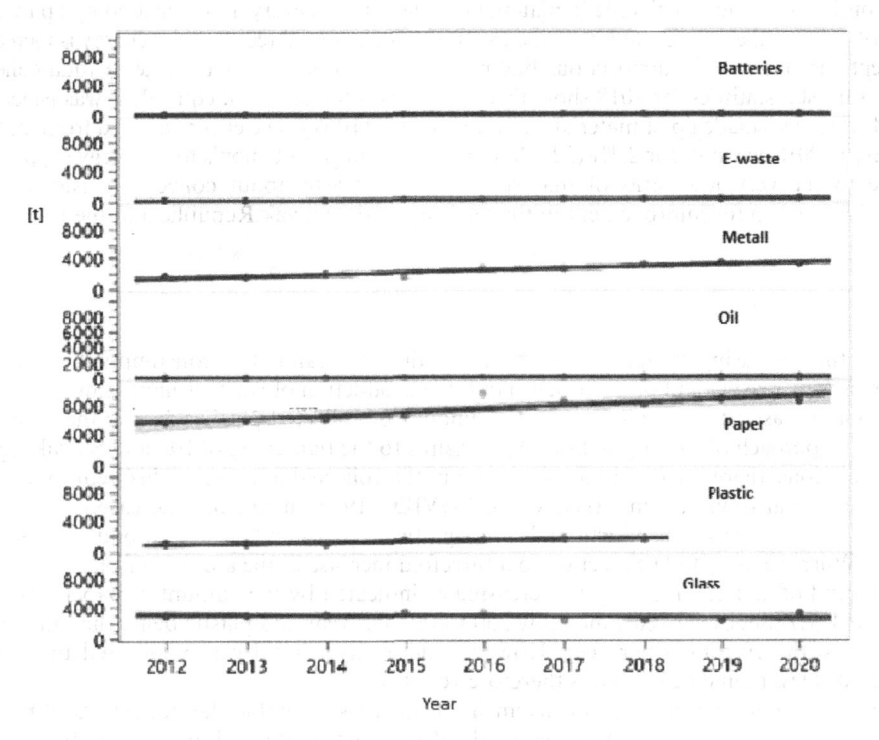

Figure 4.   Trend of the different components of collected waste.

Source: Own processing according to internal materials of KOSIT a. s., 2021

The growth of waste can be caused by various factors such as:

- increasing population,
- environmental considerations,
- the amendment and creation of waste collection and management measures, decrees, regulations and laws of the Slovak Republic and the European Union.

According to Potočár (2021), who researched and reacted to the issue of waste on the Waste Portal website, examining its development, he came to several results that point towards the increase in the amount of waste in Slovakia. It also states that Slovakia, as one of the V4 countries and an EU member state, produces the most waste and according to projections, waste production will continue to increase.

We dare to say that the claim we have found about the increase in waste is identical to that of Mr Potočár, whose research claims were based on data from Eurostat and the claims of the analyst Eva Sadovská.

2. Material recovery is increasing

As well as an increase in all waste collected, the amount of recovered waste collected is also increasing. The commodities with the most significant year-on-year growth trend in material recovery are:

- Paper (427.7 t/year),
- metal (250 t/year),
- plastic (119 t/year).

However, the ratio of total waste collected to material recovered is still low. Materially recovered waste accounts for less than 0.023% of the total waste collected.

According to Levaggi et al. (2020), material recycling, i.e. recovery, has increased by up to 200% since 1995. Also, the source states that the trend of using material recovery for energy is increasing but kept very low which supports our finding of low ratio of recovered waste to total collected waste. Eurostat statistics for 2018 show that 40.4 million tonnes of oil equivalent was generated, half of which was made up of material recovered waste (MRW). The energy derived from material recovery in 2018 accounts for 2.4% (22.7 MWh) of the European Union's total energy supply.

Due to the very low ratio of material recovered waste about collected waste, there is a significant room for improvement in the territory of the Slovak Republic and the EU.

4 CONCLUSION

Due to the increasing human population, on the one hand, the consumption of natural resources is increasing and on the other hand, the production of waste is increasing.

The main reason for the increase in the amount of collected plastics is, like the company, the active approach of the population. Also thanks to the tightening of EU and Slovak legislative regulations, there is a continuous increase in the collected amount of this item. According to the European Environment Agency, the COVID - 19 pandemic has increased the amount of production of plastic products and will significantly strengthen the amount of collected plastic. Wurpel et al, (2011) expect up to a threefold increase in the amount of plastic by 2050.

The trend of material recovery is increasing as indicated by the amount of paper recovered by up to 427.7 tonnes per year, metal by 250 tonnes per year and plastic being the third strongest item with 119 tonnes per year. However, the ratio of total waste collected to material recovered is less than 0.023% and is therefore very low.

There is room for continuous improvement of waste issues within the framework of EU and Slovak legislation, but it is also in the hands of the municipalities, but first and foremost of the people themselves, who can eliminate waste by their behaviour and attitude.

REFERENCES

Smernica Európskeho Parlamentu a Rady č. 852/2018/EU, ktorou sa mení smernica 94/62/ES o obaloch a odpadoch z obalov Spoločenstva v oblasti morskej environmentálnej politiky (rámcová smernica o morskej stratégii)

Smernica Európskeho Parlamentu a Rady 2019/904/EU o znižovaní vplyvu určitých plastových výrobkov na životné prostredie

Vyhláška Ministerstva životného prostredia Slovenskej republiky č. 371/2015 Z. z. ktorou sa vykonávajú niektoré ustanovenia zákona o odpadoch

Wurpel, G., Van den Akker, J., Pors, J. & Ten Wolde, A. 2011. Plastics Do not Belong in the Ocean – Towards a roadmap for a clean North Sea. *In IMSA Amsterdam*. IMSA, Amsterdam, p. 104. Dostupné na internete: <http://circular-future.eu/wp-content/uploads/2015/08/PML100_report-plastics-do-not-belong-in-the-ocean-DEF.pdf>.

Vyhláška Ministerstva zdravotníctva Slovenskej republiky č. 550/2007 Z. z. o podrobnostiach o požiadavkách na výrobky určené na styk s pitnou vodou

Vyhláška Ministerstva životného prostredia Slovenskej republiky č. 410/2012 Z. z., ktorou sa vykonávajú niektoré ustanovenia zákona o ovzduší

Interné materiály spoločnosti KOSIT a.s. Vydané v roku 2021.

Levaggi, L. et al. 2020. *Waste-to-Energy in the EU*: The Effects of Plant Ownership, Waste Mobility, and Decentralization on Environmental Outcomes and Welfare. [online]. Italy: Faculty of Science and Technology, University of Bozen, 2020. Dostupné na internete: <https://www.mdpi.com/2071-1050/12/14/5743/pdf>.

Living Well, within the Limits of Our Planet. Available online: https://ec.europa.eu/environment/pubs/pdf/factsheets/7eap/en.pdf (accessed on 10 January 2020).

Potočár, R. 2021. Produkcia odpadu na Slovensku raketovo rastie. Prognóza do budúcnosti nikoho nepoteší. In *Odpady-portál.* Available online <https://www.odpady-portal.sk/Dokument/105826/produkcia-odpadu-na-slovensku-raketovo-rastie-prognoza-do-buducnosti-nikoho-nepotesi.aspx>.

Sustainable Economic Development. Available online: https://www.vlada.gov.sk//sustainable-economicdevelopment/(accessed on 15 September 2019).

Entrepreneurship in the Raw Materials Sector – Bartha et al. (Eds)

Applying real-life problem-solving learning methodologies to train entrepreneurship students in the raw materials sector

A. Arroyo Muñoz & J. Mendibil Eguiluz
Tecnalia Research & Innovation, Spain

ABSTRACT: The competency requirements of the global markets, companies and other business players are significantly changing. The industry 4.0 implementation and the claim for shifting toward the circular economy pose new challenges for the higher education. The specialization in a thematic field, a technology or a production process in raw material could limit the possibility to create new innovations if students don't have the skills and the mindset oriented to problem-solving and to understand customers' needs and use open innovation in all its potential. In this paper we describe the process and analyze the satisfactory results of the application of a real-life problem-solving learning methodology to develop innovation and entrepreneurial skills in university students, involving also industries as problem owners, and researchers and teachers as mentors.

1 INTRODUCTION

The competency requirements of the global markets, companies and other business players are significantly changing. The industry 4.0 implementation and the claim for shifting toward the circular economy pose new challenges for the higher education. Today many professions which do not exist yet will be among the topmost wanted ones after 10 years. In most cases the most useful solution is to develop the key competencies of the future employees which are the information technology skills and also transversal skills as teamwork, cooperation, innovation, leadership and communication.

A T-shaped skillset must constantly become broader (general knowledge) and narrower (specialized knowledge) as the world becomes more complex, nevertheless having T-shaped skills is one of the biggest competitive advantage an employee can have in the creative society when contributing value for the markets or when achieving goals (Kos 2015).

The project LIMBRA explores the framework for new innovative education models. These models create strong bonds between the educational process and the real industrial needs of the companies. The involvement of students and Higher Education Institution (HEI)'s staff in the Multidisciplinary Real-Life Problem-Solving (RLPS) projects allows direct contact with real work life environment and facilitate gaining of new competencies from practice them in relevant project challenges. Students have the opportunity to gain new multidisciplinary and entrepreneurial thinking and skills in an international work environment. All this enabling better compatibility with the new work life requirements.

This paper describes the process of organizing the implementation of the RLPS program used in LIMBRA project for Real life Problem Solving and some conclusions after the two editions in 2019 and 2020.

LIMBRA project (2019-2021) is part of the European Institute of Technology of Raw Materials, which is the largest and strongest consortium in the raw materials sector

DOI: 10.1201/9781003259954-14

worldwide. EIT RawMaterials is the EU organization which mission is to boost the competitiveness, growth and attractiveness of the European raw materials sector via radical innovation and entrepreneurship. The project has been carried out by a consortium of University of Miskolc, Technical University of Kosice, AGH University of Science and Technology, VŠB – Technical University of Ostrava, the applied RTO Tecnalia, and Tecnalia Ventures, S.L.

2 REAL LIFE PROBLEM SOLVING (RLPS) METHODOLOGY

The Real-Life Problem-Solving program has been part of the activities done in the project LIMBRA. RLPS program is an international learning experience in which the topic is given by and industrial company. RLPS program has had two editions, involving in each edition 16 students, 4-8 staff member from 4 different HEIs (4 different countries), and company representatives. Students form international teams meet at Innovation & Entrepreneurship intensive week at the hosting HEI.

The intensive week contains tailored lectures given by company representatives and/or HEI experts based on the needs and the topic of the project. At the end of the project the results are presented by the teams and the company representatives choose the most appropriate solutions for them. The company has the rights on the solutions and may utilize the results of the project in its future products or services. HEI hosting universities have been University of Miskolc (Hungary) and AGH (Poland) in the editions of 2019 and 2020 respectively.

2.1 *Background*

In the last 15 years, we have observed an evolution and revolution in education methods for different ages: from school to HEI. Current trends on education are based on Problem Based Learning (PBL) method. Since PBL origins (back in the late 60s, there has been a lot of literature on the subject. The most common approaches currently used to integrate theory with practice are the case method, internships, and problem-based learning (PBL), being the latest the best one to adapt to a practical learning context (Perusso and Baaken 2020). In LIMBRA Problem-Based Learning (PBL) is a teaching method in which problems/challenges are used as the vehicle to promote student learning of concepts and principles as opposed to direct presentation of facts and concepts. In addition to course content, PBL can promote the development of critical thinking skills, problem-solving abilities, and communication skills. It can also provide opportunities for working in groups, finding and evaluating research materials, and life-long learning (Utecht 2003).

2.2 *Skills developed*

This method allows participants to enhance their talent and develop the following skills needed for creating innovative projects:

– Understanding real life industry challenges and applying problem solving strategies
– Ideation process to create innovative solutions to solve customers' needs, problems, challenges
– Applying the Lean Start up methodology and related tools
– Being aware of the importance of having a clear business model, considering the market needs and the customer development process
– Communicating the value proposition
– Practicing transversal skills such as leadership, agile teamwork, and effective communication.
– This open innovation practice brings fresh ideas and new approaches.

2.3 Experiential learning

An action and reflection model applied continuously provides a change in the learner mindset, who starts to see learning opportunities in any situation.

To have a significant learning experience all the concepts selected should be somehow put into practice and reflect on the action. This is known as Kolb learning cycle that follows the following four steps (Kolb 1984).

1. Concrete Experience. This is the practice, the activity of doing and having the experience, hands on the situation. It could be a new one or a reinterpretation of existing experience.
2. Reflective Observation. This is the time of thinking and reflection about the action itself, its process, outcomes, looking for any divergence or inconsistency between the doing and understanding of the action.
3. Abstract Conceptualization. With open mind analyses and make sense of the experience, what new ideas or concepts. This is learning from the experience.
4. Active Experimentation Plan and put in practice what one thinks that have learnt. Apply the knowledge derive from them to the world around them to see what results.

2.4 RLPS process

The RLPS process starts with the presentation of a real industry challenge to the students/participants. Working on this task should lead to the creation of a prototype or final delivery to the industry (solution, device, procedure...). Students in teams work on the challenge: analysis and understanding of the problem, analysis of the technologies involved or potentially involved, generation of ideas, defining a solution or prototype of a solutions that can be tested with the industry. This means that the delivery of the students will be presented at different moments to the industry to get feedback and learn more about the problem. In different moments, students have feedback from the company, teachers, experts, etc. This helps to refine ideas or adapting approaches for prototyping solutions.

2.5 Features

In the RLPS program we promote active learning vs the traditional teaching concept. The action of teaching doesn't imply student learning. The downloading of theoretical knowledge from a teacher in a classroom is no longer valid. The objective is to shift form a passive behavior as in traditional lectures to an active behavior of participants.

Blooms learning levels are considered when talking about this shift. It shows us how a person relates to the different levels of learnings based on its implication in the action of learning. The more involvement with the action, the more our brain connects with the reality of the subject. Teaching methods based on lectures are related to the lowest learning levels (Armstrong 2010).

The approach of this program has the following ingredients:

– Learning by doing. Action and reflection learning model. Both action and learning from results obtained come together. Experiential learning in a "safe" context is a very powerful training method. Students will learn by solving the problem and working in projects, from the action, from direct contact with industry, users or stakeholders.
– Experimental learning (Active learning) learners must be proactive in setting goals, choosing paths and searching for the right tools and skills needed to develop in solving the problem.
– Learning with others. Students will work in teams while solving the problem. Learning in teams, from peer and from industry allows a faster learning process. Students and industry will experiment open innovation processes while developing high impact solutions. to professionals and the understanding of real needs that manufacturing companies demand at this present moment.
– Meaningful learning. Participants will work on challenges/needs connected with the actual and future professional development. New technological trends and processes will be

central in the solutions and they will be defined considering the feedback of raw material companies.

– An integrative approach across disciplines. Students will work in teams from different disciplines offering the power of diversity to solutions.

3 RLPS IN PRACTICE

The Real-Life Problem-Solving program has been part of the activities done in the project LIMBRA. RLPS program is an international learning experience in which the topic is given by and industrial company. RLPS program has had two editions, involving in each edition 16 students, 4-8 staff member from 4 different HEIs (4 different countries), and company representatives. Students form international teams meet at Innovation & Entrepreneurship intensive week at the hosting HEI. HEI hosting universities have been University of Miskolc (Hungary) and AGH (Poland) in the editions of 2019 and 2020 respectively.

The intensive week contains tailored lectures given by company representatives and/or HEI experts based on the needs and the topic of the project. At the end of the project the results are presented by the teams and the company representatives choose the most appropriate solutions for them. The company has the rights on the solutions and may utilize the results of the project in its future products or services.

The RLPS at LIMBRA has been defined to run over 6 months, but this timeframe may vary. The topic of the challenge or industrial need is a technical subject related to EIT Raw-Materials themes of interest, which are raw materials resource assessment, mining, new mineral and metallurgical processes, recycling methods, substitution of critical and toxic materials and substitutions for optimized performance, and design of products and services for the circular economy (Hanghøj 2015).

The 2019 edition challenge was formulated in this way: towards a sustainability and circularity of the sand blasting process - How to valorize the by-product of the sand blasting process 100 tons of industrial sand?

And the 2020 edition challenge was: Opportunities to source and use alternative raw materials for the production of cement clinker, - The possibility of obtaining and using alternative raw materials for cement clinker production.

3.1 *Preparing the implementation*

This phase is, on one hand, to engage companies in defining their industry challenges and on the other hand, to engage participants to solve the challenge. Here are listed the steps to take.

3.1.1 *Setting industry challenges*

– Set clear expectations and define a problem.
– Clarify the role of industry: visits to their premises, explain the challenge to students, listen and feedback to solutions.
– Attend both to the presentation of final solutions and presentation of the process.

3.1.2 *Get mentors on board*

– To name a mentor as a technical advisor. This mentor should be involved in the project where participant's activities take place. Mentor is expected to follow up participant's project development from a technical point of view.
– The communication will be settled at the beginning of the project. A recommended practice is short meeting (1 hour or 30 minutes) every two weeks to do the follow up (feedback on activity done, knowledge generated, next steps, ideas contrast, etc. . .).
– Mentors could be teachers at the university.

3.1.3 *Marketing and recruitment: Selection of participants*

- Target candidates: first define the profile. RLPS can be oriented to undergraduates, graduate, master/PhD students, junior researchers, or even a mix of all of them. When marketing the RLPS program, it's important to consider that different target groups might need the different messages when doing the recruitment.
- Multidisciplinary teams. RLPS can offer to solve the challenge with teams where participants have different backgrounds. Also, in an international context, multiculturality is a benefit for participants, mainly to develop transversal skills like teamwork, creativity and leadership.
- Open call process (web site with registration form) with selection criteria and dates
- Receive candidates' application and a first selection of candidates (Interview the most appropriate ones based on CV and the coincidences of participant's interest and industry wishes.
- Communicate the result of the selection process to the candidates.

3.1.4 *Choosing the right problem*
When approaching an industry and trying to identify relevant needs or challenges the most important thing is to find the right problems to solve.

- The use of the correct format to facilitate the formulation of the industrial company problem is suggested. In LIMBRA we have used the so-called Request For Proposals/ format (RFP) but another format can be used as far as it includes a description of the need (not the solution that the client seeks), looks beyond the fields of knowledge and competences of the team and it is formulated in a simple way.
- The problem must motivate students to seek out a deeper understanding of concepts. Concepts could be technical, but also related with transversal or business skills.
- The problem should need a level of complexity to ensure that the students must work together to solve and require students' problem-solving skills.
- The problem should incorporate the content objectives in such a way as to connect it to previous knowledge.

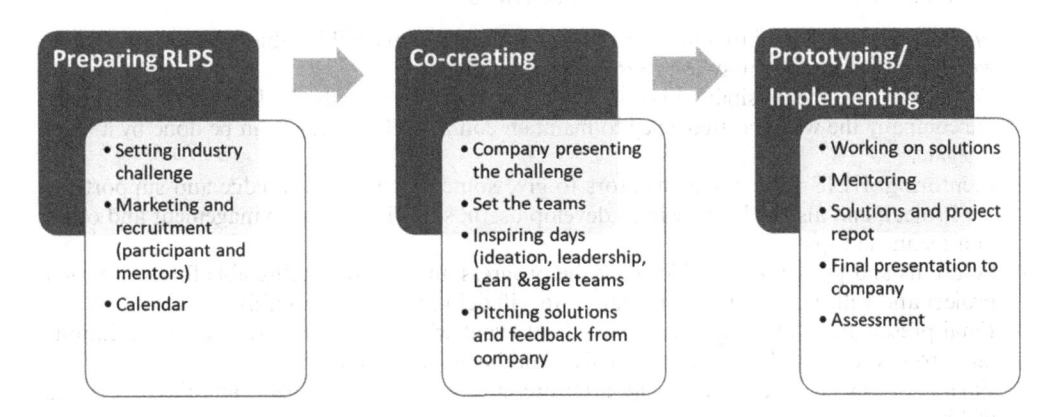

Figure 1.   RLPS process.

3.2 *Co-creating*

At the core of the creation phase is the "intensive week" where all participants join to have the first contact with the problem.

During an intensive week, students listen to the company presenting the challenge, visiting their premises if possible. Also the teams are created, there is a presentation of the methodological approach, not as a lecture, but in a practical way, getting to know the format and other tools they will use to generate the first ideas, to pitch to the company a solutions and to collect first feedback from the industry.

This week also needs its preparation. The week can have different designs, but it will include several sessions which need special consideration:

- Company presenting the challenge
- Setting the teams
- Inspiring days (with methods or contents like ideation, leadership, Lean &agile teams, etc.)
- Pitching solutions and collecting relevant feedback from the company

In this week the teams receive a lot of information about the industrial problem, and the methods to use for the problem solving. The facilitation is very important to succeed in this process. The facilitators must assure that the teams go through the following stages:

1. Understand the problem
2. Evaluate approaches for the potential solutions (like different technological approaches)
3. Ideate and prioritize (first ideation and exchange and combination of ideas)
4. Prototype solutions (materialize the ideas into something that can be explained to the company and that can be used to learn more about how far the team is from solving the problem)

3.3 Prototyping solutions

After selecting the most promising idea, teams will have between 2-4 months, depending on the global schedule, to deep into all the aspect of the solution and prepare a report of the detailed solution and prototyping it. Several prototypes or versions can be presented as the feedback received from the industry helps to redefine it.

It's important to highlight that when we speak about prototypes, these are the simplest version of a solution, that can be used in a visual way, to demonstrate to the company that the main requirements are achieved. And also, it can help the team to learn faster about the problem and if they are on the right path. At the end of the process, maybe after several prototypes, a final presentation to the industry is done.

Then this part goes through the following activities:

- Working on solutions Students works on solutions: Teams will be able to meet online and work together or separately to progress in the challenge.
- Teams will have the possibility to contact the company to get feedback. They will stablish with the company the way and frequency to maintain contact. This contact can be done by a team delegate.
- Mentoring. HEIS will provide mentors to give some technical knowledge and support for the Project, and also to help them to develop useful skills in Project management and other non-technical topics.
- Solutions and project report. To track the progress and mentors being able follow up each project and will support the team, teams are will deliver a report monthly
- Final presentation to company. There's final event where all teams present their solutions and prototypes in a plenary format. This could be in a contest format.
- Final Assessment: At the final event, after presentations are done, teams and their solutions will be assessed

3.3.1 Reporting

Students send partial reports 3 times during the semester to the supervisors/ mentors:

- 1st Report: it's the results of the intensive week. There should be clearly defined tasks and the name of student(s) who are responsible for that task to be solved. There also should be a kind of time schedule, with tasks, part tasks, how many times will be necessary to solve that problem, when should be there a result, etc.
- 2nd Report: it's a part-results report that contains the status of the work: what have you done during the past month?". Which are the results so far?

- 3rd Report: an almost finished report. Supervisors can see if the group needs help, some corrections can be done till the final deadline.
- Final report: A final and complete report, with each task solved.

3.3.2 *Evaluation*

Evaluation of the work done is very important. That is why supervisors and the representative of the company will evaluate the work of the group. The viewpoints of the evaluation will be defined after the first report. Supervisors and the company representative define the viewpoints of the evaluation.

In this case, the evaluation was based on two main aspects, the report and documentation (representing the 60% of the total value points) and the presentation done to the company (40% of total value points).

The report evaluation criteria were several like the style and uniformity of the report, the quality of the work delivered, the technical solution, the economical viability, the potential implementation, literature reviewed, and research done.

The presentation evaluation criteria were: The style of the presentation, the effectiveness, the participation of all group members, good communication and answers given to the company replies and questions.

In LIMBRA we have used some existing tools and formats like the NABCH format to summarize the solution and to communicate the value of the proposal to the customer and audience. Here are the basic rules to prepare this communication.

- N (needs). Problem or need that the solution addresses. Target customers and users. Relevance of the need for the potential customers.
- A (approach). Explain the solution. Its singularity. Why is different from other existing solutions. How you provide the solution. How you make the solution sustainable/ feasible.
- B (benefits). Specific benefits the solution provides. Advantage generated compared with what the customers does about the existing need. Strong points and pertinence.
- C (competitors). Other existing solutions that currently are used to cover the need. Why users would appreciate your solution.
- H (hook). Clear sentence that summarize your solution highlighting the most relevant aspects. Try to get attention and be memorable.

Other results and developments that the team has achieved can be provided to the company, like a canvas with the business model of the solution, research related to other alternatives, references, calculations, and supporting documentation.

3.3.3 *Program facilitation*

Facilitators are in charge of the main activities of the program and can come from the university or from external organizations. In the case of LIMBRA, TECNALIA, as project partner, provided experienced facilitators who played this significant role, which means an involvement in:

- Selection of candidates
- General presentation to the process (rights and duties, learning contract, operative meetings, follow-up, technical expectations, etc.
- Organization of the workshops (agenda, logistics, presentations) and coaching the participants in their work and use of tools (as the business model template), manage the online learning platform, communication with the participants.
- Evaluation of the process
- Delivering Diplomas to participants.

Supervisors or mentors played an important role in the follow up and communication among students and the company.

There are some lessons learned after the two editions of the problem-solving projects as practical methodology of innovation and entrepreneurial skills development in the raw materials sector.

There are some common elements of RLPS program in LIMBRA project that have been identified and shared by mentors, organizers and project partners in general, as good practices, as well as some potential ideas to improve the implementation of this methodology in the future. These elements are related with different aspects of the RLPS and are described in the following lines.

With regards to the involvement of the company it's very relevant to select companies which really appreciate ideas coming from people who are not everyday in the business, and might want to explore opportunities that the company does not tackle because they are not in the core of their business or because of lack of time or resources. To look for companies that have a close relationship with the University might be more accessible to participate in this collaboration. There is a mutual benefit, both for students who experience real problems with a business orientation and for companies. Also, this experience is a way to meet students or researchers with talent and potential that could work for the company in the future.

The communication between students and companies is very important as said by some participants and can be an aspect to be improved. Maybe creating more possibility to meet with the company in unofficial way can help in this sense.

The open innovation basis of the program helped to break some mind boundaries inside the company, however it should be said from the beginning that some ideas from students could not be feasible to implement. It's important a regular feedback by some person from the company over partial results in various stages of the solution.

Moreover, it has been highlighted that working in international teams at least in the on-site workshops it's a very powerful tool and a learning opportunity. Small teams of four to five students work well. On the other hand, it's more effort to manage intercultural aspects and also organizational aspects to facilitate the interaction among participants from different countries. And also makes it harder for some students that need to overcome the language barriers.

The 2021 edition was done online due to the COVID-19 restrictions and this was taken as an opportunity to test online workshops, but in general the results were not as fruitful as in the 2019 on-site edition. The online learning and interaction environments will need to be further explored, but in this occasion, we were not fully prepared for that change. The face to face edition allows the formation and crystallization of international teams and helps the teams to dig into the industrial problem, having the possibility to visit the company and to understand better the context. Also face to face meeting organized at the end for presenting the results to the company and final evaluation of the presented results is a strong element. A virtual visit at the company could be done, but these virtual activities need a very good preparation in terms of tools to be used that make the experience close to a face-to-face experience.

In relation with the Involvement of the students the students were eager to work in the problem, but in some cases their only motivation was the scholarship. In other occasions they felt overloaded with many schoolwork and homework, and only a little time for dealing with the project. Also, the task of answering to an industrial need was seen as a difficult task and participants felt sometimes lost or hardly dealing with uncertainty. For example, supervisors might help them by creating smaller tasks to solve with real deadlines during the project.

Also, the satisfaction on the skills development is a very strong point of this program. Some students say that hardly have a chance during their studies to work on a real industry problem and also to work in groups. Definitely the teamwork, leadership and innovation skills of the students were improved. Also, some universities appreciate the chance for students to work in international groups using English to communicate.

Finally, there are some elements that make this program attractive for the students, as it can be a chance for them to participate in an "International project work", and in some cases some universities have provided the opportunity to write papers on the project and send to a journal/conference.

5 CONCLUSIONS

The application of the RLPS program and the theoretical concepts behind have provided good results in terms of satisfaction from students, from university mentors and also from the industrial companies involved. When considering the development of competencies, such as critical thinking, effective communication, and collaborative problem-solving, we are facing a big paradox and a challenge of developing some of the most important skills for the present and future workers (also in the raw materials sector), while universities sometimes do not have the methods, or the preparation, or the recognition, or the resources, and also students underestimate the importance of such skills when they have a scientific or technical background.

RLPS program shows that it would be good to spread this type of experiences, where academia and industry/business worlds meet, and where students can live the kind of problems that industries normally face. Students might not be aware but when they work in teams in those real problems, they are living real experiential learning that probably will not forget as easily as when they receive a master lecture.

REFERENCES

Armstrong, P. (2010). Bloom's Taxonomy. Vanderbilt University Center for Teaching. Retrieved [todaysdate] from https://cft.vanderbilt.edu/guides-sub-pages/blooms-taxonomy/

Hanghøj, K. (2015) EIT RawMaterials. Brussels https://eit.europa.eu/eit-community/eit-raw-materials

Kolb, D.A. (1984) Experiential learning: Experience as the source of learning and development. New Jersey: Prentice Hall.

Kos, B. (2015) T-shaped skills in every area of your life. AgileLeanLife https://agileleanlife.com/t-shaped-skills-every-area-life/

Perusso, A. & Baaken, T. (2020). Assessing the authenticity of cases, internships and problem-based learning as managerial learning experiences: Concepts, methods and lessons for practice. The International Journal of Management Education. 18. 10.1016/j.ijme.2020.100425.

Utecht, R. J. (2003). Problem-based learning in the student-centered classroom. Retrieved from www.jeffutecht.com/docs/PBL.pdf

Use of augmented reality as a support for the visualization of urban data

F. Beneš, J. Švub, V. Holuša & S. Matušková
VSB - Technical University of Ostrava, Ostrava, Czech Republic

ABSTRACT: The involvement of citizens and residents of the participating part of the city in the decision-making process of urban planning is becoming an increasingly topical issue. Until recently, there were no ergonomic visualization tools for this purpose, and citizens could only get acquainted with the city's development plans through maps and technical drawings, which were not always understandable to everyone. In our article, we will try to describe our results in the field of data visualization using augmented reality, which we utilize to link the real world with added content related to the selected location. The first attempts in this area focused on blending of the historical state of the selected site with the present, or projecting the construction plans of the planned construction on the area where the building is to be built. We conducted a survey of the acceptance of this application by the general public as part of the Researchers Night event, which we accompanied with a questionnaire survey to find out how the outputs of the presented application affect citizens, whether they find it useful, simple and comfortable. The results of the survey show that the application is well received, the solution is evaluated as useful and meaningful. However, there is also a wide additional application potential. As part of the discussion of the results of the questionnaire survey, the follow-up directions of future research are indicated.

1 INTRODUCTION

1.1 State of the art

In recent decades, many scientists have been concerned with the use of virtual and augmented reality techniques in virtually all fields of human activity. They designed systems, algorithms, and procedures for the implementation of these technologies in industry, entertainment, the military, but also in the field of education.

For example, Vergara et al. (2019) described in their study the spread of virtual reality learning environments in schools and described the processes by which these didactic tools can improve the effectiveness of the educational process. According to my analysis of the answers, a total of 103 students in the knowledge test are the most important for his work. The analysis reveals how the step-by-step virtual reality teaching system has helped to improve students' knowledge and motivation and attention after one year of using these didactic tools compared to without these technologies. Thus, this study not only demonstrates the importance of using modern teaching tools, but also presents them as a suitable method to improve the process of acquiring and long-term preservation of knowledge.

In his work, Manuel Fernandez (2017) presents and discusses the role of virtual and augmented reality in education. However, it also addresses specific challenges in adapting these technologies to help improve students' learning outcomes as much as possible. The author

DOI: 10.1201/9781003259954-15

presents the possibilities of incorporating experiential regimes as a means to improve the acquisition of students' knowledge.

Yi Wang (2017) examined the impact of integrating augmented reality into the curriculum of a particular university course. The results demonstrated the potential of augmented reality to support students' motivation to learn. According to the author, content based on augmented reality could be used to better support the absorption of learning material.

Augmented reality technology also found its place in displaying facility layout planning, where it was able to put the planned elements into a real environment, as described by the team of Tan et al in their work (2021).

The research team of Wu et al (2021) dealt with methods of image analysis from a mobile phone camera and insertion of 3D models of buildings directly into urban terrain. Wright et al (2020) dealt with the use of virtual reality in urban planning and data visualization for the inhabitants of the region.

In our work, we focus mainly on augmented reality and how it would be perceived by the public.

1.2 *Research goal*

The LIMBRA project is focused on improving students' skills regarding starting a business career. The city of Ostrava has a rich history associated with the mining and processing of minerals. This history is captured in a large number of historical photographs. Since one of the business plans is focused on the use of augmented and virtual reality, we designed and implemented an application on which we were able to display urban data using augmented reality. In order to get feedback from residents on the use of this technology, we have conducted a demonstration to blend the real world with historical photographs using augmented reality application. We created the application as part of the Researchers night event, which is an event directly related to the LIMBRA project. Thanks to the high attendance of this event, we also had the opportunity to get relevant feedback on how this application is perceived by the general public.

2 VISUALIZATION OF URBAN DATA VIA AUGMENTED REALITY

However, in order to perceive augmented reality, mere eyes are no longer enough, but to display this information we must have a device, in this case a camera (sometimes also a mobile phone, projector, smart glasses, etc.). The information added by augmented reality does not occupy a dominant position in the whole space, it is usually information on the edge in terms of topology and meaning, which should not distract from reality, but only complement it appropriately.

At this point, it is worth mentioning the difference between augmented reality and virtual reality, in which all displayed content is already artificially created. In virtual reality, the user is convinced throughout the scene that he is in a different place and in a different space than he actually is. His senses are deceived by virtual reality glasses, or gloves or other devices to fool other senses.

If we want to display an application in augmented reality ourselves, we only need a mobile phone. It contains a camera capable of capturing the surrounding world, a sufficiently powerful processor and software background, as well as a display on which the connection between reality and added elements is displayed. To simplify the process when a mobile phone has to analyze a changing environment, we can use a visual marker. It often has contrasting colors such as black and white ensuring good visibility in various lighting conditions, as well as basic geometric shapes to make it easier to calculate the change in the angle of view of an object relative to the camera. The result is then the display of a 3D object on the marker. However, we do not have to use only mobile phones and tablets to display augmented reality, we can encounter various forms of transparent displays, which can be, for example, part of the windshield of a car. These glasses are also equipped with augmented reality glasses.

The third way to display and perceive augmented reality is a surface projection directly on the object, or holograms projected into smoke and fog, for example. This method has a great advantage because it does not actually impose any requirements on the viewer. The viewer does not need a tablet or glasses and can see the augmented reality with his own eyes.

Figure 1.   A view of VSB-Technical University of Ostrava in our augmented reality application.

In our application, we took advantage of the fact that the city of Ostrava has a rich history, captured in many historical photographs. So, we have created an application that can open an imaginary window into the past in some places. For visitors of the Researchers night event and Ostrava residents, we have prepared a smaller exhibition right on the streets of the city. All you have to do is have a mobile phone in your hand, stand in the right place and look around it. Thanks to this, the user is allowed to look at historical photographs that exactly fit into the relief of the surroundings. For the simplicity of the application, we used visual markers and placed them in the vicinity of the VSB - Technical University of Ostrava.

Figure 2.   A view of Ostrava city building in our augmented reality application.

The user could download the application to their mobile phone or borrow our tablet with the pre-installed application. After reaching the place, he may point his smartphone at the object and could look around the place in the past. The illusion of immersion in historical photography is, of course, limited by photography width itself. However, the edges of historical photography fit to the edge of the real-world surroundings.

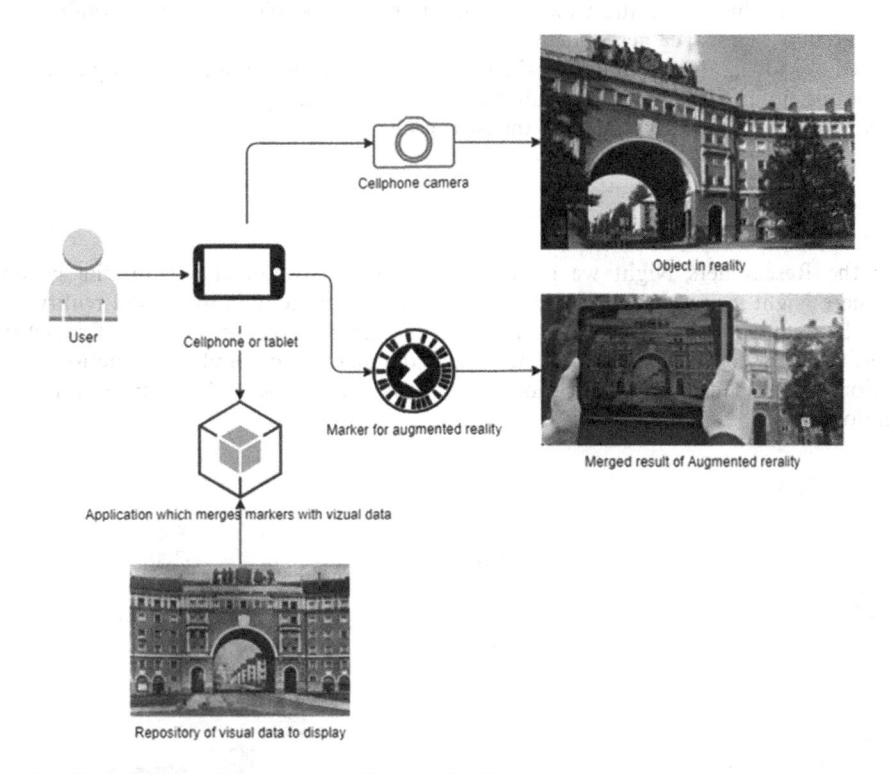

Figure 3.   The principle of augmented reality visualization.

Figure 4.   Augmented reality used for future construction plans.

The application works on both Android and iOS mobile phones. The application uses the camera of a mobile phone to obtain an image of the surroundings. The image is then analyzed and the presence of a visual marker is sought in it. If a marker is found, the application reaches its database and displays the appropriate visual element overlaying the marker. The result is a visual illusion for the viewer on the user's mobile phone display, combining the added content with a real camera stream.

We tried to show that we can look to the future in the same way and, for example, have life-size plans for future construction visualized on an empty grassy area and see how the construction would affect the peculiarity of the surroundings.

3 SURVEY AND RESULTS

During the Researchers Night we gathered data of 50 respondents from the group of Researchers Night visitors to get feedback about the experimental augmented reality application. The data were connected to the abilities of general public in the area of smart technologies, abilities to interpret classic technical documentation and construction planes, perception of the presented application as well as further possible optimization of the application.

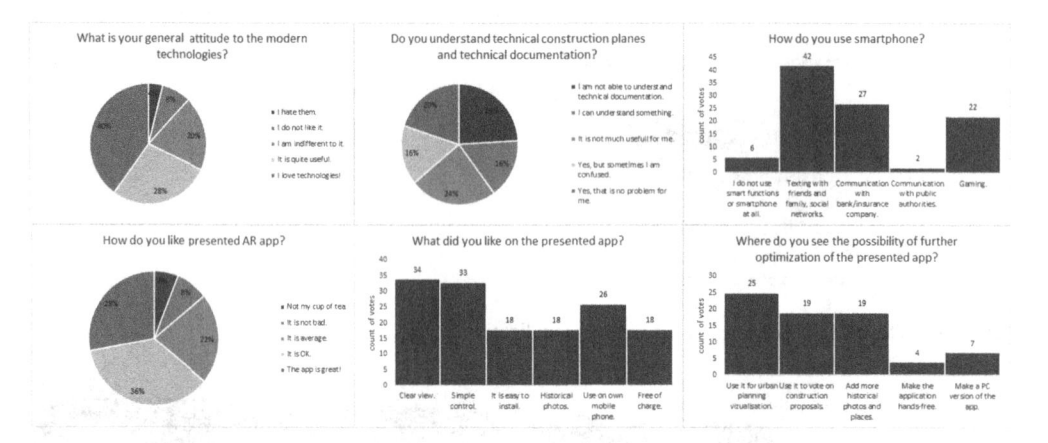

Figure 5. All age groups together.

According to the analysis of the gathered data we found a significant differences between age groups, so we decided to split the results and describe each age category separately.

As we can see on the graph (Figure 6) the respondents in the age group 0-6 years are very open to new technologies although they are not able to understand technical documentation. They also often do not use smartphones but when they do, they use it for gaming or for social networks browsing. Despite all possible problems this age group generally likes the new application.

As we can see on the graph (Figure 7) the respondents in the age group 7-20 years are also open to new technologies, but they are better in understanding of technical documentation of construction. In addition to previous age group, they use smartphones often for social networks, communication with friends, family, and sometimes public institutions like banks. This age group also generally likes the new application; however, some respondents found the app not so interesting. This age group also recommends using similar applications for urban planning visualizations as well as to add a voting function.

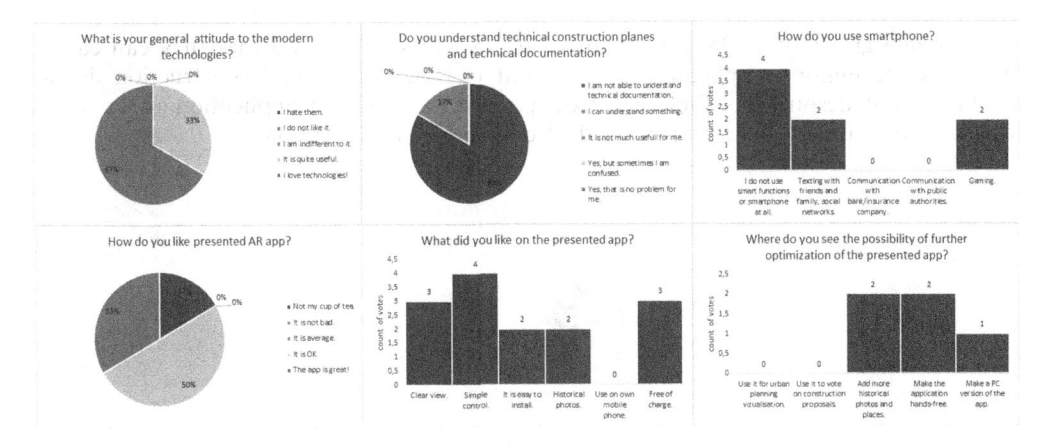

Figure 6.   Age group 0-6.

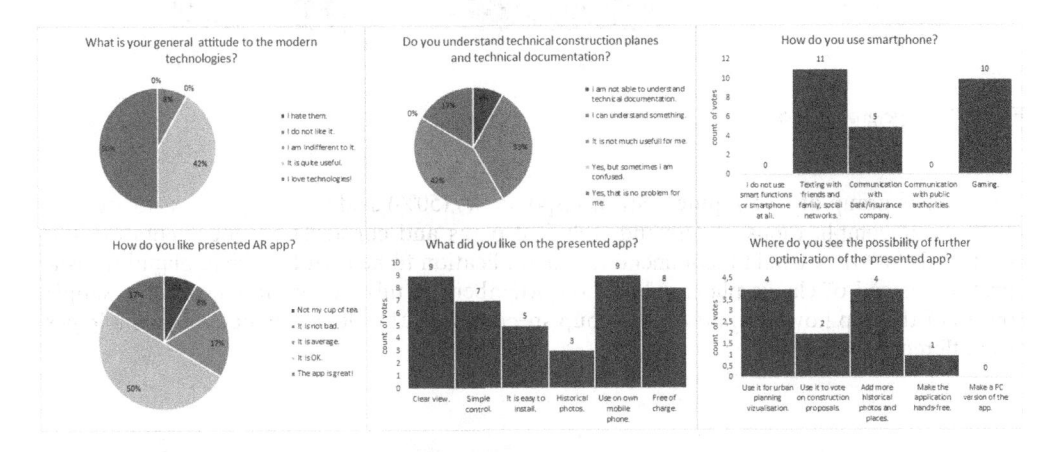

Figure 7.   Age group 7-20.

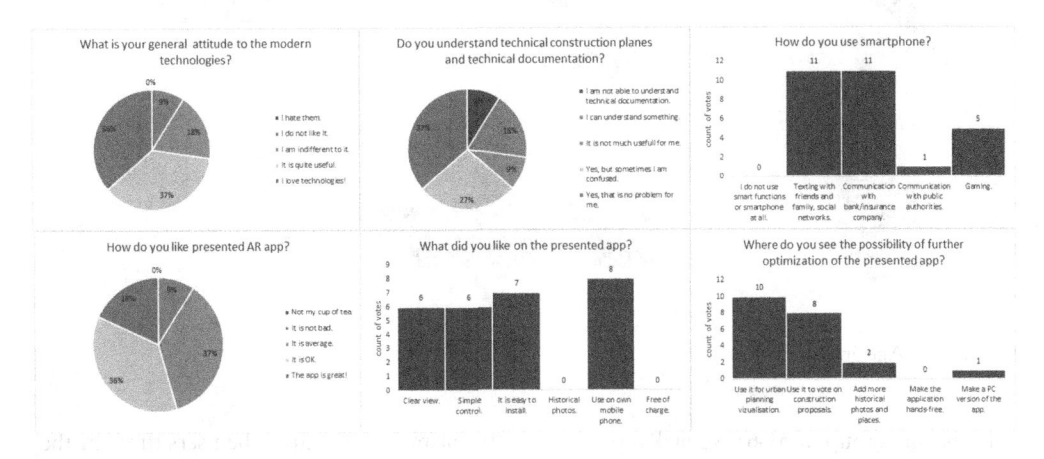

Figure 8.   Age group 21-35.

In the age group of 21-35 quite a lot of respondents (64%) said that they can easily or with some minor complications understand technical plans and construction documentation but despite this fact they would recommend tested application to be used for urban planning visualization instead of classic plans publication.

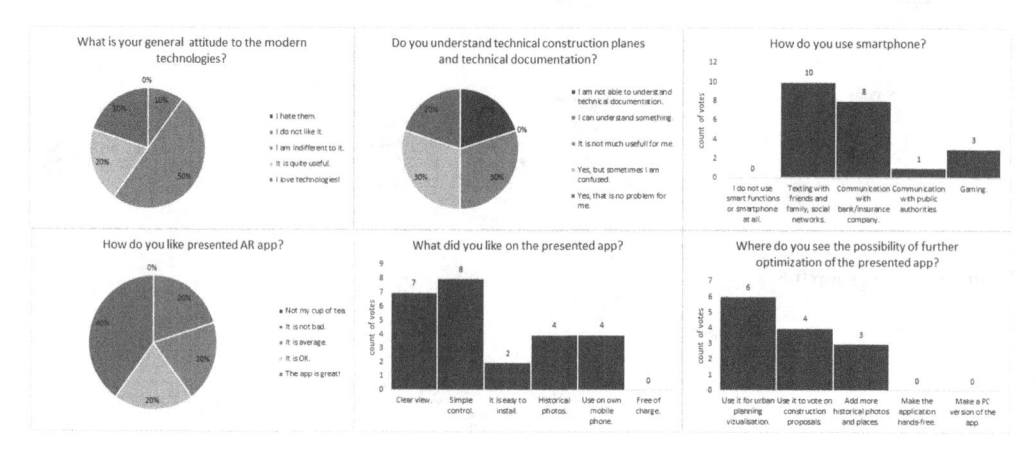

Figure 9. Age group 36-50.

In the age group of 36-50 quite a lot of respondents (50%) said that they can easily or with some minor complications understand technical plans and construction documentation but despite this fact they would recommend tested application to be used for urban planning visualization instead of classic plans publication. Members of this age group enjoyed the simple control of the app however half of the group specifies it's attitude to the modern technologies as indifferent.

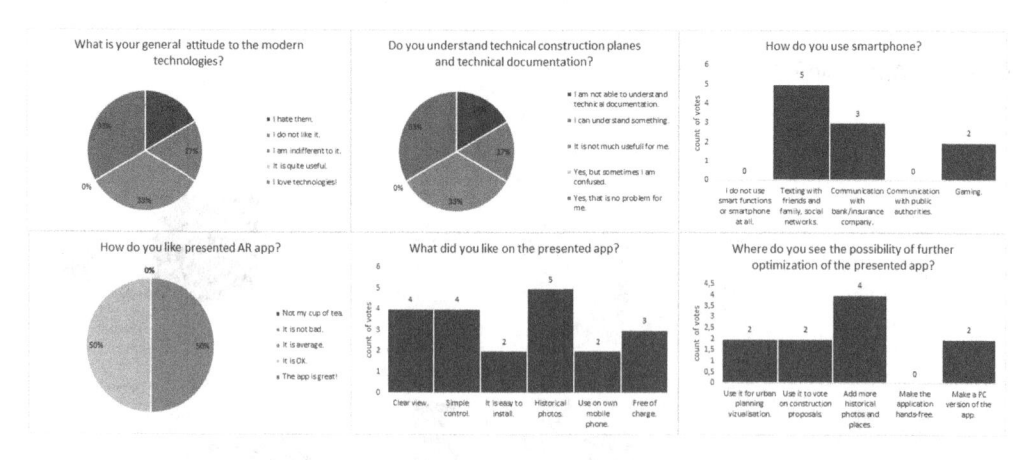

Figure 10. Age group 51-65.

In the age group of 51-65 we lack a previous enthusiasm with the app, the users thought the tested application is average or "Just OK", but as a new phenomenon they enjoyed the fact that the app is free to try and that it has some historical photos that remind them their past years. They also suggested to develop these historical photos aspect in particular.

As we can see on the graph (Figure 11), with the last age group we got back to the stage when not much smart functions on phones are used (only social networks and communication with friends). The application was still accepted well especially for its clear view and simple controls. Historical aspect was favorited even more here as well as the possibility to add more such historical backgrounded pictures.

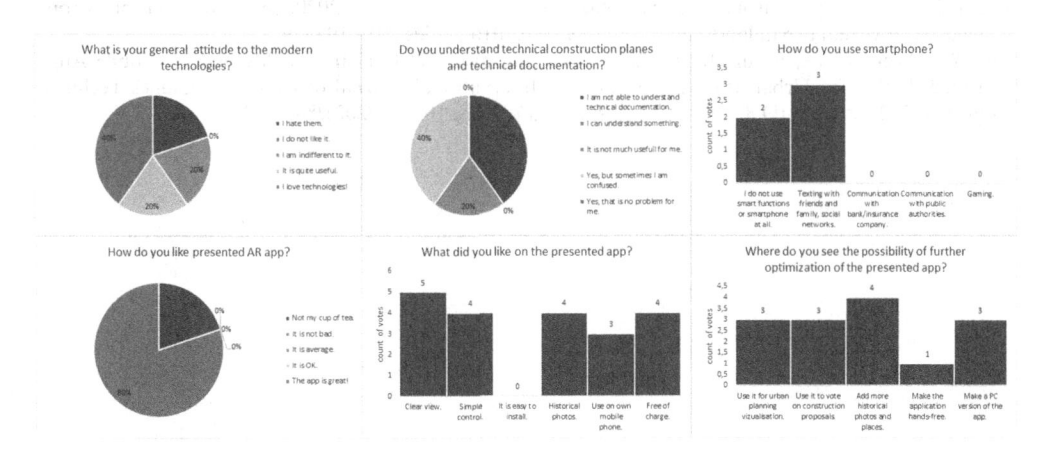

Figure 11. Age group 66+.

4 DISCUSSION OF RESULTS AND CONCLUSION

The results of the questionnaire survey showed that the offered method of displaying augmented reality is generally well accepted among the visitors of VSB-TUO part of Researchers Night. People welcomed the use of their own mobile phone as a tool to investigate the augmented reality layer. Respondents find the application clear, simple, and easy to use, even for older age groups. They could imagine that with a similar application, they would be able to look at real land use plans. They would also welcome the opportunity to vote on the possibilities of the planned construction. According to the respondents, such a vote should have an advisory power in the actual decision-making of the city or regional council.

However, markers used in this implementation, do not exist in the ordinary world, so we would like to extend this application in another direction. In the future the image database could be loaded based on the GPS position of the mobile phone, and a constant visual element in the shot would serve instead of a marker to merge the augmented reality with the surroundings. Further steps in solving this issue would lead to cooperation with city districts and the submission of a joint project to visualize land use plans using augmented reality with the possibility of participation of citizens living in the locality in the choice of modifications and expansion of urban development by voting directly in the application.

Probably since the Moravian-Silesian region is historically associated with mining activities, it was often said that this method could be used to visualize plans for reclamation of the landscape after coal mining and the decline of heavy industry in general.

REFERENCES

Fernandez, Manuel. 2017. Augmented-Virtual Reality: How to improve education systems. Higher Learning Research Communications. 7. 1. 10.18870/hlrc.v7i1.373.

Tan, C.H., Yap, H.J., Musa, S.N. et al. 2021 Augmented reality assisted facility layout digitization and planning. J Mech Sci Technol 35, 4115–4123. https://doi.org/10.1007/s12206-021-0823-6

Vergara, Diego & Extremera, Jamil & Rubio, Manuel & Dávila, Lílian. 2019. Meaningful Learning Through Virtual Reality Learning Environments: A Case Study in Materials Engineering. Applied Sciences. 9. 1–14. 10.3390/app9214625.

Wang, Yi. 2017. Using augmented reality to support a software editing course for college students: Augmented reality for educational applications. Journal of Computer Assisted Learning. 33. 10.1111/jcal.12199.

Wright, Jessica & Gopal, Sucharita & Ma, Yaxiong & Phillips, Nathan. 2020. Seeing the invisible: From imagined to virtual urban landscapes. Cities. 98. 10.1016/j.cities.2019.102559.

Yong Wu, Weitao Che, Bihui Huang. 2021. "An Improved 3D Registration Method of Mobile Augmented Reality for Urban Built Environment", International Journal of Computer Games Technology, vol. 2021, Article ID 8810991, 8 pages, https://doi.org/10.1155/2021/8810991

Coal-fired power plants in the crossfire of the European Union's energy and climate policy

Á. Horváth, A. Takácsné Papp & P. Bihari
University of Miskolc, Miskolc, Hungary

ABSTRACT: For decades, the European Union has taken decisive actions through its energy and climate policy in order to shift its energy mix from fossil fuels to renewable energy sources. In 2017 the policymakers decided to remove coal from the energy mix in order to achieve the climate goals. Most member states have already announced the last date of coal phase-out. In the year of the Paris Agreement (2015) the EU28 had 292 coal-fired power plants working with 758.5 million tonnes of CO_2 emission in a year. (CarbonBrief.org) According to our calculation, four large companies are responsible for 40.5% of CO2 emission. Our article focuses on the effects of the coal phase-out on the operation and future strategy of these companies, used mostly the annual reports as sources. Our findings are summarised in case studies. Although coal phase-out severely affects these companies, it does not shake their operation. The strategies using by the companies are mostly proactive and similar in the main principles. They want to be leaders rather than sufferers of the transformation of the energy system.

1 INTRODUCTION

Nowadays anthropogenic activity causes an enormous environmental and climate pollution that has catastrophic consequences for our planet. Humanity has reached a significant turning point. In order to leave a liveable Earth for our children, an urgent change is needed in people's mind and behaviour. The Paris Agreement (which was signed in 2015) is a milestone in climate protection. 195 countries expressed their commitment against global warming (UNFCCC 2021). Energy production and consumption can play a significant role in achieving these goals because these sectors account for more than 75 percent of the total CO_2 emissions, most of which are emitted by oil and coal combustion (Eurostat, 2021)

From the countries who signed the Paris Agreement, only the European Union took decisive actions regarding the coal phase-out process, so this paper focuses only on EU 28.

The policymakers of the European Union decided to remove coal from the energy mix in order to achieve the climate goals a couple of years ago. According to the Powering Past Coal Alliance (PPCA) launched at COP23 in 2017, a coal phase-out is needed by 2030 in the OECD and in EU28, and by 2050 in the rest of the world (PPCA, 2021). As one of the pioneers of climate protection, the EU has set increasingly ambitious goals in its energy and climate strategy for 2020, 2030, and finally to achieve carbon neutrality by 2050. Most member states have already announced the final deadline for coal phase-out. In August 2021, nine member states had no carbon in their energy mix or had already reached the coal-free status. Seven countries in the EU plan to phase-out coal from their electricity generation by 2025 and another five by 2030. Germany, however, has set a deadline for 2038, probably they will try to

DOI: 10.1201/9781003259954-16

Table 1. Summary of national coal phase-out announcements in the EU member states - as of August 2021.

Category	Number of countries	Country names
Coal-free	3	Belgium (2016), Austria (2020), Sweden (2020)
Phase-out by 2025	7	Portugal (end-2021), France (2022), United Kingdom (2024), Hungary (2025), Italy (2025), Ireland (2025), Greece (2025)
Phase-out by 2030	5	Denmark (2028), Finland (mid-2029), The Netherlands (end-2029), Slovakia (2030), Spain (2030)
Phase-out after 2030	1	Germany (end-2038)
Phase-out under discussion	4	Czech Republic, Slovenia, Romania, Croatia
No phase-out discussion	2	Bulgaria, Poland
No coal in electricity mix	6	Cyprus, Estonia, Latvia, Lithuania, Luxembourg, Malta

Source: Europe Beyond Coal, 2021a

finish the phase-out process sooner. Negotiations regarding decarbonisation are still ongoing in four member states, and there are only two countries where the issue has not been discussed yet (Europe Beyond Coal, 2021a).

In the year of the Paris Agreement (2015) the EU28 had 292 coal-fired power plants working with 758.5 million tonnes of CO_2 emission in a year. Thanks to Europe-wide regulations in the last 5 years, 61 power plants were retired from operation and a lot of them were upgraded so the yearly emission decreased to 338 million tonnes of CO_2.

However, some of the countries still have a big chunk of coal plant based energy in their energy mix (Germany or Poland), although their effort to reduce the environmental impact is undeniable.

2 LITERATURE REVIEW

The literature review shows that the topic is quite current and popular among the authors. Numerous papers deal with the analysis of the legal and political framework and impacts of the coal phase-out in different countries (Lund, 2017 (Finland), Heinrichs and Markewitz, 2017 (Germany), Rentier et al., 2019 (UK, Germany, Spain and Poland), Akerboom et al., 2020 (The Netherlands), Osorio et al. 2020 (Germany), Brauers-Oei, 2020 (Poland), Brauers et al. 2020 (UK and Germany), Markard et al. 2021, (Germany)). Each country had different starting point in terms of its energy mix, available energy sources and the targets set, etc.) and had diverse motivations and legal frameworks for implementing the coal phase-out plans.

Several articles attempted to estimate and quantify the environmental, economic and social impacts of the coal phase-out. One of the important questions is, how could the so-called "waterbed effect" could be avoided. This may occur, when the sale of emission allowances from CO_2 savings increases CO_2 emission elsewhere, so the overall CO_2 emissions will not decrease. The thoughtful design of the EU-ETS rules (especially the regulations on the emission ceiling and the market stability reserve) play an important role in the mitigation of these effects. (Osorio et al. 2020) In addition to the environmental impacts, the analysis of the social and economic effects is also very important. Coal phase-out has significant costs and burdens, but perceptible cost savings and economic benefits can also be realized. Analysts come to different conclusions when analyzing the costs and benefits of the coal phase-out, if they take into account not only the costs but the social impacts in their calculations. Such social impacts can be eg. the saving of environmental and health costs through avoided CO_2 emissions, or addressing employment problems in coal regions, etc. Studies show that it would be important, but at the same time it is difficult to find a balance between environmental, economic and social aspects. The coal phase- out must be implemented keeping the principles of the just transition (Van den Bergh-Botzen, 2015; Chan et al., 2017; Akerboom et al., 2020; Keles-Yilmaz, 2020; Heinisch et al., 2021).

Other studies focus on the profitability of power plants, and the impacts of coal phase-out on profitability. Carbon Tracker (2018) analyzed the profitability of 6,685 coal-fired power plants worldwide and highlighted that approximately 42 % of the plants operated at a loss in 2018. The authors estimated the proportion of loss-making coal-fired power plants at 56 % by 2030 and 72 % by 2040. A similar conclusion was reached by Edis-Bowyer (2021) who argued that by 2025, the economic viability of several Australian coal-fired power plants would become questionable as a result of increasing renewable energy production, so shutdown could be an attractive or even inevitable option for these power plants. In 2020 Gillich et al. analyzed the effects on the contribution margins of power plant owners, separating the effects of coal phase-out, CO_2 prices and the growing share of various renewable energies. One of the main conclusions of the study is that "Contribution margins can vary greatly between technologies and plants using the same technology" (Gillich et al. 2020, p. 9), the scenarios examined by the authors showed a difference of up to 9.5-fold in the cumulated contribution margin in the period 2020-2050 between old and new power plants. In addition, the study found that "The influence of a coal phase-out on the cumulative contribution margin of a power plant in real value can be between 5 and 47%, depending on the extent of the renewable energy expansion and the level of the CO2 price." (Gillich et al. 2020, p. 9)

3 METHODOLOGY

The cumulated relative CO_2 emission of the power plants was investigated in breakdown by owners in the European Union in 2015, in the year of the Paris Agreement. The analysis is based on the European Coal Plant Database, which contains data of 292 coal-fired power plants (EU28). The results of the study made it clear that only four large companies (with their 60 coal-fired power plants) are responsible for 40.5% of the CO_2 emissions in Figure 1. This research examines these companies through the review of their annual reports and other official documents, which are available on their official website.

The methodological framework of our study is basically descriptive and uses case study method.

The focus of our data collection was on the following points:

- the main activities of the companies,
- countries, where the company is active,
- energy mix and power plant portfolio of the company – installed capacity and power generation by sources,
- number of hard coal- and lignit-fired power plants,
- market conditions – challenges on the energy market,
- context of the mention of coal phase-out,
- regulatory environment (EU regulation and country-specific regulation),
- strategies and schedule for coal phase-out in case of power plants,
- CO_2 emissions,
- profitability and financial situation of the company, especially for conventional power generation,

Because of the different structure and content of the annual reports, it was difficult to use the same approach in a consistent way for all of the companies. The research questions were:

- how their operation was affected by the coal phase-out plans and the ongoing energy transition in the European Union,
- what pathways and solutions they have chosen,
- what strategy they have created to ensure their future survival,
- and last but not least, whether is there any shift in their emission levels compared to 2015.

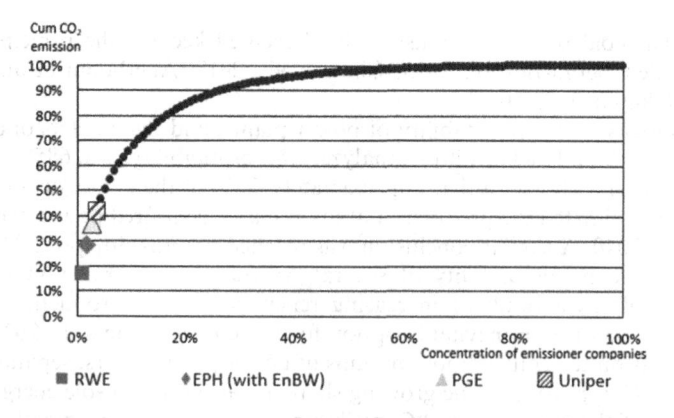

Figure 1. Cumulated relative CO_2 emission of the power plants by owners (n=126) in 2015.
Source: Own elaboration based on Europe Beyond Coal 2021b

4 CASE STUDIES

The International Energy Agency's report on the electricity market 2021 highlights that despite numerous revenue generation opportunities (forward contract, day-ahead and intraday markets, market balancing and capacity remuneration) energy companies owning coal-fired power plants faced a number of difficulties in recent years. The ever-changing legal framework and market conditions make the operation of coal-fired power plants difficult. These processes are increasingly affecting power plants operating with less efficient and emission-intensive technology. On the other hand, coal-fired power plants have an increasingly important role in the system stability because renewable energy generation alone is not able to maintain system stability (IEA, 2021). This section summarises the pathways and strategies of the four most polluting companies operating in the European Union related to the coal phase-out plans.

4.1 *The RWE group*

RWE is one of the largest energy companies in Europe. It is active at all stages of the energy supply chain, including energy production, energy distribution and energy trade. The focus of its activities has been continuously changing as a result of the major energy market events of recent years and the increasingly strict climate protection regulations. By 2020, it has become one of the world's leading renewable energy companies. "Our energy for a sustainable life" is how the company defines its strategic goal. Their ambition: "We will be carbon neutral by 2040, with clean, secure and affordable energy." This idea has gradually matured into the company's main strategic goal in recent years. The power plant portfolio of the company and the energy mix of electricity generation changed significantly between 2015 and 2020. Both the installed capacities and the amount of electricity produced decreased during this time. The installed capacity of hard coal-fired power plants was significantly reduced by 2020 (Figure 1). As a result of that also the amount of electricity generated in coal-fired power plants was reduced (Figure 2). The installed capacity of lignite-fired power plants decreased to a lesser extent (see Figure 2), but it can be seen that the amount of energy they produced decreased significantly (Figure 3). This was due to the fact that most of these power plants did not operate at full capacity. Several of them operated as a reserve to balance fluctuations in the system caused by renewables, and several power plants were switched to standby operation as a result of legal regulations. The role of nuclear energy has diminished as a result of the German nuclear phase-out. The growth of renewable energy sources is remarkable - the installed capacities increased from 4,146 MW (2015) to 10,148 MW (2020) within 5 years. 84.1 % of renewable capacities are represented by wind farms (65.2 % onshore wind, 18.9 % offshore wind).

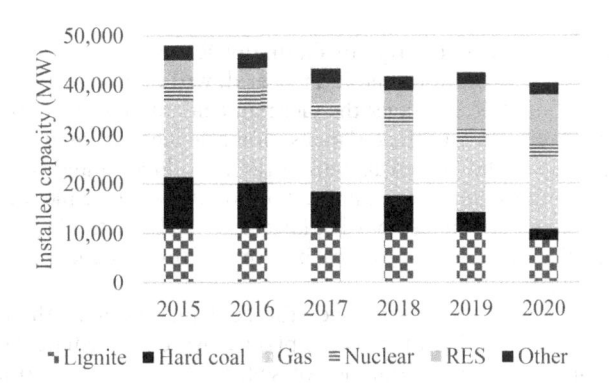

Figure 2.   Installed capacity by sources of energy at RWE, 2015-2020.
Source: Own elaboration based on the annual reports of the RWE Group 2015-2020

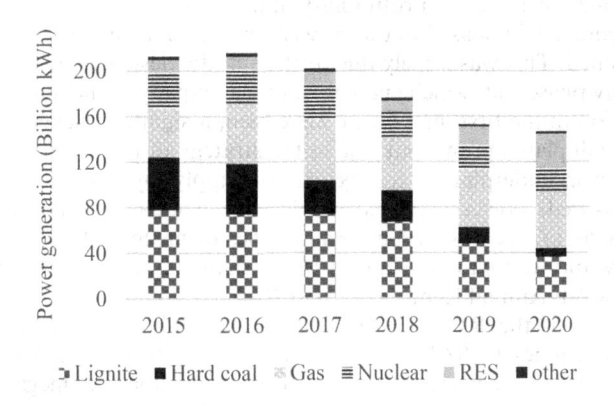

Figure 3.   Power generation by sources of energy at RWE, 2015-2020.
Source: Own elaboration based on the annual reports of the RWE Group 2015-2020

The ratio of solar energy is 2.1 %, and hydropower and biomass account for 13.8 % in the renewable mix of the company.

According to the European Coal Plant Database (Europe Beyond Coal, 2021b.) 9 lignite-fired power plants (with 42 units) and 11 hard-coal fired power plants (with 30 units) are in the ownership of the RWE Group. Geographically, the company has coal-fired power plants in Germany (56 units, of which 15 are hard coal-fired, and 41 lignite-fired), in the United Kingdom (10 units, hard coal-fired) and in the Netherlands (5 units, hard coal-fired). In addition, the Mátra Power Plant, the lignite-fired power plant of Hungary was majority-owned by RWE until its sale in 2017. Of the 72 units, 30 were already retired by the end of 2015. Between 2016 and 2020, 8 units were retired, of which 7 were hard coal-fired (Europe Beyond Coal, 2021b). By 2021 (earlier than originally planned), RWE had completely phased out the hard coal-fired electricity generation in the UK and Germany. The remaining two plants in the Netherlands are being converted to biomass (Amer 9 and Eemshaven). From 2021, lignite-fired units will also be phased out gradually, in the Netherlands by 2029, and in Germany by 2038 (RWE Annual Report 2020).

The ever stringent regulatory environment accelerated the coal phase-out process during the examined period. In addition to the Paris Agreement, EU Winter Package, EU-ETS rules, and Green Deal, a number of regulations at national level were mentioned in the RWE's annual reports. One of the important regulations is the planned criteria for power plants' GHG emission, excluding coal-fired power plants from the capacity auction market. The company faces different regulatory environments in Germany, UK and the Netherlands. Some examples can be listed for each country. In Germany RWE has had to take 5 lignite-fired power plants into stand-by operation (and later shut down) in exchange for a compensation. The Coal Phase-out Act of 2020 envisages the German coal phase-out by 2038 and determines the road map for the shutdown and the compensation schemes for lignite and hard-coal-fired power plants. In the case of the United Kingdom the introduction and operation of the capacity market and the climate change levy imposed on fossil fuels were mentioned in the annual reports. In the Netherlands coal phase-out is planned by 2030, without providing compensation to power plants. The introduction of a carbon price floor is a special idea in this country (RWE Annual Reports 2015-2020).

The company uses three types of strategies for coal phase-out in the case of its power plants. The most commonly used strategy is the plant-closure (immediately or after a standby operation period). There were also examples of selling RWE's shares to another company (e.g. Mátra Power Plant). Finally, a possible solution is to switch the plant to another alternative fuel, as in the Netherlands, the last two plants will be converted to biomass-fired. The chosen strategy and timing are influenced by several aspects, such as the regulation of the given country, the age, technology, profitability and efficiency of the power plant. As mentioned, RWE had completely phased out its power generation from hard-coal by 2021, earlier than originally planned. This was largely due to the specific design of the German compensation scheme for early phase-out, which encouraged the company to make use of the opportunities for compensation in the first line. As we have seen, a significant expansion of renewable energy production will play a prominent role in the strategy of the company. It also wants to maintain its position in underpinning the security of supply, by making available its flexible (predominantly gas-fired) power plants available. The company spends huge amounts on innovation in many areas, such as storage technologies or green hydrogen. RWE has chosen a proactive strategy and wants to be a leader rather than a sufferer of the transformation of the energy system (RWE Annual Reports 2015-2020).

The CO_2 emissions of the RWE Group decreased by about 41 percent globally, from 150.8 million metric tonnes to 88.1 million metric tonnes during the 5 year period under review. Also the specific emission (i.e. in carbon dioxide emissions per megawatt-hour of electricity generated) has been reduced significantly (from 0.708 metric tons to 0.47 metric tons) from 2015 to 2020 (RWE Annual Reports 2015-2020).

The example of RWE showed that although coal phase-out severely affects the company, it does not shake the operation of the firm and due to its graduality, did not provoke strong protests from the company. This may have been due to the fact that the period from 2015 to 2017 was critical for conventional electricity generation (RWE Annual Reports 2015-2017). The margins of power generation (wholesale electricity price decreased by cost of fuel and quota prices) was low and had a declining tendency. Some power plants could not cover their operation (fixed) costs because of low utilization and had to be shut down temporarily. Under these uncertain and insufficient profitability prospects, the company was not shocked by the requirement of the gradual exit from coal-based power generation.

The regulations affect the financial situation of the company in different ways. To name just a few examples: The lignite phase-out put a significant financial burden on the company. Although, the firm will receive a compensation of 2.6 billion euros in exchange for the early phase-out based on the negotiations, the company believes that this amount will not cover their real burden. The expected redundancies in the lignite business will affect more than 3,000 jobs in the near future, which could increase to 6,000 by 2030. The government must find socially acceptable solutions for the regions and employees concerned. In the first German coal phase-out auction RWE had a winning bid for the early shutdown of its last 2 hard coal-fired power plants, resulting in a compensation payment of € 216 million. In the Netherlands, there is no compensation for the shutting down of power plants. The last two power plants owned by the RWE Group will be converted to co-fire partly with biomass, with the help of a state aid of € 2.6 billion for 8 years. The subsidy covers investment costs as well as the differences in the cost of fuels. A full conversion to biomass would result in substantial additional burdens. As no further support is provided by the state, RWE is considering legal action to compensate for its damage (RWE Annual Reports, 2015-2020).

4.2 *EPH group*

Before the Paris Agreement came into action the Czech-based Energetický a Průmyslový Holding (EPH/EnBW company included) was the second largest company in the EU based on the annual CO_2 emission by coal-fired power plants, with its 86 million tons emission. Thanks to the regulations of the European Union, this number has significantly decreased in the last 5 years (EU-wide). However, EPH still remains amongst the top emissioners with its 55 million tonnes of CO_2 emission and with 13 operating plants.

The energy portfolio of the company is quite diversified. As Table 2 shows, the annual income of the EPH from gas and heat fired energy production had been increasing unbrokenly till 2020, when they had a sudden drop due to the pandemic, while revenues from coal-based energy production were very fluctuating.

Table 2. Annual income of EPH group between 2015 and 2020 by energy carriers (in million euro).

Energy carrier/ Year	2015	2016	2017	2018	2019	2020
Gas	1581	1675	1989	2156	2342	2201
Heat	298	358	345	354	395	329
Coal	289	268	294	337	250	210

Source: Own elaboration based on Annual reports of EPH 2015-2020

The sudden change of the revenues from coal-fired energy production in 2017-2018 can be explained by the variability of wholesale prices rather than by the decrease in the volume produced.

Analyzing the annual reports of the company between 2015 and 2020, we can see that the year by year environmental impact of their operations has been playing a more and more considerable role in their agenda. In 2015 it contained only a couple of pages about the environmental aspects of their operations and it was also mentioned that although they did not have a group-wide environmental initiative, the company was committed to meeting all the requirements of the EU and also complying with each country's regulations where they operate. In contrast, five years later, in 2020, their annual report contained approximately 30 pages about their effort related to environmental protection and they had a clear strategy for the future. „We continue to deliver on our strategy of steady carbon footprint reduction while providing flexible generation capacity and full security of energy supply." (EPH annual report 2020. p.7)

Of course, while companies are committed to decreasing their greenhouse-gas emissions, their main goal is to have a profitable business, so the economic impacts have to be aligned with the environmental protection goals. For example, in 2017 coal prices rose sharply due to the massive need for China's plants, thus energy production from coal became more expensive, giving more space to gas electricity generation in Europe.

The regulations of the European Union in the last years were also effective so the energy companies started to reduce their CO_2 emissions and invest money into zero carbon emission processes, such as biomass power plants. EPH Group is also not an exception from that. Between 2015 and 2018, they invested more than 850 million euros in zero or low carbon emission generation capacities and their Lynemouth plant belongs to the largest biomass power plants in the EU saving the globe from more than 2.7 million tons of CO_2 annually

Table 3. Most important financial KPI's and the number of employees of EPH group from 2015 to 2020 (EBITDA and EBIT are in million euro).

Key KPIs	2015	2016	2017	2018	2019	2020
EBITDA (million euro)	1637	1 520	1819	1743	2051	2150
EBIT (million euro)	1382	966	1346	1190	1396	1376
Employees	N/A	10310	10237	10711	11454	11281

Source: Own elaboration according to the Annual Reports of EPH 2015-2020

It is also important to note, that while they are investing a vast amount of money into zero carbon emission, their business could remain successful in the last years, not only financially (EBIT) but socially (number of employees) too (EPH annual reports 2015-2020).

4.3 *The PGE group*

Out of the 13 operating coal-fired power plants of the PGE Group, only 2 have a retirement date yet. One of their plants in Czechnica will be retired in 2023 (announced in 2019) and the other one in Belchatow will be retired in 2036 (announced in 2021). However, it is true that the Belchatow plant accounts for more than 50% of the CO_2 emission of the PGE's operating capacities.

This dependency can be seen in their Annual Reports between 2015 and 2020, because there is no further discussion about the Paris Agreement, nor about the coal phase-out strategy connected to their portfolio. The only highlighted information in their reports, which is related to environment protection, is that they are constantly trading CO_2 rights and they are really thorough about the financial impacts of the future price changes in ETS or in raw materials (coal) (PGE annual reports 2015-2020).

Although, they do not mention coal phase-out in their reports between 2015 and 2020, they announced their new corporate strategy in October 2020, which set the tone for the future changes with a 75 billion PLN CAPEX budget for the 2021-2030 period, of which they are planning to spend more than 50% for renewable energy sources.

As part of their strategy and in alignment with the EU expectations, they seek to decrease the company's CO_2 emission by 85% by 2030 and achieve climate neutrality by 2050. For that, it is inevitable to convert their coal heated power plant capacities to gas fired or biomass fired capacities. The main financial sources of their future plans are:

- Cohesion Policy
- Recovery and Resilience Facility
- Just Transition Fund
- React EU
- Invest EU
- Innovation Fund
- Horizon Fund
- and of course loans from private and public sources.

As it can be seen, they are highly depending on the money, which can be obtained from the European Union, and they openly admit, that at least 25% of the money has to come from funds, otherwise their operation cannot be maintained or the goals cannot be achieved (Decrease CO2 emission by 85% till 2030) (PGE Group Strategy 2030).

However, they clearly expressed their need for non-refundable money, for 2025, they are calculating with more than 5 billion PLN EBITDA/year and with more than 6 billion PLN EBITDA/year after 2030. „The goal of the PGE Group is a full use of dedicated financing options for green investments and off-balance sheet financing." (PGE group Strategy 2030 page 35.**)**

4.4 *The Uniper group*

The Uniper Group was established in 2016 when it separated from the E.ON Group. (Uniper, 2016a.) Nowadays it is one of the leading energy companies in the world's 40 countries. In 2020, it had around 12,000 employees. The company has three core business segments namely the European Generation (most significant segment), Global Commodities and the Russian Power Generation. Between 2016 and 2020 the company operated its coal-fired power plants to produce power and heat in Germany, in France, in the Netherlands, and in the United Kingdom within the border of the European Union and in the frame of the European Generation segment. A significant part of the generated energy is transferred to the Global

Commodities segment, and the other part is sold through long-term electricity and heat supply contracts. Climate change is one of the most important priorities of Uniper's strategy (Uniper, 2020a.). The European Green Deal, besides the provisions of national law, jeopardize the profitability of the company under the current operating structure because its coal-fired power plants were the fourth largest polluters in the European Union in 2015 (Europe Beyond Coal Database, 2021b). In response to the changing market and regulatory conditions, the Uniper Group decided to become carbon-neutral by 2035 in Europe, and in all segments by 2050. In 2020, Uniper announced its phase-out plan which frees the environment from 18 tons of carbon dioxide per year (Uniper 2021a.). The company marked out the path to reaching carbon neutrality by 2050. In this way, not only does European production play a prominent role, but it also covers all business segments of Uniper (Russian Power Generation and Global Commodities). First, it will decrease its CO_2 emission by 2030 compared to the 2019 level, and finally it will reach complete carbon neutrality in the European Generation segment by 2035. (Uniper, 2020b) Its carbon intensity decreased by 10%, and the direct carbon emissions from fuel combustion fell by 41% between 2016 and 2020 (Uniper, 2020a.). In the European Generation segment, nitrogen-oxide (NOx) decreased by 48%, sulphur-dioxide (SO_2) by 78%, and the dust emission by 62% (Annual Report of Uniper 2018, Uniper 2020b.)

According to Figure 4, the energy mix of the electricity production was mostly based on hard coal and lignite (43%) in 2016. This ratio decreased to 27 % by 2020 due to the circumstances mentioned above. During the examined period only one plant unit used lignite (Schkopau A +B), the other power plants burned hard-coal. The average age of the plants was 43 years.

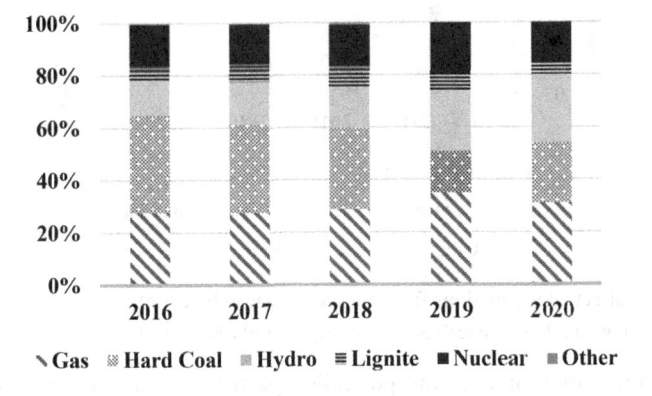

Figure 4. Uniper's energy mix of electricity production.

Source: own elaboration based on Uniper's Sustainability Reports 2016-2020

The European and national coal phase-out strategies pose a huge challenge to the company. According to Uniper's official documents, five directions of its carbon phase-out strategy can be distinguished:

- further operation (Datteln IV., in Germany)
- further operation as a reserve power plant (Heyden, in Germany)
- selling its stakes (typical in France)
- transforming its power plants to alternative fuel (typical in Germany and in the Netherlands)
- shutdown of its power plant in the frame of capacity auction (typical in Germany)

In Germany it operated seven hard coal and one lignite power plant in 2016 (Uniper, 2016b.) According to the Electricity Market Act, the lignite-fired power plants became a so-called climate reserve. Despite the German government's phasing-out decision on January 29th 2020, the company's plant portfolio was expanded by a new high-efficiency hard coal-fired power plant called Datteln 4, which will remain in operation until 2038 (Uniper, 2020a., 2020b.). According to the act the lignite and hard-coal capacity had to be reduced to 15 GW by the end of 2022, then an additional 6 GW of lignite, 7 GW of hard coal by April 1, 2030, and the rest by 2038. Kiel Power Plant in Germany was decommissioned on March 31, 2019. (Annual Report of Uniper, 2019) Hayden 4 hard-coal-fired power plant with its 875 MW capacity was the first which successfully took part in the German capacity auction. In the second auction the Wilhelmshaven 1 (757 MW) will be home to a green hydrogen plant. This power plant will be transformed into gas-fired, Staudinger 5 (510 MW) by 2025. The Schkopau lignite-fired power plant (900 MW) was sold to Uniper's co-owner, EPH in 2021. (Annual Report of Uniper, 2020) In 2019 the company sold its French interests for risk mitigation purposes. In the United Kingdom, decommissioning (Ratcliffe 2000MW) will take place by 2025. The Dutch government is required to reduce its greenhouse gas emissions by at least 25% by the end of 2020 on the 1990 basis after a lost lawsuit. With this decision, the fate of Dutch coal-fired power plants was also sealed (Uniper, 2020b.) that is why Maasvlakte 3 (1070 MW) will close down by the end of 2029. On the other hand, the compensation awarded is not considered appropriate and is therefore diverted to legal action (Uniper, 2021b.).

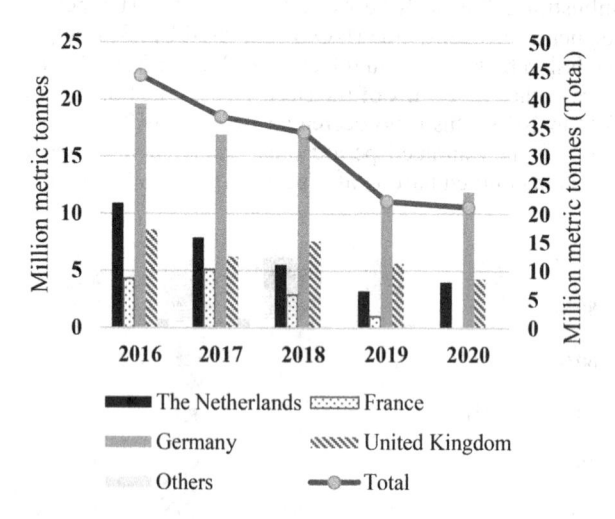

Figure 5. Uniper's direct CO_2 emissions from fuel combustion by country.
Source: Own elaboration based on Uniper's Sustainability Reports 2018-2020

As a result of the former actions and portfolio optimization, the company reduced its CO_2 emission connected to the European Generation by 52 % between 2016 and 2020 (Figure 5).

In 2016 Uniper believed that the coal-based electricity production would increase, but the changed regulation environment did not prove it. On the other hand, the company found a new opportunity in this process, so the adjusted EBIT of the company nearly tripled between 2016 and 2020, and nowadays it develops renewable capacity and invests in clean hydrogen technologies (Annual Reports of Uniper, 2016-2020).

5 CONCLUSIONS

In this article we examined the effects of coal phase-out from the perspective of power plant owners between 2015 and 2020. The extent of the impacts was influenced by a number of factors, such as the composition of the company's portfolio, the share of coal in installed capacity, and the plans to speed up exit from coal-based energy production. Using a case study method we summarised the pathways and strategies of the four most polluter companies operating in the European Union, focusing on their coal phase-out plans. The applied strategies were mostly proactive and similar in the main principles. They wanted to be a leader rather than a sufferer of the transformation. The firms' focus has moved towards renewable energy sources and the diversification of their activities, they invested remarkable amounts in technology innovations. The regulatory environment accelerated the coal phase-out process during the examined period. The ambitious energy and climate policy of the EU and the different regulations of the member states made an increasingly stringent conditions for the power plants. Although coal phase-out severely affected these companies, it did not shake their operation. This may have been due to the fact that the examined period was critical for the conventional electricity generation. Obligation of coal phase-out is put in a different light if the profitability prospects of coal-based electricity generation are considered. The margin of the power generation is influenced by a lot of factors (see Nalbandian-Sugden, 2016; Edis-Bowyer, 2021), such as the development of fuel prices (in this case coal and lignite) as well as the burdens of climate protection efforts (eg. the price of emission allowances, levies and taxes), the declining costs and rapid expansion of renewable energy production as well as the development of wholesale electricity prices. According to several studies (Carbon Tracker, 2018; Edis-Bowyer, 2021) the economic viability of several coal-fired power plants will be questionable in the future and shutdown can be an attractive or even unavoidable option for them. In order to successfully implement the coal phase-out mechanism, it is essential to adhere to the principles of just transition, as well as to ensure the stability of the energy system and supply security. The analyzed annual reports and other sources had been made before energy prices were released in 2021. Compared to the low points in 2020 (largely caused by the Covid-19 epidemic), prices soon reached their pre-epidemic levels. However, the price-boom did not stop. Natural gas prices have risen drastically, 4-6 times in recent months, but electricity prices have also risen significantly, partly due to intense increases in quota prices. There was an upward trend in the price of coal quotations too (Energy Market Report 2021). Analysts say high energy prices will remain in the long run. Next year's reports of the analyzed companies will also provide interesting lessons for dealing with the situation in the energy market.

REFERENCES

Akerboom S. & Botzen W. & Buijze A. & Michels A. & Rijswick M. 2020. Meeting goals of sustainability policy: CO2 emission reduction, cost-effectiveness and societal acceptance. An analysis of the proposal to phase-out coal in the Netherlands. Energy Policy, 138

Annual reports of EPH Group 2015-2020 https://www.epholding.cz/en/annual-reports/

Annual reports of PGE Group 2015-2020 https://www.gkpge.pl/Investor-Relations/financial-data

Annual Reports of RWE 2015-2020 https://www.rwe.com/en/investor-relations/financial-reports-presentations-videos/financial-reports

Annual Reports of Uniper 2016-2020 https://ir.uniper.energy/websites/uniper/English/3000/reporting.html

Bibert S. 2020 H1 Interim Results https://ir.uniper.energy/download/companies/uniperag/Presentations/2020-08 11_H1_2020_Uniper_InvestorPresentation_Final.pdf

Brauers H. & Pao-Yu O. 2020. The political economy of coal in Poland: Drivers and barriers for a shift away from fossil fuels. Energy Policy, Volume 144, ISSN 0301-4215.

Brauers H. & Pao-Yu O. & Walk P. 2020. Comparing coal phase-out pathways: The United Kingdom's and Germany's diverging transitions. Environmental Innovation and Societal Transitions, Volume 37, Pages 238–253, ISSN 2210-4224.

Carbon Tracker 2018. Powering Down Coal: Navigating the economic and financial risks in the last years of coal power. https://carbontracker.org/reports/coal-portal/

Chestney N. 2020 Nearly half of global coal plants will be unprofitable this year: Carbon Tracker. Reuters, 8. April. 2020

Edis T. & Bowyer K. T. 2021. Fast Erosion of Coal Plant Profits in the National Electricity Market, IEEFA

Energy Market Report 2021: Energiapiaci összefoglaló 2021/18. Energymarket24 Kft. https://energymarket24.hu/

ENSZ 2020. Fenntartható fejlődés energetikai vonatkozásai https://www.un.org/sustainabledevelopment/energy/

Europe Beyond Coal, 2021a: Overview: National coal phase-out announcements in Europe https://beyond-coal.eu/wp-content/uploads/2021/08/Overview-of-national-coal-phase-out-announcements-Europe-Beyond-Coal-3-August-2021.docx.pdf

Europe Beyond Coal, 2021b: European Coal Plant Database https://beyond-coal.eu/database/

Eurostat 2021: CO2 emissions from energy use clearly decreased in the EU in 2020, 07/05/2021 https://ec.europa.eu/eurostat/web/products-eurostat-news/-/ddn-20210507-1

Gillich A. & Hufendiek K. & Klempp N. 2020. Extended policy mix in the power sector: How a coal phase-out redistributes costs and profits among power plants. Energy Policy, Volume 147, ISSN 0301-4215

Global Energy Monitor 2021. https://globalenergymonitor.org/projects/global-coal-plant-tracker/summary-data/

Heinisch K. & Holtemöller O. & Schult C. 2021. Power generation and structural change: Quantifying economic effects of the coal phase-out in Germany. Energy Economics, Volume 95, ISSN 0140-9883.

Heinrichs H.U. & Markewitz P. 2017. Long-term impacts of a coal-phase out in Germany as part of a greenhouse gas mitigation strategy. Appl. Energy, 192, pp. 234–246,

IEA 2021. Electricity Market Report July https://iea.blob.core.windows.net/assets/01e1e998-8611-45d7-acab-5564bc22575a/ElectricityMarketReportJuly2021.pdf

International Trade Administration 2021 Energy sector of Poland https://www.trade.gov/country-commercial-guides/poland-energy-sector

IRENA 2017: REthinking Energy 2017: Accelerating the global energy transformation https://www.irena.org/publications/2017/Jan/REthinking-Energy-2017-Accelerating-the-global-energy-transformation

Keles D. & Yilmaz H. Ü. 2020. Decarbonisation through coal phase-out in Germany and Europe — Impact on Emissions, electricity prices and power production. Energy Policy, Volume 141, ISSN 0301–4215.

Lund, P.D. 2017. Implications of Finland's plan to ban coal and cutting oil use. Energy Policy, 108 pp.78–80

Markard J. & Rinscheid A. & Widdel L. 2021. Analyzing transitions through the lens of discourse networks: Coal phase-out in Germany. Environmental Innovation and Societal Transitions, Volume 40, Pages 315–331, ISSN 2210-4224.

Maubach K. & Tuomela T. 2021a, b: 3M 2021 Interim Results Interim Results presentation Uniper-presentation https://ir.uniper.energy/download/companies/uniperag/Presentations/20210506_Q12021_UniperInvestorPresentationF.pdf

Maubach K. & Tuomela T. 2021b,c: H1 2021 Interim Results presentation Uniper-presentation https://ir.uniper.energy/download/companies/uniperag/Presentations/2021-08 11_H1_2021_Uniper_Investor_Presentation_Final.pdf

Nalbandian-Sugden H. 2016. Operating ratio and cost of coal power generation, IEA Clean Coal Centre

Osorio S. & Pietzcker R. C. & Pahle M. & Edenhofer O. 2020. How to deal with the risks of phasing out coal in Germany, Energy Economics, Volume 87, ISSN 0140-9883.

PGE groups strategy 2020. https://www.gkpge.pl/investor-relations/PGE-Group/pge-group-s-strategy

Rentier G. & Lelieveldt H. & Kramer G. J. 2019. Varieties of coal-fired power phase-out across Europe. Energy Policy, 132, pp. 620–632,

Ron Chan H. & Fell H. & Lange I. & Li S. 2017 Efficiency and environmental impacts of electricity restructuring on coal-fired power plants. Journal of Environmental Economics and Management, Volume 81, Pages 1–18, ISSN 0095-0696

Sustainability Reports of Uniper 2016-2020 https://ir.uniper.energy/websites/uniper/English/3000/reporting.html

UNFCCC 2021: The Paris Agreement https://unfccc.int/process-and-meetings/the-paris-agreement/the-paris-agreement

Uniper 2016a. Sustainability Report 2016 Short version https://ir.uniper.energy/download/companies/uniperag/Sustainability/Uniper_SR16_short.pdf

Uniper 2016b.: Lists of Assets https://ir.uniper.energy/websites/uniper/English/3000/reporting.html

Uniper 2020a.: Uniper strategy highlights Andreas Schierenbeck, CEO Uniper Fortum Capital Market Day, December 3, 2020 https://ir.uniper.energy/download/companies/uniperag/Presentations/2020-12-03_Uniper_Strategy_Schierenbeck.pdf

Uniper 2020b: Quarterly Statement Q1-Q3 Financial Result https://ir.uniper.energy/download/companies/uniperag/Quarterly%20Reports/DE000UNSE018-Q3-2020-EQ-E-00.pdf

Uniper 2021a.: Fact Sheet https://irpages2.eqs.com/download/companies/uniperag/factsheet_17739_English.pdf

Uniper 2021b. Half Year Interim Report 2021, Financial Results https://ir.uniper.energy/download/companies/uniperag/Quarterly%20Reports/DE000UNSE018-Q2-2021-EQ-E-00.pdf

Van den Bergh J.C.J.M & Botzen W.J.W. 2015. Monetary valuation of the social cost of greenhouse gas emissions. Ecological Economics, 114, pp. 33–46.

Spent pickling liquor as industrial waste recover opportunities

H. Zakiyya & T. Kékesi
Faculty of Material Science and Engineering, University of Miskolc, Hungary

ABSTRACT: Pickling is one of the essential steps in galvanizing industries in which hydrochloric acid (HCl) is used as the main composition to clean up the steel surface. This HCl lost its pickling efficiency because of decreasing in its concentration as well as increasing metals content because of dissolution processes. Recovery processes could be done to this kind of waste, so circular economics and a nearly zero waste cycle industry can be established. Processing SPL by electrodeposition is possible to recover pure metal from the waste solution. However, the presence of iron in the zinc chloride solution changes the nature and the conditions. It was found that the effect of iron concentration on the polarization curves is complex. Initially it has a negative effect on the generated cathodic current because of the enhancement of hydrogen bubble formation. Further increased iron concentrations may make the composition of the Zn-Fe deposit dominantly in favour of iron, resulting in a hydrogen dominated cathodic mechanism. Controlling the parameters such as Zn and Fe concentration, and the electrolyte's agitation intensity could play essential impacts on the electrodeposition of zinc from chloride media. Nevertheless, separation is still essential; thus, introducing the anion exchange separation to prepare the electrolyte is needed to achieve an acceptable quality of zinc deposition. In the relatively low concentration of HCl, Zn tend to be retained in the resin as its more likely to produce chloro-complex. As in the higher concentration of HCl (>1), Fe-(III) distribution fucntion in HCl will increase thus the Fe may retain in the resin. However oxidation state control can be the answer of this problem by reducing Fe(III) to Fe(II) or in order to optimalize the separation process partially precipitation of Fe might be an option.

Keywords: Spent Pickling Liquor (SPL), Zn-Fe recovery, liquid waste, electrowinning

1 INTRODUCTION

Preventing corrosion on the surface of metals is one of the necessary steps in the metal production. One of the most common corrosion control methods is coating the surface by a passivating layer, like in the case of hot dip galvanizing, where the surface of the steel object is protected by a zinc layer. This process consists of subsequent steps, where pickling is an important for preparing the surface (Agrawal et al. 2009; Regel-Rosocka. 2010; Csicsovszki et al. 2005). In this step, some acids, namely hydro chloric (HCl) or sulfuric (H_2SO_4) acids are applied to remove the oxide layer (Abad et al. 2017; Regel-Rosocka et al. 2010). In practice, quite a large proportion of the products with faulty zinc coatings are returned to this step, which results in the enrichment of the pickling liquor in also zinc, beside iron, and the acid concentration decreases at the same time. At a level of 15 – 30 % of the original acid concentration, the solution is categorized as spent, i.e. no longer serviceable, while the metal content, primarily Zn (II) and Fe (II) is increased to 150-250 g/dm^3 (Regel-Rosocka 2010). In this condition, the rate of oxide dissolution by acid is getting slower. Sonmez et al. 2003 has found

DOI: 10.1201/9781003259954-17

that the zinc concentration of the solution increased faster than that of iron when H_2SO_4 was used. Due to the heavy metal content, spent pickling liquor (SPL) is categorized as a hazardous waste, and need to be treated before disposal.

An ideal treatment of this liquor can be not only satisfactory for the environment but can also serve the economy by recovering valuable metals, Zn and/or Fe in this case. Due to environmental protection regulation, the processes of Zn recovery from various industrial wastes are lately becoming progressively more attractive. If the metals can be extracted at a high purity level, the processing of the waste material may offer some extra economic benefit (Kekesi et al. 2002). The price of zinc, as of all the metals, strongly depend on purity. For example, the 99.999% (5N) purity zinc (available as a special material) may cost almost 4000 times more than the common commodity at the metal markets. Therefore, treating such waste materials may become more promising if the recovery process is capable of reaching higher purities. This is one of the goals of the envisaged research challenge.

1.1 Spent Pickling Liquor (SPL) treatment

It has been reported by European stainless steel and alloyed steel companies that approximately 300 000 m^3 of spent pickling liquor is produced every year. This stream is neutralized to produce 150 000 t/y of sludge, which is stored (Frias et al. 1997). Neutralization with an alkaline agent is widely used in spent pickling liquor treatment due to its simple and economical procedure to treat relatively dilute low-cost heavy metal solutions. According to the restriction by the Environmental Protection Agency (EPA) for steel pickling plants, the HCl limit in the air is 6 ppm for continuous and 18 ppm for batch processes. Also, the European standards state that the metal and chloride ion contents after neutralization must not be higher than 2 mg/dm^3 Zn, 10 mg/dm^3 Fe and 1 g/ dm^3 Cl⁻ with the acidity range between 6 and 9. Thus the effluent has to be treated to meet these regulations and to prevent environmental pollution.

The properties of the neutralization product depend on the composition of the SPL, which varies according to the plant of origin. Table 1 is one of the example of SPL composition, a wider survey (Regel-Rosocka. 2010b) suggests the following characteristic ranges of composition for the SPL obtained from pickling applied before hot dip galvanization: 30 ~ 80 g/ dm^3 Zn, 50 ~ 150 g/dm^3 Fe and 40 ~ 160 g/dm^3 HCl. However, the Zn content greatly depends on how the recycled products are treated. If removal of the faulty zinc layer is carried out separately, stripping solution of higher Zn concentration also arises. In other cases, the SPL carries the whole of the stripped zinc.

Table 1. Chemical composition of hot-dip galvanizing waste.

Waste	Process	Phase	Chemical composition	
			Cu	0.56 mg/dm^3
			Co	1.99 mg/dm^3
			Ni	10.70 mg/dm^3
			Pb	18.68 mg/dm^3
Spent Pickling Liquor (Sonmez et al. 2003)	Pre-treatment (Pickling)	liquid	Cd	1.36 mg/dm^3
			Cr	3.07 mg/dm^3
			Mn	230 mg/dm^3
			Cl (total)	185 g/dm^3
			Fe^{2+}	45.83 g/dm^3
			Fe^{3+}	6.49 g/dm^3
			Fe (total)	52.32 g/dm^3
			Zn	95.45 g/dm^3
Stripping Liquor (Hluchanova et al. 2012)	Special pre-treatment	liquid	Zn	97 %

Beside the main components – zinc and iron (with the predominance of the Fe(II) form) – the spent solution left over from hot-dip galvanizing contains also a little amount of lead, chromium and some other metals together with hydrochloric acid. The concentration ranges from plant to plant relatively wide, which makes it difficult to use a universal method. The regeneration of the pickling liquor is the first idea coming up to minimize the pollution and to reduce the costs incurred by the fresh acid requirement.

Some recycling processes have been developed to turn spent pickling liquors into valuable secondary resource but the process to generate both acid and metal in an economical and practical way, still needs further research. The main problem is the physico-chemical complexity of transition metal ions in hydrochloric acid effluents (Regel-Rosocka 2010). Consequently, it is difficult to choose the proper method to be used. Nowadays, a number of technologies such as precipitation, membrane separation, ion exchange, electrowinning, pyrohydrolysis, liquid-liquid extraction, diffusion dialysis, hydrolysis, solvent extraction and oxidation are combined to get a better results (San Román et al. 2012). Table 2 describes the advantages and disadvantages of various traditional technologies in SPL regeneration.

Table 2. Various technologies of SPL treatment (Regel-Rosocka. 2010b).

Technology	Efficiency	Advantage	Disadvantage
Spray roasting		Effective for large amount	Limited by Zn concentration
		Reduce wastewater and sludge	High operating cost
		Cost covered by the result Applied	Complex installation High NO_x release
Precipitation/ Neutralization		Low operating cost	Large consumption of chemical
		Neutral by-product	No acid recovery
		Simple technique and equipment	Expensive sludge storage
		Can be applied in the small industry	Hazardous precipitate High nitrogen content
Retardation/ ion-exchange	Recovery of metal salt 50-55%	Effective Zn retention	Limited metal ion concentration
		Effective selectivity	High volume of waste
		Low operation cost	High volume of diluted solution
		Little equipment and space	High consumption of fresh water
		Applied in industry	
Solvent Extraction Solvent Extraction	91 % of extraction Fe 91 % of extraction Fe	TBP is effective for wide range of Zn concentration in feed	Organic impurities in aqueous phase
		Good selectivity with TBP Acidic extractant permit Zn up to 100 g/dm^3 after stripping	Extractant loss
			Stripping problem from certain extractant
		High production with compact equipment	Co-extraction of Fe(III) with Zn Phase separation after stripping
			The greater the feed concentration the higher treatment cost

Membrane technologies combined with electrowinning is one of the promising directions of research where Zn(II) ion can be separated from Fe(II) before further recovery of either of these two metals. Separation is performed to prevent the contamination of one recovered metal by the other ion in electrowinning. It has to be carried out also because hydrolysis of a metal may locally disturb the conditions of the electrodeposition of even the more noble metals (Díaz et al. 2002).

1.2 *Electrowinning of zinc from SPL and its challenges*

The application of electrowinning is possible by depleting metal from the solution through cathodic deposition. Electrochemical separation of various metals in the solution can be done due to relative potential differences. Through electrochemical processes metal ions in HCl solutions are electrodeposited to the cathode of an electrolytic compartment. This technique is believed to be economically friendly. In hydrometallurgy, electrodeposition is often applied together with other predominant techniques of solution purification, such as membrane separation, ion exchange and solvent extraction. As a result, this technique offers pure metal and acid regeneration form SPL.

Zinc recovery from SPL through zinc electrodeposition still faces some challenges, one of which is the energy consumption due to the competition between zinc and hydrogen ions at the electrolyte/electrode interface. As reported in many studies, zinc deposition is often coupled with the evolution of hydrogen. Due to the readily formed zinc-chloro-complex species (Kekesi 2018; Kekesi et al. 2002), the metal deposition must be preceded by the dissociation of the complex structure, liberating the electro-active cation:

$$[\text{ZnCl}_x]^{(2-x)-} = \text{Zn}^{2+} + x\text{Cl}^- \tag{1a}$$

$$\text{Zn}^{2+} + 2e^- = \text{Zn} \tag{1b}$$

This mechanism has a natural inhibiting effect at the cathode, but also some bubbles are produced by hydrogen evolution at the same time:

$$2\text{H}^+ + 2e^- = \text{H}_2 \tag{2}$$

The complex form of the dissolved zinc even in weak HCl solutions may be a reason why the ion supply to the cathode surface is hindered. This case has also been found with tin in HCl media (Kulcsar et al. 2016). However, the inhibiting effect of the preliminary complex dissociation may have a beneficial effect on the structure of the formed cathodic deposit.

Besides the types of crystal growth, another challenge in zinc electrodeposition from a Zn-Fe mixed chloride solution is the interference of the main cathodic process caused by the side-reactions with the iron species. The redox potentials of the Fe^{2+}/Fe and the $\text{Fe}^{3+}/\text{Fe}^{2+}$ couples are -0,44 and +0,74 V, respectively (Kekesi. 2018). These potentials directly indicate the stability of the Fe^{2+} oxidation state if metallic iron is present in the system and oxidation by as strong agent (like oxygen in the ambient air) can be excluded. Zinc, with its more negative standard electrode potential of the Zn^{2+}/Zn couple, will also directly reduce the Fe(III) species, if present. However, the oxidation by air or also by the anode can always generate the ferric species, which – coming in contact with the deposited metal – may cause cathode corrosion:

$$2\text{Fe}^{3+} + \text{Zn} = \text{Zn}^{2+} + 2\text{Fe}^{2+} \tag{3}$$

$$\text{Fe}^{3+} + \text{Fe} = 2\text{Fe}^{2+} \tag{4}$$

Although, the formation of the respective chloro-complex species:

$$\text{Me}^{z+} + x\text{Cl}- = [\text{MeCl}x]^{z-x} \tag{5}$$

may influence the Me(Z)/Me formal potentials, where z is the charge of the aquo-ions, Z is the valence of the oxidation state and x is the coordination number of the chloride ions in the complex species formed (Csicsovszki et al. 2005; Kekesi. 2018). As the concentration of HCl is limited to a low level by keeping the pH in the electrolyte preferably above the 2-3 value, the formation of the complex species will depend only on the free Cl⁻ ions dissociated from the added chloride salts used in preparing the tested synthetic electrolytes. There may also be a difficulty in terms of energy consumption because of the competition between zinc and hydrogen ions at the electrolyte/electrode interface. Zinc deposition is expected as the dominant cathodic reaction. However, Fe impurity content in the electrolyte may promote also the hydrogen ion reduction, because the overpotential of hydrogen on iron is lower (by ~ 400 mV) than on zinc(Kekesi. 2018).

Anion exchange, offers a clean separation of iron in the Fe(II) state from zinc. Figure 1 shows the known and relevant anion-exchange distribution functions, which can be used for devising the separation procedure.

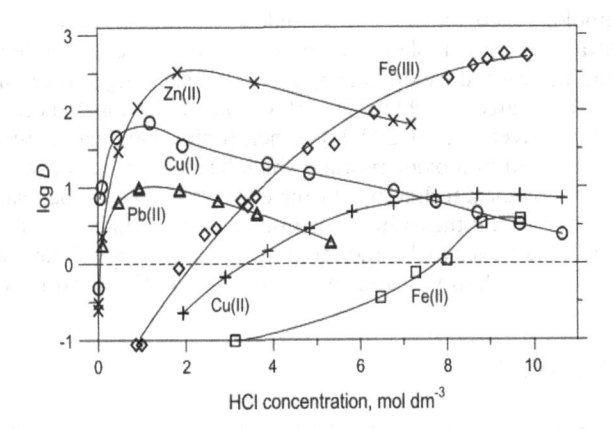

Figure 1. Anion exchange distribution functions of Zn and Fe (a) and those of the Sn species (b) determined by batch equilibration. (Kekesi et al. 2002).

The most important task is the elimination of iron, separation of iron requires a preliminary reduction of the trivalent species according to Eq. (4) by stirring iron chips in the mixed solution of the SPL. We have performed this step in the laboratory, and the efficiency was found satisfactory within several minutes. The solution was not re-oxidized if kept still in a closed container within any appreciable time. Feeding the original SPL into the anion-exchange column, Fe(II) is directly eliminated in the first effluent, containing the original concentration of HCl too, while zinc is fixed in the resin bed. Elution of the purified zinc is possible by a low concentration (1 0.01 – 0.05 M) HCl, just to prevent any hydrolytic precipitation. If separation of tin is also required, the zinc elution process needs to be further refined.

Separation of metals as dissolved ions in the solution by anion-exchange can be extremely efficient if the tendencies of chloro-complex formations are appreciably different for the metals in question. The resin may contain mobile counter-ions (A⁻ anions) worked as the exchanger for corresponding anionic complex ions of the metals in solution (Kékesi. 2002; Kekesi et al. 2003). This separation can be carried out by adjusting the chemical properties of the aqueous solution, i.e. the concentration of the complexing ions, to match the favorable condition of either sorption or elution in contact with the strongly basic anion exchange resin. The purification of the solution can be done through feeding the appropriate eluent to either bacth or vertical column containing anion-exchange resin at controlled rate. If the distribution coefficients are largely different, as in the case of Zn(II) and Fe(II), the separation can be executed also by a batch procedure where the two phases are simply mixed for a certain time and then separated. Chromatographic separation, however, in a vertical bed of the resin in a column (of a length of approx.. 10 times tits diameter) may offer separation of species showing less difference in their distribution coefficients.

In view of the possibilities related to investigate the best method to recycle the liquid waste of hot-dip galvanizing, the spent pickling liquor (SPL), our main purpose is to determine the conditions and the suitable processes of an efficient zinc extraction procedure offering a pure metallic product, while allowing the residual liquor to be used for regenerating the HCl content too. Thus the waste could be transformed into a valuable resource.

1.3 *High-value materials prepared from SPL*

There are various metal ions in SPL which can be considered as a resource of high value materials such as ultra high purity iron or iron oxides, high purity zinc or zinc salts. Another prospective product is ultra high purity iron that is also promising commercial product for semiconductor grade silicon, it was proved by Kekesi et al (Kekesi et al. 2002), that a two-step anion exchange technology – combined with the redox conditioning of the chloride solution of proper HCl concentration - is suitable to eliminate the other metal ion contamination. Iron yields over 80% could be reached by optimizing the anion-exchange procedure controlling the oxidation states and the degrees of chloro-complexation of the ionic species to be separated under optimum condition (Kekesi et al. 2002). Further, it may significantly increase the value of SPL by producing nano-sized iron oxide powder which has wide range application on magnetic recording material and biological technology (Tang et al. 2016).It may be related to the preliminary solution purification step if the cathodic deposition of pure zinc is the main objective. The value of these products may overwhelm the economical advantage of eliminating the costs of incurred by the otherwise mandatory treatment and handling of the hazardous material.

2 MATERIAL AND METHOD

In this preliminary research two main processes were carried out to confirm the possibility of producing pure Zn from SPL by combining electrowinning and anion exchange. Electrodeposition is the essential technique to recover Zn from the SPL. The preliminary separation process to purify the SPL is a necessary part of the scheme, as pure zinc cannot be obtained from a solution heavily contaminated by iron. Therefore, solution purification by anion-exchange in this case, has to be included. In all the experiments so far, model solutions prepared from reagent grade chemicals have been applied. The potentiodynamic experiments to characterize Zn deposition from SPLwere performed with 85 cm^3 volume of the solutions. The initial cathode was made of copper plate with the active surface of 2 cm^2 and the anode was made of a pure zinc rood of 5 mm diameter. The cathode surface was polished with an 800 grit SiC paper giving a uniform surface, then washed with distilled water and acetone, finally dried before setting into the cell. All the runs were carried out at room temperature with 40 mV/s continuous polarization speed – giving the widest range of clear results - and with 10/s sampling rate. The composition of the Zinc deposit was determined by Atomic Absorption Spectrophotometry (AAS) using zinc hollow cathode lamp at 213.9 nm wavelength. While the iron determination were did by ratio of weight of total deposits.

3 RESULT AND DISCUSSION

In the first series of the experiments, our aim was to identify the dominant cathodic process in different ranges of the examined parameters. Zn deposition was investigated from pure "synthetic" Zn chloride solutions by the potentiodynamic technique, applying a specially developed potentiostat that could follow the rapidly changing surface conditions by increasing the current in the required pace. The deposits were observed to form irregular growths of dendrites and loose crystals as can be seen in the Figure 2.

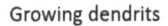

Growing dendrits

General deposit growth pattern:

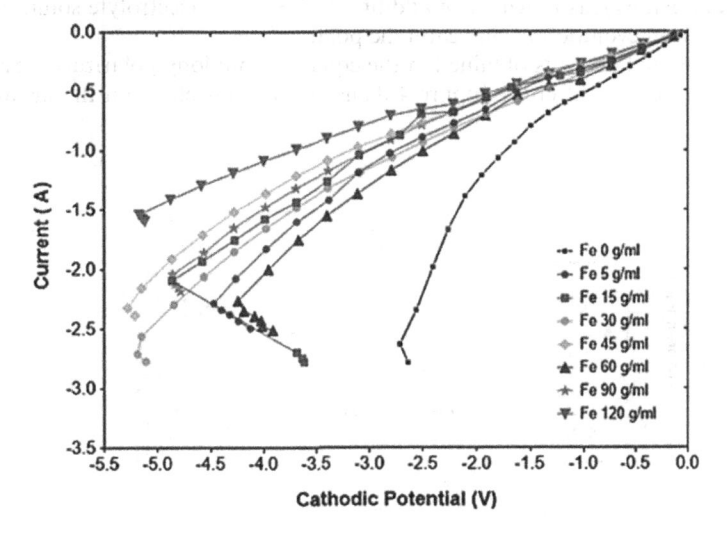

In the solution

Figure 2. The changes of the cathode surfaces during potentiodynamic polarization start with (a) Cu starting surface, (b) uniform densed deposition, (c) black spongy deposit and (d) dendritic deposition. (1 min runs at 40 mV/s polarization speed).

Acceptable deposition of Zn on the cathode mainly depends on the composition of the bath, in which various agents may influence the deposition process and the structure of the final deposit. Chloride solutions offer higher rates of zinc deposition on the cathode surface compared to that of sulphate systems. However, it is hard to obtain smooth and compact deposits. From the result it seems that deposit tend to be fine-grained at the initial phase where the current relatively observed low and the active surface relatively constant, as more deposit colected on the surface of the cathode the more active cathode was developed and the deposit more likely to be sponge-like and dendritic. Besides the evolution of hydrogen obtained along with metal deposition also effect the morphology of the deposit. So the hydrogen ion concentration in the chloride solution has to be controlled.

In correlation with the visual observations. It is observed that the generated current tends to be decreased by increasing iron concentration in the $0 - 45$ g dm^{-3} range. This infers a lower deposition rate as more iron is in the solution (Figure 3). However, if the iron concentration was increased further to 60 g dm^{-3}, the tendency changed and the current increased. As the iron concentration got high enough, hydrogen evolution dropped in favour of metal deposition and the surface was less blocked by initiated gas bubbles, thus also enhancing zinc deposition. The latter

Figure 3. Cathodic polarization curves at different Fe concentrations (0 r.p.m.) (1 min runs at 40 mV/s polarization speed).

is characterised by a stronger dendrite formation. Further increasing the iron concentration, as far as 120 g dm^{-3}, however resulted in the overwhelming dominance of iron deposition. It mostly produces powdery deposits, and the iron particles are easily detached, therefore the picture shows smoother surfaces, but the solution becomes turbid with the dark iron powder mixed in. The backdrop potentials were also shifted to more negative values, confirming that less metal could be deposited at the lower ranges of polarization without agitation because of hydrogen blocking. It also proves that iron in the solution promotes hydrogen evolution at the cathode.

Another remarkable difference is found in the changing of the slopes during polarization. In the case of the pure zinc solution and also if the added iron concentration was very low, the slope of the curve could get much steeper as the cathodic polarization was increased. This reflects a stronger formation of dendrites, i.e. a faster growth of the actual surface. However, if iron is added at higher proportions to the solution, the slope virtually remains constant, although the Buttler-Volmer-Erdey relationship (Kekesi. 2018) suggests that with constant surfaces the curve should be exponential. This discrepancy can be explained by the blocking effect of the evolved hydrogen bubbles adhering for some considerable time to the cathode surface. Thus the more constant the slope of the polarization curve is the more dominant the hydrogen reduction can be. It can be seen in the case of the highest concentrations of iron in the electrolyte.

A further difference in the shapes of the polarization curves may be expressed by the observed voltage ranges and the finally occurring potential backdrop forming a virtual hook. As the potentiostat is capable of supplying a total voltage of only 10 V, the conditions may also be limited at the end of the polarization runs by the voltage drop required to drive the current through the main cell from the counter electrode (anode) to the work electrode (cathode). If the polarization curve can span only a short potential range, the resistivity of the complete electric circuit may be high. With the applied constant anode-cathode distance, it is also a good indication of the resistivity of the solution. In the case of iron addition, the hydrolytic conditions expressed by the following reaction

$$FeCl_3 + 3/2H_2O = Fe(OH)_3 + 3HCl \qquad (4)$$

resulted in a more acidic solution (pH 1 ~ 1.3), which allowed the relative potential of the cathode to develop further. In the case of the pure zinc solution, on the other hand, the actual surface of the cathode was quickly change for a larger area by the effectively developed dendrites requiring less polarization potentials, but the whole electric circuit reached the maximum voltage supplied by the instrument as the solution was closer to the neutral state (pH 4 ~ 5). This is an obvious reason why iron addition to the $ZnCl_2$ electrolyte solution was found to enhance hydrogen evolution during cathodic polarization.

Comparing the final deposits obtained in the equally 1 min long polarization runs, it is evident, that the masses are different. Figure 4 demonstrates this effect on the metal deposition

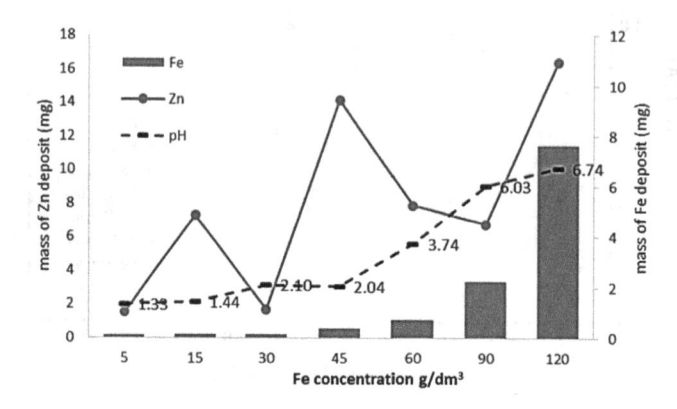

Figure 4.   Deposit composition obtained from solutions of 90 g/dm^3 Zn with various concentrations of Fe.

from the mixed electrolytes, which requires more experimentation for its elucidation. There-fore, polarization experiments were carried out in the same mixed solutions with copper sub-strates as starting cathodes of carefully measured masses.

The highest mass of zinc in the deposit was obtained in the range of 45 to 60 g/dm^3 Fe in the solution. The acceleration of Zn electrodeposition by the Fe content of the solution is also shown by the results in Figure 4. In these experiments the obtained and dried deposit was weighed, followed by a complete dissolution in 1 M HCl from the copper substrate, and finally the iron mass was calculated from the analyzed concentration. The deposited mass of zinc was determined by subtracting the iron mass from the total mass of the deposit.

The columns in Figure 4 show that the amount of iron deposited from the mixed solution is increasing quickly as the Fe concentration is increased beyond 30 g/dm^3. However, zinc depos-ition is also increased concomitantly. It is also seen that the intensity of stirring has a strong effect on the rate of zinc deposition. It can be also seen for iron in the 45 – 90 g/dm^3 Fe con-centration range of the mixed solutions. At the highest iron concentration, however, stirring seems to lose its relative importance. Comparing the positions of the curves (indicating the Zn deposit) and the bars (standing for the Fe deposits), it is seen that from stirred solutions of 90 g/dm^3 Zn and various Fe concentrations the purest Zn deposit can be obtained at the lowest iron concentrations. If however, the solution is stationary, and there is little iron in it, the deposit was too small in mass to make accurate measurements.

With increasing contamination of Fe in the electrolyte solution, hydrogen evolution will increase because of its lower overpotential to Fe. The generated gas bubbles give an extra stir-ring at the surface of the cathode, enhancing the transport of the zinc ions. It may increase the rate of Zn deposition as seen in the 30 – 60 g/dm^3 range of iron concentration. With even more iron in the electrolyte, the mechanical effect of hydrogen evolution is outweighed by the chem-ical effect of strongly increasing local pH. It may trigger a local formation of hydroxide par-ticles. Thus an inhibiting layer can be formed hindering the deposition of the less noble zinc. Therefore, in the 30 – 60 g/dm^3 Fe range, where Zn deposition is enhanced, the increased rate of iron deposition results in more contaminated zinc deposits. This is especially true if the solution is not stirred intensively. At higher iron concentrations, even more contaminated zinc deposits can be obtained. Therefore, in order to obtain pure zinc from the SPL, it is necessary to apply the planned preliminary purification of the solution, removing iron as much as possible.

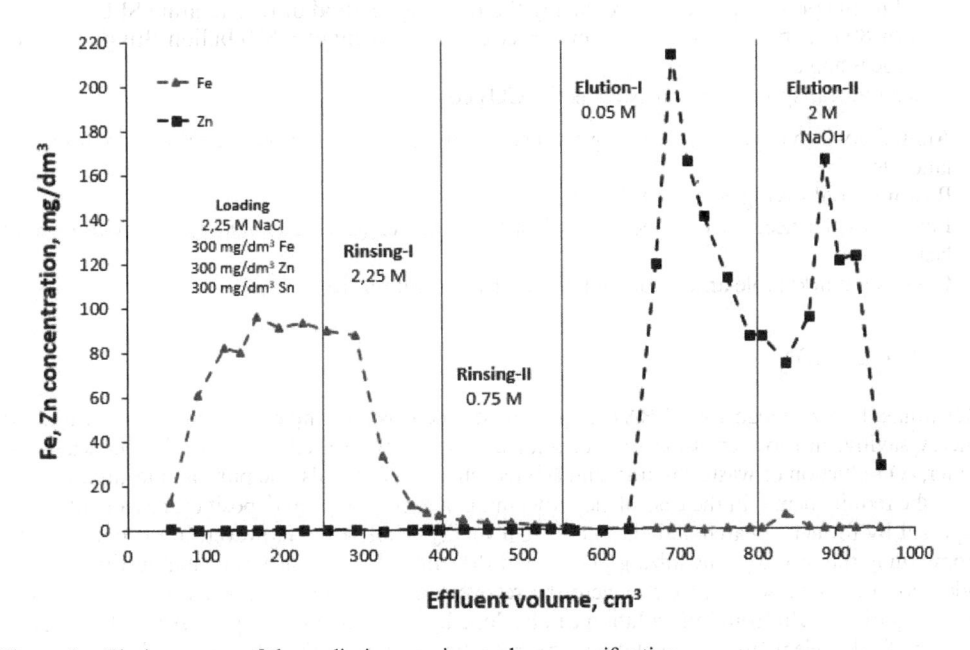

Figure 5.   Elution curves of the preliminary anion exchange purification.

Anion exchange is one of the best technique as suggested in former experimental results (Kékesi 2002; Kekesi et al. 2003;Uchikoshi et al. 2004) if high purity is aimed. In the case of SPL, the anion exchange method not only offers a perfect separation of the impurities but also helps in regenerating the acid in a further process. The first effluent will contain almost the whole HCl loaded with iron (and some minor impurities of Ni, Co or Mn) as the metallic content. This solution can be evaporated to regain the pure HCl and the residue can be processed to obtain the metals in either metallic or compound form. The results of the devised procedure can be seen in the elution diagram of Figure 5. The devised anion exchange procedure could selectively remove Fe from the solution, mostly during the loading step. The removal of iron is continued as the mobile phase in the resin bed is replaced by a pure NaCl solution of the same concentration. Rinsing was continued with 0,75 M HCl just to see if any Fe(III) could be present mostly depressed to the bottom of the resin bed, and to remove any incidentally precipitated iron hydroxide. It proved that the initial reduction of iron to the Fe(II) state by stirring the solution with iron chips was virtually complete. Reducing the chloride ion concentration to 0.05 mol/dm^3 could initiate a sharp peak of zinc elution.

In this case, HCl was used to prepare the eluent, so as not to risk any precipitation of zinc in the resin bed. This step also removed some tin, which must have been present in the divalent form. it may be just negligible in real SPL solutions, but a second anion-exchange step under oxidizing conditions could eliminate also this minor leakage. The recovery of zinc by the 0.05 M HCl elution may not have been complete, but applying a longer elution with this eluent and somewhat slower flow rate could improve it in practice. Another way to improve the recovery feature in the elution step can be a moderate decrease in the applied HCl concentration as far as e.g. 0.01 M HCl. The residual zinc was finally removed by applying 2 M NaOH in a secondary elution step.

3.1 Benefits of the process

Every year, 300 000 m^3 of discarded pickle liquor are produced in Europe, leading in costly and energy-intensive handling, treatment, and disposal. The offered technology solves the problem of waste disposal, resulting in significant savings in operating, environmental, and capital expenditures. As well as the costs of manufacturing hydrochloric acid to replace the spent liquor solution. The benefits of the purposed method are decribed as follow:

- Domestic energy savings of about millions barrels of crude oil equivalent per year compared to the present process by replacing the roasting method of regenerating SPL
  - For 800 m^3 per day SPL, this new process offers saving of ~ 870 billion Btu per year of processing energy.
  - saving transport energy as well as the CO_2 cost.
- Annual cost savings in by avoiding the need to neutralize and bury waste pickling liquor in landfills.
- Raw material saving cost for HCl regeneration
- Eliminates the need to bury neutralized pickling waste, which has significant environmental benefits.
- Creates a marketable and valuable product by on-site service

4 CONCLUSION

Regarding to six categories of BAT requirement, such as: (i) implementation in industry, (ii) energy saving, (iii) low emission of green-house gases, (iv) reduced use of fresh chemicals and water, (v) reduction of waste streams, and (vi) recycling of chemicals, the purposed technology can meet the requirements. In the case of electrowinning, a successful iron deposition has already been reported by former research activities at the University of Miskolc. However, in the current SPL from Hungarian hot dip galvanizing plants, and the implied economical potential justify the consideration of a reversed approach where the recovery of pure zinc is targeted in the first place. Recovery of pure Zn from SPL solution can be done by electrodeposition process but the contamination of other elements in the solution, especially Fe, decreasing the efficiency of the process. As a result, in order to acquire pure zinc from the SPL, the solution must undergo the specified preliminary purification, removing as much iron as feasible. Anion exchange separation can perfectly remove iron in the Fe(II) state. As the testing of the devised procedure proved, relatively low concentration of chloride ions, naturally present in the treated solution form anionic chloro-complex species of zinc, thus it is strongly fixed in the resin bed of strongly basic anion-exchange resin in the chloride form.

With the new method, the cost of waste processing is eliminated, as is the cost for purchasing raw materilas of the fresh pickling reagent. By-product sales of pure metals (Zn) used for industrial need are an additional economic benefit of the novel technique. However, further investigation is required to develop a better understanding of the whole process.

REFERENCES

Agrawal, Archana. et al. 2009. "An Overview of the Recovery of Acid from Spent Acidic Solutions from Steel and Electroplating Industries." *Journal of Hazardous Materials* 171 (1–3): 61–75. https://doi.org/10.1016/j.jhazmat.2009.06.099.

Carrillo-Abad, J. et al. 2017. "PH Effect on Zinc Recovery from the Spent Pickling Baths of Hot Dip Galvanizing Industries." *Separation and Purification Technology* 177: 21–28. https://doi.org/10.1016/j.seppur.2016.12.034.

Csicsovszki et al. 2005. "Electrodeposition of Iron from Spent Hydrochloric Pickling Solutions Containing Fe(II) and Zn(II)." *Unpublished Manuscript, University of Miskolc.*

Csicsovszki, Gabor. et al. 2005. "Selective Recovery of Zn and Fe from Spent Pickling Solutions by the Combination of Anion Exchange and Membrane Electrowinning Techniques." *Hydrometallurgy* 77 (1–2): 19–28. https://doi.org/10.1016/j.hydromet.2004.10.020.

Díaz, S. L. et al. 2002. "ZnFe Anomalous Electrodeposition: Stationaries and Local PH Measurements." *Electrochimica Acta* 47 (25): 4091–4100. https://doi.org/10.1016/S0013-4686(02)00416-4.

Frias, Carlos. et al. 1997. "Novel Process to Recover By-Products from the Pickling Baths of Stainless Steel." Project Funded by the European Community under the Industrial & Material Technologies Programme (Brite-Euram III), Project BE-3501, Contract BRPR-CT 97-0407, 1997–2000. 1997. https://doi.org/https://cordis.europa.eu/project /rcn/37577_en.xml.

Hluchanova, J. et al. 2012. "Solid Wastes Originated From Hot-Dip Galvanizing Process." In *ISDM 2012 - FREIBERG*, 282–86.

Kekesi, Tamas et al. 2002. "The Purification of Base Transition Metal." In *Purification Process and Characterization of Ultra High Purity Metals.* Berlin, Heidelberg: Springer.

Kekesi, Tamas. 2018. *The Fundamentals of Chemical Metallurgy.*

Kekesi et al. 2003. "Anion Exchange for Ultra-High Purification of Transition Metals." *ERZMETALL* 56 (2): 59–67.

Kékesi, Tamás. 2002. "International Motivation and Cooperation for Research in the Ultra-High Purification of Metals." *European Integration Studies* 1 (2): 109–26.

Kekesi, Tamas. et al. 2002. "Ultra-High Purification of Iron by Anion Exchange in Hydrochloric Acid Solutions." *Hydrometallurgy* 63 (1): 1–13. https://doi.org/10.1016/S0304-386X(01)00208-0.

Kulcsar, T. et al. 2016. "Complex Evaluation and Development of Electrolytic Tin Refining in Acidic Chloride Media for Processing Tin-Based Scrap from Lead-Free Soldering." *Transactions of the Institutions of Mining and Metallurgy, Section C: Mineral Processing and Extractive Metallurgy* 125 (4): 228–37. https://doi.org/10.1080/03719553.2016.1206693.

Regel-Rosocka, Magdalena. 2010a. "A Review on Methods of Regeneration of Spent Pickling Solutions from Steel Processing." *Journal of Hazardous Materials* 177 (1–3): 57–69. https://doi.org/10.1016/j.jhazmat.2009.12.043.

San Román, M. F. et al. 2012. "Hybrid Membrane Process for the Recovery of Major Components (Zinc, Iron and HCl) from Spent Pickling Effluents." *Journal of Membrane Science* 415–416:616–23. https://doi.org/10.1016/j.memsci.2012.05.063.

Sonmez et al. 2003. "A Study on the Treatment of Wastes in Hot Dip Galvanizing Plants." *Canadian Metallurgical Quarterly* 42 (3): 289–300. https://doi.org/10.1179/cmq.2003.42.3.289.

Tang, Jianzhao. et al. 2016. "The Recycling of Ferric Salt in Steel Pickling Liquors: Preparation of Nano-Sized Iron Oxide." *Procedia Environmental Sciences* 31: 778–84. https://doi.org/10.1016/j.proenv.2016.02.071.

Uchikoshi, Masahito. et al. 2004. "Production of Semiconductor Grade High-Purity Iron." *Thin Solid Films* 461 (1): 94–98. https://doi.org/10.1016/j.tsf.2004.02.076.

Author Index

9781032195964